MALE AND FEMALE

To my parents

MALE AND FEMALE:
AN APPROACH TO
THOMAS MANN'S DIALECTIC

by

INTA MISKE EZERGAILIS

MARTINUS NIJHOFF / THE HAGUE / 1975

PRINTED IN BELGIUM

CONTENTS

CHAPTER I

INTRODUCTION: THOMAS MANN'S DIALECTICS

Most critics see dialectical patterns in Thomas Mann's work. So does the author himself.[1] The structure of his works, as well as their statement, makes that pattern so evident that there is no need to prove its existence. Some dialectical pattern may indeed be inherent in all art. Susanne Langer [2] envisages dialectical rhythms as the essential identification of "living form" in art, as they are in life. While undialectical thinking tends to be abstract and to lack the vital impetus to unite its antinomies, a synthesis is not a mechanical thing but rather a *coincidentia oppositorum* in an almost mystical sense, or perhaps an organic process.[3] But it is not my intention to add to the philosophical elaboration surrounding the idea of the dialectic itself. I mean rather to pursue one dialectic in Thomas Mann's work—the polarity of male and female principles—one which stands at a point of convergence of several others and illuminates many of them.

[1] In comparing his *Doctor Faustus* to Hesse's *Magister Ludi*, for instance, Mann sees the absence of dialectical structure in the latter as the major difference. *The Story of a Novel. The Genesis of Doctor Faustus,* transl. by Richard and Clara Winston (New York, 1961), p. 75.

In the "Snow" chapter of *The Magic Mountain* Mann appears to reject dialectical thinking and indeed he subtly undermines it throughout the Settembrini-Naphta argument. But, like Hans who cannot maintain the synoptic vision he briefly glimpses, his creator is wont to return to a dialectical view, as he does emphatically in *Doctor Faustus.* "Polarity" is a more common term in discussions of Mann's oppositions. Thus, Manfred Dierks (*Studien zu Mythos und Psychologie bei Thomas Mann,* Thomas-Mann-Studien II, Bern: Francke Verlag, 1972) refers to the opposi- tions "paternal/maternal", "male/female" as polarities and as orienting constellations for the author's complex conceptual antitheses. (p. 160)

[2] *Mind: An Essay on Human Feeling* (Baltimore, 1967), p. 324.

[3] I owe these associations to Alfred Baeumler whose lengthy introduction to a selection of Bachofen's works I will have occasion to cite later in another context. Here, he is paying tribute to Hegel's thinking as well as Bachofen's *Der Mythus von Orient und Occident. Eine Metaphysik der Alten Welt* (München, 1926), ccxci.

If it is agreed that Mann's work is dialectical, unanimity disappears in an attempt to define the fundamental dialectic. One reason for that difficulty is the shifting nature of the pattern, which has led some critics to excessive frustration and hence to premature capitulation. Hans Egon Holthusen [4] defines Mann's dealing with ideas as "superessayism" and accuses him of "an unbounded, unscrupulus lust for making new associations or combinations, an ambiguous and subtle art of distorting and confusing concepts . . . ." In his irritation, he is ready to abandon any attempt to work with Mann's ideas as ideas.

> Regarding Thomas Mann's concepts, it is easy to sink into a bottomless pit if one wants to fix, circumscribe, and place one of them. His concepts have no definite boundaries, no locus, no region where they obtain without ambiguity. As concepts they are not to be taken at all seriously, they are to be understood only as continuously varying atmospheric values and psychological stimulants.[5]

We will brave the pit. First of all, pits can be a wholesome experience, as Thomas Mann's Joseph finds out when they twice save him from himself and effect a rebirth of what is best in him. Also, if one is willing to jump, one may find that there are no bottomless pits. Holthusen overstates his case. One should also remember that the ambiguity of art is not that of discursive writing. In literature, clear intellectual distinctions may not always be necessary or even desirable, and the ambiguous becomes not a measure of failure but rather a richness fully intended and needed. In *Death in Venice,* we are told that the greatest happiness for a writer is a thought that manages to become wholly feeling, and the feeling which, without residue, becomes thought.[6] This statement illustrates the special way in which an artist usually treats ideas. It also shows one of our difficulties. As statement of a dialectic, it gives a false impression of antithesis, at least in its resolution. To convey more precisely what the author himself does in his work, it would be much more accurate to say that, in both cases, feeling and thought coalesce to form a new synthesis, the special totality of the artist—felt thought. The explicit statements that Mann makes usually emphasize polarity and antithesis at the expense of potential synthesis. It is left to the artistic portrayal of reality to provide the synthesis. In this sense, Lukács[7] is correct in cautioning critics against considering the author's explicit theories and

---

[4] "The World without Transcendence," In *Thomas Mann: A Collection of Critical Essays,* ed. Henry Hatfield (Englewood Cliffs, 1964).

[5] Holthusen, p. 128.

[6] *Death in Venice,* p. 92.

[7] Georg Lukács, *Essays on Thomas Mann* (New York, 1964), p. 16.

the philosophy implicit in his work as alternate and identical statements, with each reinforcing the other in interpretation. Lukács also stresses the realistic novelists' concern with the dialectical process rather than with stationary antithesis. Mann's preoccupation with the development of man and society shows his interest in the process. Most of his work deals with it, but the novel of education, *The Magic Mountain*, is interested exclusively in development through synthesis.

The "ambiguity" that derives from the medium of the artist, then, is a necessary one. Total exactitude is attained by a process of progressive abstraction, by sacrificing the special physiognomy of a thing to obtain an equation or a model which retains a minimal structural description of it. An artist cannot make that sacrifice—he needs to be concrete even in his abstractness. Yet, even while granting him that general immunity of the artist, commentators frequently accuse Mann of a special personal ambiguity. His dialectics are not clear-cut and abstract—they shift constantly. Contents and values change. Thus, there are antitheses of life and death, of artist and burgher, of disease and health, East and West—(along with North and South), of spirit and nature, and many others. It is evident to anyone at all familiar with Mann's work that even seemingly literal and straight forward oppositions such as the geographical ones or the contrast of health and disease carry a heavy load of emotional and broadly philosophical overtones. Thus, artist and burgher are not representatives merely of social classes but rather of totally different ways of existing, thinking, and feeling, some of which may be traditionally associated with the artist and the burgher, others not at all. Once the paradigm is established by Mann, however, his reader orients himself within it and can invoke the necessary associations at subsequent mentions of "artist" and "burgher". That is true also of the other oppositions. The contrast of East and West, for instance, might carry certain cultural associations for a relatively wide group of readers, as may certain temperamental attributes frequently connected with the North or the South. And, to a large extent, Mann utilizes these associations. To illustrate a recurring situation, Tonio Kröger's temperamental mother brings the seed of artistic tendencies (and decay) into the father's Northern German burgher family. Significantly, this configuration also shows how the categories connect and overlap—a connection, if not an equation, has been set up between North/burgher and South/artist. The links multiply and become more complex when one realizes (and this can be seen from the early novellas on) that the "artistic" qualities, which often include broadly intellectual ones, are also connected with disease, while the "burgher" stands for a "health" which by this time has clearly become a symbolic state, though it is still usually represented concretely as physical health and opposed to various carefully chosen physical diseases—tuberculosis and syphilis most prominently.

The dialectical pairs are not on the same level of analysis. In addition to the larger North/South, East/West polarities the ocean is set off against the mountains as a symbolic landscape, replete with various psychological and metaphysical associations. On the other end of the scale, perhaps the most inclusive appears to be the antithesis of spirit and nature (*Geist* and *Natur*). This heads a list included in the notes for the projected essay "Geist und Kunst", later to be attributed to Aschenbach's fictional pen and likened to Schiller's essay on "Naive and Sentimental Poetry". The list is entitled "Antitheses" ("Gegensätze") and reads as follows:[8]

> Spirit and Nature *(Geist und Natur)*
> Spirit and Art *(Geist und Kunst)*
> Culture and Nature *(Kultur und Natur)*
> Culture—(civilization)—and Art *(Kultur-(Zivilisation)-und Kunst)*
> Will and Idea *(Wille und Vorstellung)*
> Naive and Sentimental *(Naiv und sentimental)*
> Realism and Idealism *(Realismus und Idealismus)*
> Paganism and Christianity (Platonism) *(Heidentum und Christentum (Platonismus))*
> Plasticity and Criticism *(Plastik und Kritik)*

It is evident from this catalogue that one concept can serve as the opposite of several others, and that, in each new opposition, a different aspect of its nature is emphasized. Spirit enters into one opposition as the antithesis of nature, suggesting in this perhaps a kinship with art, while in the next it is seen as antithetical to art, pointing to Mann's distinction of the poet (*Dichter*) and man of letters (*Literat*). The sweeping ambition of Mann's categorizing is also apparent, as Schiller's "naive and sentimental" polarity is included along with such philosophically charged terms as realism and idealism. In another note,[9] yet more interconnections are established among items on the list: there spirit is

---

[8] Paul Scherrer/Hans Wysling, *Quellenkritische Studien zum Werk Thomas Manns* (Bern und München, 1967), p. 218. I listed the original German which in some cases may seem superfluous, but in others the terms are either charged with traditional meaning or not easily translatable into English of the same connotation, or are associated with particular philosophies.

[9] Wysling, p. 219, No. 134.

aligned with Christianity and Platonism, sensuality and plasticity with paganism.

Not only do the values and weights placed on the members of the pair shift, then, but the various antitheses themselves tend to flow into each other. Together, they map out a field of sensed essential differences in the world and in the self. If they overlap, it is because they are the categories of an imaginative writer, not of an analytical philosopher. Some confusion results when one tries, as Mann himself does, to compare or align them with other established categories, such as Apollonian/Dionysian or naive and sentimental. As Hans Wysling points out,[10] such connections are usually not convincing. Even if the other typologies affect Mann's own scheme, set beside the latter as equivalents they make it difficult to see the distinctions clearly. Apellations such as Hans Egon Holthusen's "bottomless pit" or Wysling's own "typological jungle" [11] result not only from a demand for methodological rigor hardly applicable to an artist but also from the seemingly (and often misleadingly) close relationship between Mann's categories and those of other artists and thinkers.

I will not try to sort out or analyze the associations of Mann's dialectics with those of Nietzsche or Schiller though it may be rewarding enough to follow the changes the concepts have undergone in time and in Mann's usage. Instead, I will attempt a clarification of that usage in another way, one which to some may at first appear designed to deepen the pit or proliferate the jungle, or, else, to oversimplify the issues. I will stress one dialectical opposition above others—that of male as against female principles. It is a distinction deeply embedded in Mann's work. It is also a good choice because, as a general human category, it does not imply the rigorous philosophical consistency which the mere naming of many of Mann's other polarities suggests. In its very statement, emphasis is placed on the dynamics of dialectical opposition—on tension, attraction, and repulsion. Thus, in explaining the opposition of animus and anima, Jung comments: "Their opposition is that of the sexes. They therefore represent a supreme pair of opposites, not hopelessly divided by logical contradiction but, because of the mutual attraction

---

[10] Some, like Horst Daemmrich, argue for an almost total acceptance of Schiller's aesthetic categories by Mann, though he might then imbue them with modern ambivalence and scepticism. Wysling, I think correctly, emphasizes the importance of Schopenhauer's and Nietzsche's dialectics in modifying Mann's consciousness so that a literal adherence to the Schillerian categories becomes impossible.

[11] P. 140

between them, giving promise of union and actually making it possible".[12] In this context also, the male/female dialectic can represent the potentiality (in love) of a productive synthesis which is inherent though not immediately apparent in all the other oppositions.[13] And it can serve as a summation of the other polarities. Through association with it, Mann can endow them with a concreteness and density they may not otherwise have. (Though, in turn, "male" and "female", in becoming principles, lose some of their concreteness in the process and at times approach metaphysical distinctions.)

The male and female opposition, then, is not only a simplification. It is a key to most of Mann's other antitheses. Others have tried to extract a hierarchy from the various explicit and implied lists of opposites in Mann's writing. A plausible candidate, for instance, for such an inclusive dialectic that might summarize most others is form and dissolution.[14] Though it has generality, it lacks the other advantages of the male/female opposition. The latter could easily [15] be introduced into Mann's list of fundamental opposites. Thus, spirit (in its opposition to nature) is clearly male, and nature is female both in its contrast to culture and to spirit; the naive artist is female as against the male sentimental one. One might go on at will with such schematizing. What is valuable about the flexibility of the sexual dialectic, however, is its close relationship to life and its inherent dynamism. It can serve as a link between other sets of antitheses, but, more importantly, it can enhance an appreciation of the artist's work in all its concreteness, showing similarities within variety and variations within apparent sameness, enriching the reader's understanding of substance and structure.

A special ambiguity of the male-female dialectic is its lack of correspondence with men and women. Women may represent the female principle better, but they do not do so exclusively. For this assertion, we will see much evidence as we go on. It is, then, impossible to identify the female principle with a summation of the qualities of the women in

---

[12] See the views of C.G. Jung on the potency of this dialectic, which are discussed in the conclusion.

[13] There is a movement in Mann's work, from seeing these pairs of concepts as more or less stationary oppositions, to an increasingly dynamic and dialectical perception of them. Wysling also attests to such a development.

[14] Erich Heller. *Thomas Mann: the Ironic German* (Cleveland, 1961), p. 186.

[15] For some pairs, more information might be needed, a further explication of the meaning of the terms, expanding the rather laconic statement of them in the list and based on Mann's statements elsewhere.

Mann's work. For Mann, sex is not a firm and circumscribed thing. It is rather a continuum. Joseph, thinking about the sexlessness of Potiphar, sees his "zero" condition as the opposite of a totality which he calls "man-womanliness". A perfect combination of masculine and feminine qualities is the lot of gods, but the closer to myth a fictional figure comes the more bisexuality there is in him. After Rachel dies, she appears at times in Jacob who feels his double role of both father and mother to Joseph quite literally, but she is incorporated even more noticeably in Joseph. The less myth or art is associated with a figure, the less he is capable of uniting in one body a mixture of the two sex aspects. But he has to be one or the other; to be truly human, one has to be male or female—as it is divine to be half one and half the other, so it is sub-human to be neither.

But the sexual continuum is not that simple. Even in the middle realm of the human, there is a mixture of masculine and feminine qualities. Pure masculinity, Mann tells us in *The Beloved Returns (Lotte in Weimar)*,[16] is unnatural. Men have some characteristics that are considered feminine, and women may get quite masculine at times. By creating the "double image", a pair of characters who are really one entity, Mann illustrates the insufficiency of those who are sexually onesided. Some of the double images consist of a man and a woman who together may form one full person. Where the pair consists of two men, one of them usually shows some aspects of the female principle. It should, then, be remembered that when we speak of women in Mann's work we are not exhaustiing his treatment of the female principle.

The relationship of the male and female principles can be both an antithesis and a continuum because it is a dialectic—a series of actions which consists of alternating contraries,[17] both antithetical and a continuum. The dialectic is a process—it describes the whole distance between the two extremes—, and thus the continuum does not contradict it. When men and women are portrayed in real situations, the continuum tends to prevail. Synthesis is implicit under such conditions. But as soon as character or narrator speculates about manliness and womanliness as qualities, the dialectic comes to the foreground. If the dialectical view seems prevalent in this discussion, it is because this is a conscious attempt to categorize. There may be an implicit unity in phenomena, but when it is perceived by the dialectical mind it is seen as a strenuous

---

[16] P. 285.
[17] Langer, p. 324.

overcoming of opposites, a new totality arrived at by reconciling antitheses.

Let us first take a preliminary look at the substance of the female principle, with the expectation that the content of the male principle will at first emerge antithetically.

In a brief sketch of 1893, Mann describes a vision.[18] A girl's hand rests dreamily in front of a crystal goblet. It is motionless, open, fingers surrounding the glass rather than grasping it, but pulsating life can be sensed in the bluish vein meandering across the whiteness. The arm is relaxed, passive. As yet it remains a "sweet mystery"—beyond the wrist where hand will grow into arm the vision blurs. Thus, though we know that it belongs to a woman, we never find out who she is. It is not an individual arm. As a vision, it is an arrested moment, suspended and beyond the flow of time.

When Mann shows the whole woman, these are still the qualities that most persistently accompany her, as long as she is an incorporation of the female principle: a special kind of passivity, a tendency toward anonymity or antagonism to rigid individuation, and a privileged relationship to time. All of these assertions need to be proved both by what the author says and what he does. A good theoretical statement is a discussion about women in one of the final chapters of *The Magic Mountain*.

Hans Castorp, disappointed after a long wait for her, finally meets Clavdia Chauchat again, but she is accompanied by a new lover, Mynheer Peeperkorn. He asks Clavdia if she loves the other man. "He loves me," she answers. This prompts Hans to think about women, and we hear the results of his ruminations in the course of a long talk with Peeperkorn. Whether his opinion is correct, we will have to determine —Hans may be merely reassuring himself about his failure. "Women," he says, have no initiative. They "are creatures not of action but of reaction ... inactive in the sense that they are passive." [19] Women do not choose a mate but wait to be chosen, and then give themselves to the man either in gratitude for his having picked a lowly creature such as they, or in appreciation of their excellent taste.

"Passive," Hans calls Clavdia, and "inactive." The latter is a translation of the German "lässig." Why use two distinct but associated adjectives for this aspect of Clavdia? Assuming that it is indeed one

---

[18] The title is simply *Vision*.
[19] *The Magic Mountain*, p. 602.

aspect, passivity describes its negative side—it characterizes Clavdia by telling us what she is not. The quality of "Lässigkeit," on the other hand, is a more positive one. It is one that recurs again and again in connection with Mme Chauchat. Miss Engelhart who sits next to Hans at table and also admires Clavdia describes her as "lässig," clearly thinking it to be something of an accolade. Clavdia is charming not in spite of this quality but because of it. A more emphatic word, and a related one, is sometimes used to describe the disturbing yet attractive negligence of door-slamming, round shouldered Clavdia—"Nachlässigkeit." Passivity, then, as implied by this description, can receive positive or negative coloring. Another word, one that Mann does not use so often but that is of the same family, may best show the wider implications of its fellows —"Gelassenheit." It indicates not only calmness, imperturbability, and poise, but also a quality associated with mystics which describes mainly their openness to higher inspiration and a consequent willingness to relinquish or suspend the self. I postulated a tendency toward anonymity, the will to surpass individuality, as the second of the fundamental shared qualities of women in Mann's work. It is closely related to the first.

Sometimes the anonymity becomes complete, and the author speaks of "women" collectively, without distinguishing them individually, a practice that has frustrated those who would make an exact count of his female characters.[20] In any case each of the primary female characteristics modifies the other, so that passivity becomes colored by the special relationship of the female principle to the self, to identity. The categories themselves—selflessness, passivity, a special status in time—are working concepts. They may be added to or modified as the argument progresses. The proportions in which they appear vary greatly too. Not all of the representatives of the female principle are equally passive, timeless, and beyond individuation.

The passivity of the female principle, however, like the attitude of the seeker of mystical union, contains an invitation, a potential direction. In the conversation with Hans, Peeperkorn sees feminine receptivity as the holy duty of man. Man often appears as awakener. Women who have to wait long to be awakened demonstrate this need most vividly. Delayed and violent flowering can be seen, for instance, in Ines Rodde in *Doctor Faustus*, and especially in Potiphar's wife in the Joseph-novels. Women

[20] Erna H. Schenck, "Women in the Works of Thomas Mann," unpubl. diss. (University of Wisconsin, 1928). Condensed version in *MDU*, 32: 145-164 (April 1940).

are potential; they are constantly described as "ready." This readiness is perhaps the most conspicuous characteristic of Rachel, and it is her tragedy that God seems reluctant to let her make use of her willing eagerness which is described as "readiness for life." Later in the story, we see the same quality in Joseph's betrothed Asenath:

> ... the large, beautifully painted eyes had that peculiarly fixed and expectant gaze which is typical of the deaf; but Asenath was not deaf, her gaze only reflected her inner expectancy. It was as though, with conscious readiness and acceptance, she was waiting for the hour of her destiny to strike.[21]

Similarly, Lotte (in *Lotte in Weimar*) irritates her daughter by what the latter feels to be an excessive openness to people's advances, a "ready willingness." Her potentiality is also a good example of the female principle. When she met Goethe, she had just changed from half-child into a desirable young woman. In the course of her reminiscences, we discover that she credits her fiancé Kestner with bringing out the attractions that ensnared young Goethe—they were the fruits of Kestner's "warming, awakening look."

Once carriers of the female principle (and here we are speaking primarily of women) are "awakened," can they still be called passive? Potiphar's wife becomes a raving, pursuing maenad, driving off Joseph who was hardly unaffected at first, by her sheer aggressivity. Yet even here an essential passivity is preserved. The naarator tells the reader repeatedly that Eni could not help herself, that the pursued is herself pursued by all the furies, a woman possessed.

The passivity of the female principle is, then, a special kind of passivity. The characters that incorporate that principle may precipitate events in a story and thus be quite "active." But, as we will see, they serve this purpose more through what they are than through what they do. To say that they are passive is, in any case, not to consider them unimportant. But it does raise the question of their function in a work of art. One might well ask what role a passive character plays in the thematic and structural development of the work. As passive figures, they are used mostly as vessels to contain thematic content, the substance of thought and feeling that the work carries. The male characters, on the other hand, advance the events in the novels, make things happen, and actively express, in mediation or conversation, the ideas and themes involved.

Rarely is a woman the central character of a work, though male figures in whom the female principle predominates may well be. When the hero

---

[21] *Joseph the Provider*, p. 267.

of a novel is given "female" characteristics, this is done for a special purpose. Since this depends on the substance of the female principle, only conjectured so far, the discussion of such male characters should be delayed. But some generalizations about the overtly female figures might be ventured. Their function can at first and most simply be seen in their relationship to the male hero. Often, they precipitate significant changes in him; at other times they may appear to be mere sounding boards. Thus, Lizaweta seems like a conveniently projected alter-ego of Tonio Kröger. Yet one senses real personality, and, against the effusive speeches of her friend, her remarks are sharply insightful and benevolently ironic. Still, her insights are there to serve Tonio—to help him understand himself and come to terms with his art. Women often serve men. Unselfish maternal women appear frequently. They are not necessarily mothers, and not all mothers are warm and accepting. Substitute mothers, such as "mother" Schweigestill in *Doctor Faustus*, may surpass the real mother in motherliness. Mrs. Schweigestill is one of several ministering women who surround Adrian in the years of his worsening sickness and growing genius. These, though they are individually distinguished, often appear together, forming a warm, supporting and caring feminine background (similar to that of Jesus, whom Adrian's physical appearance increasingly resembles).[22]

Two of these women are always mentioned together—the pair of Nackedey and Rosenstiel, one a gentle but persistent spinster piano teacher, the other—owner of a sausage casing factory. They are introduced as "caring women." A more interesting friend of Adrian, but one who also fits into this category, is Jeanette Scheurl, like Lizaweta an artist in her own right.[23] She has charm, eloquence, and intelligence, but, as with Lizaweta, who must have had artistic and personal problems of her own that are never mentioned, what is stressed is her special talent as confidante. When female artists appear in Mann's work, the brief characterizations of their work usually indicate more elegance and psychological acuity than genius. In a discussion of the female principle,

---

[22] The reference is also one to Nietzsche's life, especially in a description that Mann read while he was working on *Doctor Faustus*:—Hellmut Walther Brann, *Nietzsche und die Frauen* (Leipzig, 1931). Mann refers to it in *The Story of a Novel*, p. 19.

[23] Brann, p. 170, describes some authoresses of Nietzsche's acquaintance in similar terms. They are "authoring women." Brann quotes from a letter that Nietzsche wrote to his sister: "Do read the novellas of my Berlin devotee Fräulein Glogau; they are much praised for their 'psychological refinement.' "

this peculiarity will eventually have to be faced. For the moment, we can say that their work does not seem to interest Mann.

What matters is the women's relationship to men. Nurturing alone does not exhaust it. Erotic attraction plays a large role. The physical characteristics which make for such attraction are described in meticulous detail. Yet even beautiful Gerda Buddenbrook is most important functionally as an objectification of Thomas "unorthodox" leanings and, secondly, though not at all in the way hoped by the family, as mother of future Buddenbrooks. Clavdia, in *The Magic Mountain*, is a love object, but she also serves as a symbolic representation of larger values —love generally, death, disease—before Hans learns to comprehend them intellectually. Even Potiphar's wife in her loving pursuit of Joseph simply fulfills her role in bringing him to the necessary next stage of his predetermined career.

If this is what women such as Gerda, Clavdia, and Eni do, then their function is much like that of the ministering women. They are more similar than might appear at first. Hence, though it may be easy enough to place Mann's women into groups such as "demonic" and "maternal,"[24] it is more fruitful to disregard such facile classification and to look for common qualities. It is imperative to do so once we have accepted the overflow of the female principle into characters overtly male. Function, then, is an outgrowth of these qualities. Thus, the passivity of the female element brought with it a subsidiary, facilitating role. Women characters, the more readily identifiable representatives of the female principle, are frequently assigned such a function. Their entrances and exits are not determined by the exigencies of the plot,[25] but by the needs of the male hero's growth.

In order to fulfill this function, women must have influence over men. At times that is achieved by making female characters sexually attractive. But not even the ministering women are entirely passive. Nackedey and Rosenstiel are aggressive and competitive in proffering their affection to Adrian. The love of the true mothers, though not devouring and diminishing, as that of Adrian's own mother turns out to be, is an active love. The confidantes need to inspire confidence to receive it. Thus, the

---

[24] Most critics who deal with Mann's women at any length categorize the figures occasionally. One analysis that limits itself to classification is Paul Albert Graber's, "Female Characters in the Early Works of Thomas Mann," unpubl. M.A. thesis (State University of Iowa, 1939).

[25] Schenck, *op cit.*, accuses Mann of using his female characters for mere plot purposes.

first thing we find out about Jeanette is that she is "worthy of confidence," and her relationship to Adrian is summed up as follows: "He was then and remained for many years trustingly attached to her."

More active yet than trustworthiness is the quality of understanding, the special gift and talent of Else Schweigestill. Mrs. Schweigestill's "gift of understanding" is a large part of the attraction that draws Adrian to the village of Pfeiffering. Understanding of others' weaknesses is an important component of it. She can be quite pitiless in her common sense, in her direct and perspicacious diagnosing of those weaknesses. But her understanding which is a mixture of intuitive insight and emotional acceptance is just as direct. Knowing neither pity nor condemnation, it is both sensible and practical. Though Adrian is not the only recipient of this understanding, he is the one most desperately in need of it. She herself best expresses the scope of her acceptance when Adrian collapses into a paralytic seizure that leads to his final madness. The crowd of friends surrounding him hesitates for a moment. Mrs. Schweigestill has been standing farther away than the others, but it is left to her to go to him, cradle him in her arms, and drive the gapers off.

> Let me see the backs of ye, all and syndry! City folk all, with not a smitch of understanding, and there's need of that here! Talked about th'everlasting mercy, poor soul, I don't know if it goes 's far 's that, but human understanding, believe me, that doos![26]

Such simple, encompassing acceptance is rare, and, among the large group of friends and well-wishers around Adrian none other has it. That it is a woman who is capable of it may indicate an openness that is well nigh selfless. Even the importance of mother figures, however, tends to derive from an interest in the mother-child relationship rather than in the mother herself. This is true especially in *Doctor Faustus* where the focus is on Adrian's need for mothering and the attitudes of the various mother-figures toward him.[27]

In the same work, there is a figure who epitomizes total self-effacement. It is a woman who is willing to put her whole wealth at Adrian's disposal but herself wishes to remain unknown. In Frau von Tolna, we can see some of the qualities of the ministering women at their best—she asks

---

[26] *Doctor Faustus*, p. 503.

[27] The ambivalence of the relationship with his own mother especially emerges clearly in the epilogue. There, the mother is said to feel some satisfaction at the failure of her son's Icarus-flight and at his forced return to her protection. And, what is more, Adrian, even in his madness, feels this satisfaction and resents it.

nothing, not even the right to be with Adrian. Rich, sensitive, cultivated, a woman of the world, she prefers to remain a shadow. She fosters the acceptance of his work, and thus her admiration has a practical, tangible cast, like that of "mother" Schweigestill. Zeitblom ponders her relationship to Adrian—does she wish to fit into the role of mother or shadowy mistress? We do not know. Neither is any hint given of her physical appearance. Most of the women in Mann's works, even figures such as Nackedey and Rosenstiel, are meticulously tagged with a physical description. Yet it is perhaps her very facelessness that makes Frau von Tolna a better representation of the female principle. At least, the narrator Zeitblom describes this woman's sphere as that of love and faith—the "eternal feminine." [28]

This benefactress of Adrian is a good example of the function of the female principle in Mann's work because she *is* pure function. It is less evident in other female characters. Yet even when they seem more individual, women are frequently just such catalysts, precipitators, and facilitators in the life of the central male. Thus, as we said, Clavdia mediates between some insights and Hans, who is not yet ready to receive them in intellectual form; her second appearance on the mountain is more significant because she leads Hans to acquaintance with the "personality" Peeperkorn than for its own sake. Thus, if women need men to come into their own as women, men need women in a similar way. But whereas a man's touch is needed to make a woman receptive, women seem to be not so much awakeners as indicators of the degree of wakefulness the man has reached at any particular time. They are barometers, or better, perhaps, considering the imagery of heat and cold that is persistent in Mann's work and especially Hans' world of disease, thermometers. Thus Clavdia is there as an embodiment of Hans' changed attitudes—he is ready to choose a woman like her. Similarly, Thomas Buddenbrooks' choice of Gerda Arnoldsen, the exotic, musical beauty from Amsterdam, shows his townspeople how "decadent," in their opinion, his tastes have become. Gerda, thus, shows them and us how Thomas has changed at this point in the novel, but she does not get him there. These women, in helping the author to show the readers what the male hero is like, serve a function similar to that of the female confidante.

---

[28] *Doctor Faustus,* p. 390. As all of Zeitblom's utterances, this should be read with an eye to the ironic treatment of the narrator by the author. The generalization suggested by him is worth examining but cannot be accepted as a final evaluation.

The woman who listens to man and helps him may not only be unselfish—she may be selfless. And in this she foreshadows an important aspect of the female principle, perhaps the most important one—its special relationship to individuation. The understanding helper, the confidante, even the lover whose main function is to be a catalyst or a thermometer, imply a negation of their own individuality. One might object that, with the exception of mysterious Frau von Tolna, we always know what the women look like. Lisabeta is briefly but graphically described. We find out what Gerda looks like as soon as we first meet her at boarding school. Hair color, eyes, face structure, posture, and specific parts of the body—especially hands and arms—all are described as soon as the reader is introduced to a woman. Even clothing is rendered in realistic detail. Yet it is precisely the faceless presence of Frau von Tolna that is described as the realm of the "eternal feminine." [29] We will see that, even where physiognomy is given in loving detail, facelessness is still sought. But in this general discussion, let us first take a brief look at what is said or implied in a general way about women's individuality.

The question is whether the female principle differs from the male in identity, not qualitatively but quantitatively. Nietzsche has Zarathustra say: "Surface is woman's soul, a mobile, stormy film on shallow water." [30] For different reasons, Thomas Mann might agree. That is, he might agree if the statement were combined with another, one that Nietzsche makes contrastingly of man's soul—"... its current gusheth in subterranean caverns...." [31] The important question, however, is where does it cease being *its* current—a personal, differentiated identity—and become a common anonymous flow.

There is a persistent cluster of images, from the earliest to the latest of Mann's works, which indicates that the individuality of the "female" (including its male representatives) is indeed shallow, and that the anonymous current begins just under the surface. A pulsating vein attracted attention in the 1893 vision of a girl's arm. Such visible veins constantly accompany his physical descriptions of women. In *Tristan*, Gabriele has a small pulsating vein that becomes visible when universal emotions such as laughter or love tax her small strength. In *The Magic Mountain*, Hans' erotic vision of Clavdia is again focussed on her arms, and again a vein pulsates inside her elbow. It is in this way that Mann

[29] *Doctor Faustus*, p. 390.
[30] Friedrich Nietzsche, *Thus Spake Zarathustra* (New York, 1911), p. 76.
[31] *Zarathustra*, p. 76.

concretely portrays the common flow, the anonymous and undifferentiated blood stream of humanity. Vividly, we are shown that individuality is only skin deep with women. The male embodiments of the female principle may occasionally have such marks, but they are rarely so obvious. Since they are physically male, their share in the female element usually has to be shown in other ways. And the purely male, we will see, are also distinguished by recurring physical qualities, such as closed and rigid posture, indicating their high degree of individuation, their imprisonment in personality.

There are other evidences, in portrayal as in direct statement, to show the tendency to efface the individual in women. In the Joseph-novels women are referred to as creatures of the primeval swamp. It is granted that woman can also be the virginal moon priestess that Eni almost succeeds in being, but that is again a role which surpasses her own individuality. In any case, the moon is not necessarily employed as a polar contrast to the swamp. Joseph's adoration of the moon, for instance, brings him out of himself into an orgiastic, trance-like state rather than into any transcendental and spiritual purity. In his correspondence with Mann, Karl Kerényi compliments his friend on his image of Eni as a swan.[32] Femininity, he feels, is thus connected with the similarly irreducible archetypal unity of "the swanlike" ("the swanlike or the swampbirdlike," he writes, thus connecting the image definitely with the chaotic but fertile swamp). The lesser definition of the female principle is also invoked by Potiphar when he complains of being trapped in the role which he has to play in life.

> For a man might be many other things than precisely that which it is his lot to be or to represent. He may often marvel at the absurd playacting he has to do in his allotted rôle; he feels stifled in the mask life has put on him, as the priest may at times feel stifled in the mask of the god . . . .[33]

Eni, he says, may not understand him because women are not as confined to an individual role as men are.

> Probably women have less understanding of such a feeling. For the Great Mother has granted them a more general sense in respect of their being more women and image of the Mother, and less this or that individual woman. For instance as though you were less bound to be Mut-em-enet than I am to be Petepre because I am conditioned by the sterner father-spirit . . . .[34]

---

[32] Thomas Mann-Karl Kerényi, *Gespräch in Briefen* (Zürich, 1960), p. 72.
[33] *Joseph in Egypt*, p. 402.
[34] *Joseph in Egypt*, p. 402.

This is what Mann means when he says that a pure embodiment of the male principle is monstrous. Potiphar is "male" to a high degree in this sense, though he is castrated. By that, and by the empty ceremonial quality of his office and marriage he is cut off from any real relationship with the world. Not all male characters are so isolated. For some, there are ways to open the prison of the self. But whereas the representatives of the female principle possess this capacity as a birthright, the others have to either be mythical figures or to battle very hard for it. As a mythical character, Joseph has that capacity and he also has a great infusion of the female principle. After trying to find out his identity, Cha'ma't, one of the Potiphar's scribes, in utter frustration compares Joseph to a set of multicolored balls. He is, however, not a ball but the arc that the balls form in the air. As a representative of the female principle, he is also in some ways a function or process rather than a thing or a clearly circumscribed entity. If one incorporates more of the male principle, one needs to unlock his "I" to accomplish such a transformation. This release from confining individuality is felt to be a positive value. Feelings of happiness are persistently associated with empathy —"compassion," "sympathy," or "all-sympathy," even "all-infatuation." They all go beyond the self. Perhaps this is why the female arm is so important—the arm reaches out beyond its owner, the arms open to receive child or lover.

Youth is also associated with the female principle. There are numerous boys and adolescents in Mann's work, and they are portrayed with much care. When they are supposed to be beautiful they look feminine. In *Young Joseph* a description of the boy is followed by an explanation of this association: "But so much we must admit: that beauty in the guise of youth must always both inwardly and outwardly incline toward the feminine. That is its essence, that conditions the tenderness between it and the world; that is betrayed by its smile." [35] Individuation is not yet rigid in youth, and thus the young share the openness of the female principle. The two young men in *The Transposed Heads* are drawn to each other because they are aware of their differences (their complementarity, in this case) and yet are so newly formed that the desire for exchange and union seems capable of satisfaction. Individual feelings have not yet hardened, Mann says,—the clay of life is still soft.[36]

---

[35] *Young Joseph*, p. 5.
[36] *The Transposed Heads* (New York, 1941), p. 5.

Potiphar is not only described as being locked inside himself; he is also beyond time: "Composed, symmetrical, he sat there, without access to the world, inaccessible to the death of begetting; eternal, a god in his chapel." [37] A man like Potiphar is beyond time because he is insulated; those who participate in the female principle are more or less untouched by it precisely because they are more open to the world. Karl Kerényi sees women, in an archetypal sense, having a special relationship to time:

A woman lives earlier as a mother, later as a daughter. The conscious experience of these ties produces the feeling that her life is spread out over generations—the first step towards the immediate experience and conviction of being outside time, which brings with it a feeling of immortality. The individual's life is elevated into a type, indeed it becomes the archetype of woman's fate in general.[38]

Not all of Thomas Mann's women are thus privileged, but all who are associated with the female principle seem to enjoy a special standing in time. One indication of this special status is the recurrent characteristic of transparency. Women's clothes are often transparent; so are their skins. In the Joseph-novels we find enlightenment on one aspect of this transparency. Eliezer, the major domo of Jacob's household, has a transparent personality. In looking at him, Joseph feels he can see beyond and through the present Eliezer a whole series of his predecessors. The quality of transparency, then, is related to time. This transparency may show a mythical figure or a literary one behind the outlines of the real figure, though it need not necessarily do so.

Insofar as women do represent some aspect of the female principle, its privileged relationship to time can be shown in the way time treats female figures, and in the way they treat time. Gerda Buddenbrook does not age. Although Thomas changes and ages very noticeably in the course of a novel that spans much time, Gerda does not change at all. She seems ageless, and that quality is stressed by describing her in almost exactly the same words every time she appears. At the end of the novel, when Thomas and their child Hanno have died, she takes up her life at the point where Thomas' proposal had interrupted it. She goes back to Amsterdam to play duets with her father. In *The Magic Mountain*, Clavdia feels she can afford a similar contempt for time. She is spendthrift with it, an attitude that is ascribed to her Russian background whose spatial expanse fosters lack of economy with time. The humanist

---

[37] *Joseph in Egypt,* p. 396.
[38] *Eleusis. Archetypal Image of Mother and Daughter* (New York, 1967), xxxi. He cites Jung and Kerényi, *Essays on a Science of Mythology,* p. 219.

Settembrini condemns the Eastern influence that Clavdia represents especially for its destruction of the Western idea of time. In another way, the double image can be related to time. It is occasionally used to show a variability of male and female ingredients. But it can also embody a variation in time, such as the several mother-daughter pairs do. (In *Felix Krull* and *Lotte in Weimar*, or in Mont-Kaw's story in the Joseph novels.) Thus, the double image may be play with sex, time, or individuation itself.

Since women (though by no means all of them) are primary representatives of the female principle, a woman from one of the important novels should be examined carefully. Clavdia has already appeared prominently in this general introduction; she is a complex and interesting female figure. Hence she was chosen for this part of the investigation. To get an idea of representatives of the male principle, I have chosen two heroes—Gustave Aschenbach and Adrian Leverkühn—very different in many ways and representing works far apart in time, yet also illustrating the consistency and continuity of Mann's dialectic. We should also look at a phenomenon that has been mentioned repeatedly—the double image. In discussing the double image with its varying components, male figures in whom the female principle predominates can also be considered. This phenomenon is especially relevant since, as a pair, it is well suited to exemplify a dialectic. Another pair that merits attention is that of Goethe and Schiller, frequently treated by Mann. Though not a double image, it is seen in male-female terms. Finally, the possibility for a synthesis of the dialectical antitheses will be examined, under the heading of love. Love ought to stand for a successful synthesis when the dialectic is one that is symbolically expressed as male against female.

Another consideration that should be kept in mind is the possibility that Mann's conceptions may have changed in the course of a long career. The later works have been emphasized in the following discussion, but, wherever possible, examples are adduced from the early ones as well. There seems to be development in the nature of evolution rather than change in direction. As a concrete example of this evolution, we could recall the feminine arm in the 1893 vision. In 1954, in *Felix Krull*, the author is still interested in that arm. It is still feminine, still disembodied, still beautiful. But it is no longer the "sweet mystery" of 1893. Felix and Professor Kuckuck talk of time and space, of evolution, and of the unity of all nature. Felix would like to exempt the arm, "the charming stream-lined feminine arm" from the seemingly prosaic scheme of evolution. After chiding his companion for having a "certain cult of extremities," the Professor explains that the arm is essentially and specially a part of that totality. "It is remarkable how primitive, in contrast to the brain, human arms and legs still are. They retain all the bones you find in the most primitive land animals." [39] The arm is still the same, though it is now saturated with a meaning that has accrued through years of work and thought. Now, it represents a total, partly poetic, partly scientific conception of the universe. But the arm is still not individuated; it is passive; it belongs to a woman. Most importantly, it is associated with timelessness and has shed all other differentiating characteristics except its femaleness. Its archaism and its transparency to time belong to the female principle. Not only is this arm transparent in the sense that one can, through its structure, see the primitive formations from which it evolved. It is actually identical with these structures—it *is* the claw of the primeval bird and the pectoral fin of the fish.[40]

---

[39] *Confessions of Felix Krull, Confidence Man,* p. 270.

[40] As will become apparent later in the discussion, it is not only the structure of the arm that is important but its gesture as well, especially that of the hand. Scientific confirmation of such telling gestures as "palming" and of their correlation with mental and emotional attitudes is now found by Kinesicists, and it corroborates the artist's intuitions nicely. (See *The New York Times Magazine,* May 31, 1970— "The Way We Speak 'Body Language'" by Flora Davis.)

CHAPTER II

THE FEMALE PRINCIPLE IN A WOMAN:
CLAVDIA CHAUCHAT

Clavdia Chauchat—the name arouses and provokes the reader as it provokes Hans Castorp when he first hears it. As he does, one might well ask: is she French? She is not, though her absent husband might be. We never find out. But knowing Mann's care, wit, and subtlety in choosing names for his characters, we attend to the sound and meaning of first name and surname. In contrast to the soft sibilance of the last name, "Clavdia", especially in its Slavic variant, sounds harsh. With his sense for words, Mann must have known the commonly accepted etymology of the name. "Clavdia" means "the lame one". If we equate lameness with disease, we can see that, like her vaunted freedom, Clavdia's erotic attraction derives precisely from this quality. Why, however, a last name like "Chauchat" for a woman who seems to stand for the East, for the holy barbarism of Russia? First of all, what does it mean? Warm cat. The catlike quality of Clavdia is again and again confirmed by her catlike movements and her noiseless walk. Her feline grace is constantly emphasized. Even her speech is likened by Doctor Behrens to the miauwing of a kitten.[1]

The suggestiveness of the name's etymology, thus, already invites hypotheses about what aspect of the female principle Clavdia represents. It also puts her in good mythological company. Nietzsche especially picks up this traditional feminine association. "Oh! What a dangerous, creeping, subterranean little beast of prey she is! And so agreeable withal!", he says in *Ecce Homo*,[2] speaking of what he calls the perfect woman.

---

[1] Warren R. Maurer, "Names from the Magic Mountain," *Names*, IX (December 1961), 248-259, also makes this connection. He associates the first name with "Klauen"—claws, to reinforce the feline connection.

[2] *Ecce Homo*, in *The Complete Works of Friedrich Nietzsche* (New York, 1911), p. 65.

If the implications of the last part of the surname are evident and easily followed, though we have not as yet exhausted its significance, the first part is not as immediately transparent. Warmth may indeed be associated with the helpful, ministering quality of many women in Mann's work which we discussed in the introduction. In Clavdia, too, warmth may indicate not only the erotic effect she has on Hans, but also the more important human warmth concentrated in the Russian kiss she exchanges with him. The former influence is explicitly demonstrated and could be traced mathematically in Hans' fever curve. The more general warmth is indicated in the "humanity" she so likes to speak of (with her special pronunciation—the vowel wide open, long drawn out) and also in her association with Peeperkorn. In that relationship, Clavdia comes close to the caring women of *Doctor Faustus,* for instance.

Apart from the meaning of the name, what about its sound? The assonance, the virtual repetition of syllables, is an early example of a device Mann is to employ more frequently later, especially in *Felix Krull* where we have Loulou, Zaza, and Zouzou. It is playful; it may be ironic. As an early awareness of the possibilities of sound and a self-conscious manipulation of it, such repetition is primitive poetry. In a book review article of 1932,[3] Mann speaks of such stammering (the German "lallen" has more of a musical connotation). He thinks of it as both a primitive childish communication common not only to all individuals but all races, and as a more refined mythical expression.

The mother is called Ninmah, "almighty mistress." But by what other name is she called, at least in certain intimate moments? "Mama," "Mami"—thus one addresses her. Early mankind stammers at her feet, at her breast, as we all have stammered, as they will stammer on this earth forever. A touching symbol of the unity of all that is human, this primitive sound of innocence that is timeless and at home in East and West.
But there is a stammering more sensual than that of the toothless infant, and this too bears witness to the fascination that the mother-goddess exercises on humanity and to the universal function of this goddess. "Nana"—so too is the Beloved Lady called. One wonders whether Emile Zola was impelled by memories of the history of religion when he gave this enticing name to his symbolic heroine, that Astarte of the Second Empire. He "invented" it—whatever men think invention is.[4]

---

[3] "Die Einheit des Menschengeistes," *Gesammelte Werke,* X, 751-756.

[4] "Einheit des Menschengeistes," pp. 754-755. My translation. I have rendered as "stammer" the German "lallen" and thus lost its musical connotations. We are to meet it later. Kerényi (*Eleusis,* p. 136) mentions Nana as another name for the Great Goddess.

This will shed some light on Mann's use of names of this sort. It also puts Clavdia in a mythical context of which more will be said later.

To return to the original question—why a French name for a woman whose association with Russia is not incidental but an essential quality of her function in the novel? Clavdia speaks French, of course, and this places her socially, as indeed does her financial independence. Of Clavdia's maiden name we know only that it was Russian. Neither do we know anything of Clavdia's husband except that he is a civil servant in Daghestan. He may derive from a Napoleonic straggler. In realistic terms, such a name would not confer much respect in the Russia of that time. But what does it confer upon Clavdia? We may conjecture that Mme Chauchat is deliberately made not be a one-sided entity, not the equivalent of Asia, the East, or Russia that Settembrini wants to make her. She is not one side of the dialectic set up simplistically by the Italian, and, more complicatedly, by the author. Rather, she is already at least an approximation of a synthesis, an early embodiment of the solution Hans seeks.

Hans calls Clavdia "the genius of the place". But the place is more than place—it is disease itself and, most importantly, the state of mind that results from disease. As an incarnation of the attractions and dangers of he place, Clavdia thus becomes a double representation; her capacity to stand for something beyond herself is raised to a higher power. Yet she is an incarnation, not an abstraction, very much flesh, as Hans' reaction testifies. Since it may be her influence on Hans that is her main function, let us first see her through Hans' eyes.

Before Hans sees Clavdia, however, he hears her. His interest has been aroused earlier, in a dramatic and highly unpleasant way. On the morning after his arrival on the mountain, his cousin introduces Hans to the communal dining hall. Breakfast, like all meals, is rich and plentiful, consumed greedily in an atmosphere of false cheeriness and shallow sociability. The one jarring note is provided by a slammed door. It is a door consisting of small glass panes, and thus the sound multiplies and reverberates in the room. It also reverberates in Hans' mind. At first, his reaction seems out of all proportion. He feels the noise to be a personal insult; it is a sound he has always hated—hated to the death, we are told. This is no mere irritation at a breach of manners—his face is distorted, he is filled with hatred and contempt; he is described as being furious. Mild Hans, we are told, feels like hitting people who slam doors. Yet, though he does not yet know it, he will soon be deeply in love with this one.

Before he meets Clavdia, Hans is to hear this special motif of the slammed door once again. It is second breakfast, and Hans is staring at a Russian couple whose frequent and noisy lovemaking in the room next to his own has also badly jarred him and evoked ambivalent responses. At that very moment he hears the door slam again. Since first breakfast, however, Hans has met many people and heard about more. He has also started ruminating about time. Along with physical fatigue, these experiences reduce his reaction to a mere wince this time. He is too tired to turn his head and see the culprit. By dinner-time, however, he has recovered sufficiently to shudder at the sound again. Again, he is angry, and this time the cumulative frustration produces an explosion of uncontrollable interest.

"I must find out", he whispered with exaggerated earnestness. Miss Robinson and the schoolmistress both looked at him in surprise. He turned the whole upper half of his body to the left and opened wide his bloodshot blue eyes.[5]

Finally he sees Clavdia, noticing especially her schoolgirl's hands; he asks his table neighbor about Mme Chauchat's manners, and then, during that day, thinks no more of her.

The first encounter has, however, left a deeper impression than Hans seems to realize. A memory is stirred when he sees Mme Chauchat, and dream establishes the exact connection. The broad cheekbones and slanted eyes of a Slavic schoolboy whom Hans had loved from afar are recalled. But Mme Chauchat appears in yet another dream—a dream that recurs in the same form during the same night. She enters, slamming the door, and gives Hans the palm of her hand to kiss. On the fifth day of his stay, Hans watches Clavdia as she goes off to an excursion; he listens to her veiled voice, and confirms her similarity with Pribislav Hippe. The next day, attending a lecture on "Love as Cause for Disease", he sits behind Clavdia. Hans has just returned from a long walk on which he has vividly relived the Pribislav episode, only to face this reincarnation of his early love. Evincing the continuity of erotic attraction, Hans is painfully aware of Mme Chauchat's body. He feels her as a distraction from the lecture. In truth, she is the very embodiment of what Krokowski is saying. She represents both love and disease and their mysterious connections.

[5] *The Magic Mountain*, p. 76. The Lowe-Porter translation here tones down the dynamic emotionalism of the moment by rendering "Leidenschaftlichkeit" by "earnestness" (thus losing the connotation of passion) and "aufreissen" (to "tear open" his eyes) by the quieter "opened wide."

By the beginning of the second week of his stay, Hans' reaction to the slammed door has changed. He waits for it impatiently, yet cannot muster his indignation any more. Now, he is ashamed. And well he might be. Hans has been deriving stealthy satisfaction from discussing Mme Chauchat with his table neighbor Fräulein Engelhart who enjoys both the vicarious romance and Hans' attention which she buys by going along with the little fictions on which their discussions are based (that it is she who has a crush on Clavdia, for instance). Life has become one long meal in the hall with the seven tables, waiting for and speaking of Clavdia, trying to encounter her eyes. Between meals, Hans lies in his chair and listens to his pounding heart.

What has Clavdias' role been so far in relation to Hans and his education? Let us remember that he is still formally a visitor in the sanatorium, in the second week of his intended three-week visit. Yet we have seen him gradually being drawn into this world of disease and thinking of people and things down below with growing contempt. Mme Chauchat is not the only or even the original reason for Hans' temptation. But she greatly increases the allure of the mountain and becomes a person-ification of what it means. If the sanatorium represents distance from bourgeois life with its values of toil, punctilious moral responsibility, and narrowly prescribed social relationships, then that liberation is epitomized in Clavdia. She is "free", as Hans finds out early in his conversations with Miss Engelhart; that is, her disease has enabled her to consider even the commitments she might have made as not binding. She has a husband, but marriage can be suspended at will to take up her constant round of health resorts. As a Russian, she is outside Hans' normal world of Western morality and scruples. He feels a mixture of admiration and contempt for the Russians, the admiration rooted in personal feeling, the contempt based mainly on a consciousness that he represents Western European culture. He also feels a glow of superiority when they try to communicate in his own terms—as when Clavdia speaks German. Thus Clavdia's freedom, which results from a lack of tradition (a tradition identifiable by and familiar to Hans, in any case) and from her illness, makes her both desirable and accessible. Hans feels he does not need to go through the usual social amenities, as their relationship cannot, in any case, be socially acceptable in terms of "down below". Clavdia is to him a concentration of all the attractions of the mountain. To make this representative function explicit, she is frequently spoken of as "the Russian" or "the ill one".

Yet Mme Chauchat is more than just a synthesis of the seductions of Haus Berghof. In addition to personifying the qualities of the place, she points beyond it. Unlike most of the other patients, Clavdia is not a lifetime inmate of Berghof. She is not hermetically enclosed in the life of the sanatorium. There is truly some freedom in her life, beyond the dubious liberties of the others who may deem themselves free. She may never be well, but she is not so dangerously ill that she cannot visit her husband in Russia whenever she wants to. Also, Berghof is only one of many, though probably similar, institutions she visits. In any case, Clavdia incorporates the attractions of the mountain, but she also does something more. She gives a depth to its seductions, and we have indications of this as early as this, the second week of Hans' visit. He is thinking of his pounding heart, a condition that started immediately upon his arrival, a purely physical condition at first. With the arrival of Clavdia, it is no more merely physical:

For now he need not feel that it so beat of its own accord, without sense or reason or any reference to his non-corporeal part. He could say, without stretching the truth, that such a connexion now existed, or was easily induced: he was aware that he felt an emotion to correspond with the action of his heart. He needed only to think of Madame Chauchat—and he did think of her—and lo, he felt within himself the emotion proper to the heart-beats.[6]

Perhaps Berghof expands Hans, opens him up, and Clavdia, though also an expansive influence, provides some content to fill his widened mind and heart. But to come to any conclusion about this, we have to follow the events and meanings of their relationship.

Hans follows his own precept of keeping their association mysterious, sweetly dangerous, existing on another level than his other social contacts, even at Berghof, where his relations already are freed from most confinements to standards of down below. He carefully stages "chance" meetings in hallways, he stares at Mme Chauchat in the dining hall. More and more the resemblance to Pribislav Hippe is substantiated as he gets a closer look at Clavdia's face and hears her voice. She comes to stand for the East and becomes one of the opponents of Settembrini's world of republicanism, humanism, and rhetorical finesse (Naphta is another and a different one). This dialectical opposition is clearly indicated in the connection Hans feels between his relationship to Settembrini and Mme Chauchat and the memory of a strange experience on a Holstein lake a few years earlier.

[6] *The Magic Mountain*, p. 141.

But what—or who—was it that drew down the other side of the scales, when weighed over against patriotism, belles-lettres, and the dignity of man? It was— Clavdia Chauchat, "Kirghiz"-eyed, "relaxed", and tainted within; when he thought of her (though thinking is far too tame a word to characterize the impulse that turned all his being in her direction), it was a though he were sitting again in his boat on the lake in Holstein, looking with dazzled eyes from the glassy daylight of the western shore to the mist and moonbeams that wrapped the eastern heavens.[7]

Late on a summer evening, Hans had sat in a boat and seen simultaneously bright daylight in the West and a moonlit night in the East. The conjunction had lasted only ten minutes, to be resolved, by the nature of things, in the victory of night. To associate Clavdia with this experience is to admit that she is identified with the night and contrasted with the rational daylight world of Settembrini. It is also to admit that her influence is becoming dominant. We cannot concern ourselves here with working out all the implications of this image, but it is relevant insofar as it has to do with an important aspect of Clavdia.

Often, Clavdia is important for what Hans says to her, for what his thoughts and dreams of her show of his present state of development. But, at a very significant juncture, she directly influences Hans' decision. It is Saturday of the third and final week of Hans' visit with Joachim, and Hans, who has developed a pretty respectable fever, has to decide whether to keep an appointment he has made with Doctor Behrens, in view of his somewhat improved condition. The appointment is set for two o'clock, and as the dining hall clock strikes two, Clavdia turns her head and directs a meaningfully smiling look at Hans. The decision is made, the appointment is kept, and Hans starts his seven-year stay at Berghof. An object lesson illustrating Doctor Krokowski's lecture has occurred—Hans' unsatisfied erotic longing has literally produced his disease. Now the temperature of his daydreams and table conversations with Miss Engelhart increases, fostered by the newly confirmed feeling of an extra-social intimacy and wild complicity. Jealousy enters as Hans finds out that Clavdia receives visits from a young Russian and is being painted in oil by Behrens. Unexpectedly Hans finds himself face to face with her in the waiting room of the x-ray cabinet. Again, as in the lecture, Clavdia is associated with penetration of surface appearances— Krokowski's psychological or Behrens' merely physical transparency. As yet, they only meet in the waiting room, however.

As Hans' daydreams show, his love for Clavdia is strongly physical. The disease has emphasized her body, and Hans is constantly and

---

[7] *The Magic Mountain*, p. 160.

painfully aware of it. Yet there is more. The narrator indulges in some analysis of his own at this point of the story where the hero is beyond earshot of Settembrini's warnings against "Scythians and Parthians" and the seductions of disease. The love Hans feels for Clavdia is described by the narrator as "homeless" (*unbehaust*). It is a mixture of frost and fever, lacking a conciliating middle. On the one hand, it is desire for her body, an unabashedly open physical attraction. On the other, he intuitively feels that within Clavdia lies at least a partial answer to the questions about the meaning of life and death that he now finds himself asking. Thus, at this time his feeling for her is a strange composite of the animalistic and the metaphysical.

Doctor Krokowski would approve of the mixture, if he shared Thomas Mann's own opinion of Freud's teaching. What distinguishes it, the author believes, is a special kind of spirituality, one that is closely associated with sexuality. In setting the sex drive against the death wish as a champion of life in its instinct for higher development, Freud boldly endowed the sexual with an unprecedented spiritual or intellectual potentiality. It is intellectual because it stands for form, differentiation, and perfectibility.[8] In this impulse to development, it is well applicable to the effect that Clavdia eventually has on Hans. And, though Clavdia herself stands at times for the death wish and the obliteration of form more than for the life force, the love Hans feels for her becomes more understandable in this light. In this special sense, it is spiritual even when it seems to be at a fever pitch of sexuality.

Whatever the content of this love, it affects Hans as it might affect any impressionable young man, even "down below". He plots his chance meetings, strives to impress Mme Chauchat by his courtesy, wit, and devotion. But not directly. He tries to communicate with his eyes, or, if he speaks, then it is usually a conversation with others, held near Clavdia so she might hear and admire his audacity and spirit. "Merci", she has said to him so far, and they have exchanged good mornings on an early walk. This is the extent of their direct communication. Yet every look from Clavdia sends Hans' spirit and his fever curve soaring or plummeting, depending on whether it is kind and interested or cold and

---

[8] "Freud's Position in the History of Modern Thought," in *Past Masters and other Papers* (Freeport, 1968), pp. 196-197. Frank Donald Hirschbach, in *The Arrow and the Lyre: A Study of the Role of Love in the Works of Thomas Mann* (The Hague, 1955) also sees the combination of intellectuality and passion in Hans' feeling as Freudian, without, however, specifically linking it with Mann's essay on Freud.

contemptuous. Another exchange consists of Mme Chauchat's "Pardon" and "Pas de quoi, Madame" on the part of Hans, a feat of which he is proud. Yet he again tells himself that a normal social relationship with Clavdia is not what he wants.

Hans has heard rumors about Doctor Behrens painting a portrait of Clavdia. Finally, he maneuvers the doctor into showing it to him. As Hans looks at the painting, the mixed motives of his attraction are again evident. He is fascinated by the portrait first of all simply because Mme Chauchat has sat for it, even though the resemblance is slight. He touches the décolleté of the figure. Properly impressed, he admires the one masterly feature of the work—the rendition of the skin. It seems to breathe; it has anatomically and sensually correct texture; a vein can be detected through the semi-transparent surface between the breasts. Hans carries the painting around, even puts it in his lap—a purely physical reaction to it as a physical object. Yet the painting has served as a springboard to a scientific and eventually metaphysical discussion. Hans' interest and excitement do not diminish—they grow—as talk proceeds from Clavdia's body (there is no interest in her face—an omission that can here be explained simply by a reminder that it was badly painted) to the human body generally. Anatomy, physiology, and body chemistry are discussed, and lead to general observations that touch the central concerns of Hans' quest. Oxidation is the process of life as well as of death; thus living is dying, Hans gets Behrens to admit. And hence an interest in death might really be an interest in life.

Clavdia's body, then, is not only an object of desire for Hans—it stands for something. It is not only for titillation that he listens to Behrens' explanation of the human body and its processes and later reads thick tomes on biology and anatomy. Clavdia's picture is not only a substitute for Clavdia's body. It is also a first abstraction of the body necessary for Hans to see what it means to him in his search for ultimate answers. A second, and more radical, abstraction is to follow. As Hans asks "What is life?", in a triadic, ascending passage, he finally sees an embodiment of it, an image—"the Image of Life". It is a body furnished with all of the scientific attributes of which he has just heard and read. It is also the body of Mme Chauchat. Thus, it is described by that most persistent tag of Clavdia—"indolent" (lässig); it also has the epicanthus structure that Behrens has explained to Hans as the cause for the charming slant eyes of Mme Chauchat. It is Clavdia, and it is also a representative body. Anatomy, Hans thinks, lets him look under the skin of this body. So does art, though in a different way. Behrens' painting hovers between anatomy and art. It lets Hans see or at least feel that he saw the layers of the skin itself, a vein, even perhaps glandular structures. Finally, the skeleton appears (Hans was impressed earlier by seeing bone structures on the fluoroscope in the x-ray room), the embodiment of the aim of all this obsessive attempt to penetrate, to get under the skin. It represents to Hans the unity of all humanistic endeavor. It is lyrical (or, we might say more broadly, aesthetic)—a quality that it has acquired perhaps mainly by the origin of the speculation in Clavdia's body; it is medical—Behrens had made this abundantly clear; it is also an engineering feat—Hans' early technical education has enabled him to see the mechanical perfection of the body, and thus to connect organic and inorganic nature. To summarize, it stands for the "unity of all that is human, the unity of all disciplines". It may be a hint for us to remember when we look at Clavdia's function in the novel that Hans sees this symbolic skeleton as belonging to Clavdia. She stands for the world of disease with its erotic intoxication and death. She also represents life. The vision that started out as Clavdia becomes "the image of life".

He beheld the image of life in flower, its structure, its flesh-borne loveliness. She had lifted her hands from behind her head, she opened her arms. On their inner side, particularly beneath the tender skin of the elbow-points, he saw the blue branchings of the larger veins. These arms were of unspeakable sweetness. She leaned above him, she inclined unto him and bent down over him, he was conscious of her organic fragrance and the mild pulsation of her heart. Something warm and tender clasped him round the neck; melted with desire and awe, he laid his hands upon the flesh of her upper arms, where the finegrained skin over the triceps came to his sense so heavenly cool; and upon his lips he felt the moist clinging of her kiss.[9]

The elements of this dream derive from Hans' recent anatomical research as well as from his desire for Clavdia, and they show some traces of a scientific-aesthetic synthesis. Mann's persistent fascination with the female arm is shown again. We feel that the arms stand for something. Though sensually vivid, they are still just barely phenomena. In an earlier dream, Hans kissed the palm of Clavdia's hand. Now the arms open to him, for the moment only in dream, but soon they are to do so in reality.

When Hans has been on the mountain for seven months, he borrows a pencil from Clavdia, an act whose deep meaning has by then been made clear to the reader. It has marked the symbolic consummation of his love for Pribislav; in another dream, Clavdia had already lent him

---

[9] *The Magic Mountain*, p. 286.

one. The narrator tells us that the pencil was returned, that Clavdia has now departed from the sanatorium leaving Hans a treasured keepsake. After some teasing of the reader's expectations, he is told that the memento is an x-ray slide of Clavdia's chest.

An "inside portrait", Hans calls it, as he lovingly holds the glass up to light to trace Clavdia's bone structure and organs. He is deeply moved. "Mon Dieu!", he exclaimed on being told of the existence of the slide, and his attachment to it is not due only to its being Clavdia's but also to its particular form. This faceless image surpasses Behrens' portrait which intimated what was below the skin but did not actually show it. Why would a man in love prefer this kind of a representation of his beloved? The face of Behrens' portrait was a bad likeness; the slide has no face. The x-ray picture would be quite anonymous if it were not for Clavdia's disease. It is disease that marks her as an individual. But, versed as Hans now is in the lore of disease, he still cannot distinguish, or is not interested in, those marks. What interests him in Clavdia, if we can judge by the images on which he dotes and by the visions he has, is not what is unique and individual in her but that which is symbolic, universal, and representative.

When Clavdia returns, she is with Mijnheer Peeperkorn, a "personality" who fascinates Hans and enlists his sympathies so much that Clavdia cannot help being slightly piqued. In this triangular friction, the love of Hans for Clavdia somehow transcends itself. Earlier, he had felt it to be composed of fever heat and intellectual coldness. It alternated between fits of sexual desire and occasional flights of daring imaginative symbolism where, as we just saw, Clavdia's body became the image of the richness and balance of God's creation and human life. Now, there is a warm middle ground. Peeperkorn's presence invokes concern over a third person; it leads both Clavdia and Hans out of themselves and unites them in unselfish love for the mutual friend. They make a pact to protect Peeperkorn and seal it with a Russian kiss, an appropriate mixture of the fleshly and the holy. With Peeperkorn, on the other hand, Hans ponders feminine nature—the sacred facts of sex differences that were mentioned at the outset; the reactive nature of woman, her passivity, her desire to "choose" after she is chosen. Peeperkorn sees this as the holy duty of man the awakener. Man is intoxicated by his own desire, he says, but woman demands and expects to be intoxicated by his desire. Hans tells Peeperkorn Clavdia may never have loved him, in spite of their carnival night adventure. This is not only a consideration to spare Peeperkorn's feelings—it follows from his theoretical deductions about the female principle. Their short affair he ascribes to feminine receptivity: "The possibility of—of a twentyninth of February could only be ascribed to feminine receptivity on the basis of the man's choice already made".[10] After Peeperkorn commits suicide, Hans renounces any further suit of Clavdia. The "genius of the place" leaves again, with no talk of return and Hans does not seem to think of her any more, as he completes his stay and leaves to fight in World War I. Whatever she has meant to him has now been incorporated and her physical presence is no more necessary.

But what is the meaning of the phenomenon "Clavdia"? Most importantly for our purposes, how might she stand for the female realm in the world of this work? (This is not to say that she is the only figure in the book to represent that realm—Hans himself is in many ways an incorporation of the female principle). First of all, she looks like a woman. Not all of the women figures in Mann's work share such a strikingly feminine appearance. Clavdia is of middle height, had reddish blonde hair that she wears wound around her head in heavy braids, frequently supporting and ordering this coiffure. Hans, like his creator, has much appreciation for hands and arms. Clavdia's hands are the rough nail-bitten ones of a schoolgirl, and her arms are white and unusually beautiful. The Slavic features of her face—the high set, wide cheekbones and the slanted eyes—are constantly emphasized, as they provide the important link between Mme Chauchat and Pribislav Hippe. But it is Clavdia in movement that is most attractive. She moves noiselessly, "creeping"—often she is referred to as "the creeping one". Behrens calls her a kitten, and the slinky grace of her walk and stance warrant this comparison. This confirms the archetypically feminine aspect of her nature. One thinks of cat goddesses and the playful grace and cruelty of Nietzsche's desert maidens.[11] Vera, a character in Goncharov's novel *Obryv*,[12] whom Alois Hofman[13] has shown to have been influential in Mann's conception of Clavdia, also has the walk of a cat.

At times, as on the pivotal carnival evening, other subtle mythical reminiscences are adumbrated. In an especially seductive mood and setting, Clavdia wears a dress made of lightweight black silk that some-

---

[10] *The Magic Mountain*, p. 608.

[11] Nietzsche, "The deserts grow: woe him who doth them hide!" *Thus Spoke Zarathustra* (New York, 1911), esp. p. 376.

[12] Ivan A. Goncharov, *Obryv* (Moscow, 1946).

[13] Alois Hofman, *Thomas Mann und die Welt der russischen Literatur* (Berlin, 1967), esp. pp. 273-274.

times shows a golden brown shimmer. The Garden of Eden comes to mind, and Mann may well have intended the reminiscence, especially since Clavdia is no simple seductress. Her seductions are put in the service of Hans' growth. Like the snake, she is not offering lust but knowledge. She is not to lead him astray, but rather lure him onward on the dangerous road to life, the one that goes through death. As Clavdia leaves the room that evening, she is described as "gliding" to the door.

Gesture, then, is an important aspect of Clavdia's attraction. Yet another fascination, one that we have already mentioned, is exerted by her body as body. Her skin intrigues Hans, as do the veins one can see beneath it and her bones. As he sits in the foreroom of the x-ray cabinet staring at her, he notices mostly her knee, her rounded back, and her shoulders. The vertebrae of her neck always interest him. On carnival night, her small décolleté just shows the beginnings of the collarbone and the "somewhat prominent" vertebrae. Already in the waiting room the vertebrae deserve his attention and so does the nearly distinct backbone which, under a closefitting sweater, shares equal attention with her girlish breasts. The skeleton of Hans' vision which represented a dream of unity, an early attempt at synthesis, inevitably comes to mind. Even in the dream, the body was at least partially identified with Clavdia, and this later concentration on her bones reinforces that connection.

The skeleton was earlier described as the image of life, but one should not forget that traditionally the skeleton is a symbolic representation of death. Most of the skeleton associations—Hans' glimpse at his cousin's bones and his own hand, for instance,—are explicitly connected with death. As he looks at his hand through the fluoroscope, Hans feels he is looking into his own grave, and, in representing disease, Clavdia also stands for death. Yet the symbolism Mann intended with this figure is complex and ambivalent. When the skeleton vision is invoked later, then, both its life and death associations should echo. Seen separately, Clavdia stands more for death than life—not only because she is incurably ill, but also because the total openness and formlessness that the female principle represents when seen in its most pure and abstract distillation leads to death. But her effect on Hans is finally to show him the way to life. He has to pass through a stage of infatuation with death first. Since he experiences that infatuation through Clavdia, however, it carries within itself the seeds of the strength needed to overcome it. Death wish is combined with erotic attraction: an attribute of the life force.

Hans' obsession to penetrate the surface and to see within life's secrets is also apparent in his visual attitude to Clavdia. Transparency is one of the important characteristics of events and figures throughout the book. (In a Princeton lecture, Mann speaks of making reality transparent for the spiritual and the ideal as the basic device of the novel).[14] It is especially persistent with Clavdia. We have spoken of her skin—in life, in Behrens' portrait, and, prominent in its absence, in the x-ray slide. The impression of transparency is reinforced in another, more evident and explicit area—Clavdia's clothing.

Hans concerns himself with what Mme Chauchat wears. Even for a man head over heels in love, his interest in the color and fabric of her apparel is extraordinary. "You are well versed in my wardrobe?", asks Clavdia as he comments on the new black gown she wears on carnival night. And indeed he is. So is the reader for he is kept painstakingly informed of Clavdia's garb every time she appears. The effect is both to make her more marked individually by visual specification and to deepen her representative value. Like the shimmering carnival night dress which carried hints of the fall of man, so other costumes are used for suggestive value. As we get more deeply into the themes of the novel, such overtones become more frequent. The first time Mme Chauchat appears we are told only that she is wearing a white sweater and a colored skirt. In Hans' dream that night the sweater has found its place. During Dr. Krokowski's psychoanalytical lecture on love, Clavdia's clothing starts a whole train of thought in Hans' mind. Gauze sleeves appear on her blouse, as a prelude to the later transparencies of her skin and body. He thinks about the lack of functional justification for such seductive apparel on a woman whose illness makes it impossible for her to have children. It seems to be an erotic and perhaps aesthetic appeal, one that has lost its bourgeois moral basis and thus become sweet but reprehensible.

On the decisive day when Hans is to see Behrens and commit himself to stay, he notices (or recollects later) that Clavdia is wearing a new sweater, gold colored with large buttons and embroidered pockets. Another sweater, a white one, appears at their meeting in the x-ray waiting room, along with a blue skirt. But this is merely noted, without suggestion of further implications. A white morning robe that Clavdia occasionally wears to second breakfast in warm weather makes Hans pale with delight. White appears again soon after—on a morning walk

---

[14] "Einführung in den Zauberberg," *Gesammelte Werke,* XI, pp. 602-617.

with Joachim, Hans encounters Clavdia who is dressed entirely in white. Not only is she wearing a white sweater and a white skirt, but even her shoes are white. Walking along the reddish path, with the sun shining on her reddish hair, she presents a striking appearance. And, as on the remembered evening in the boat, sun and moon are both in the sky at the same time, except that now the moon is on the wane. Transparent covering recurs in the painting of Clavdia. Not only does the skin seem transparent, as I pointed out earlier, but shoulders and bosom are also draped with veiling. A counterpart to the vision in white is formed by Clavdia on carnival night with her serpentlike gown and the accompanying black stockings and black shoes.

After this climactic night, however, Clavdia's dress seems to have no great significance any more. She has become transparent; her significance has been for the moment fixed. The colors and textures that invoke various mythical and archetypal figures and scenes are no more necessary. By now, Hans can appreciate the lucidity and simplicity of higher abstraction—the x-ray slide, for instance—which has no equivalents for color, no concern with clothing or even skin. The vision is being stripped to its essentials.

In clothing, in appearance, and in behavior Clavdia conforms to a conventional conception of femininity. But, as in Thomas Mann's work one cannot simply equate woman with the female element and man with the male one, we have to ask what makes Clavdia a good representative of the former. In his conversation with Peeperkorn, Hans makes a statement that is dictated partly by his sly modesty, but also has direct and important bearing on this problem. He has naturally spoken of his relationship with Clavdia as of a man-woman relationship. Then he feels he must qualify:

I must say that when I refer to myself as a man, it seems to me a sort of self-advertising and bad taste—but at all events, Clavdia is a woman.[15]

An exaggerated act of self-effacement, perhaps, out of consideration for the vulnerable masculinity of the friend. Humorously intended by the author, yes, at least partly so. But the comment has a core of truth. For the moment, we can take it as a testimonial to Clavdia's female nature. This is one area where one can seek information about the relevance of Clavdia's characteristics to the larger problem of the female principle. We could call this the area of direct statement, either

---

[15] *The Magic Mountain*, p. 608.

by narrator or characters in the work, explicit remarks about femininity
and masculinity. Another source is the use of a character like Clavdia
in the work, her function in displaying its themes and structure. This
involves the association of Clavdia with the important device of transparency, for instance, of which we have spoken. What this reveals has
to do with the lesser individuation of the female principle, an earmark
which was suggested in the introduction, and which makes such a figure
especially suitable to display that theme. Along with this, the frequent
association of Clavdia with doors may also suggest the greater openness
of female figures, both in the sense of time and general receptivity.

Inanimate objects in the novel often are used expressively, to comment
on character or situation.[16] In speaking of Clavdia, doors come to mind.
She is announced by a slammed door, and the change in Hans' feelings,
their ambivalence and the fast growth of his passion is accompanied
by and often made apparent to the reader through his anticipation and
reaction to successive slammings of that same dining hall door. Another
door—that of Clavdia's own room (the magic number 7)—gets prominent
mention. As Hans calculates encounters with Mme Chauchat, he walks
through the hallway past her door. We have not heard of it yet, but
Hans has long ago familiarized himself with it—to him it is a "long
known room door". Other calculatedly spontaneous or really accidental
encounters are connected with doors. Once, Hans feels Clavdia come
up behind him at the dining hall door. He steps aside, very aware of
her passing near, receives a smile and a "Merci" which is a perfect gift
for Hans does not want an articulate, specific, and socially categorizable
relationship with his love object. It is to him an "incredible adventure",
one described in terms of a mystical ecstasy. And the experience becomes
a unique memory labelled "the meeting by the door". At the height of
their erotic relationship, on carnival eve, just after Hans' ecstatic confession of love and just before she allows Hans to come to her later
by reminding him to return the pencil, Clavdia remains for a moment
standing in the doorway. Placed at the end of this important chapter,
the tableau vivant she forms is striking, and again this moment is closely
associated with a door.

She slipped from her chair, and glided over the carpet to the door, where she
paused an instant, framed in the doorway; half turned toward him, with one bare

---

[16] Hermann J. Weigand, *The Magic Mountain. A Study of Thomas Mann's Novel
"Der Zauberberg"* (Chapel Hill, 1964), e.g., makes a good and amusing case for
chairs.

arm lifted high, her hand upon the hinge. Over her shoulder she said softly:
"N'oubliez pas de me rendre mon crayon".
And went out.[17]

After Clavdia has left Berghof, Hans once hears about her through
someone who has met her in Spain. He speculates that the austere
discipline of those regions will cure her of doorslamming. As she returns,
this prophesy is fulfilled in an ironic manner.[18] The door of the dining
hall does not slam because the new lover Peeperkorn is there to catch
and close it. Thus doors mark all the high points of Hans' relationship
with Clavdia. But why concern ourselves with that? First of all, the
open door may furnish some proof of the openness of the female principle
as opposed to the male. The openness means that the female character
is not as imprisoned in the individual self as is the male. Those who
represent this principle are not obsessed with penetrating the skin and
breaking through the frontiers that separate one self from another because
it is easier for them to do so. Thus, Hans asks for Clavdia's x-ray picture,
while Mme Chauchat is not at all interested in seeing his of which he is
himself so proud.

In addition to the inter personal openness suggested by a door, a way
out of one's self into another, it is also a way to the outside world
generally, and, most importantly, to knowledge. As a tool of Hans'
education, Clavdia does symbolically open doors for him. We have
associated her with the biblical snake, and this earlier connection
harmonizes well with the open doors of knowledge. As snake, or as Eve
(or Lilith, as we will see), Clavdia is definitely associated with Hans'
search for knowledge.

A third source of knowledge about the contribution that an examination
of Mme Chauchat can make to the understanding of the female quality
appears in looking through the various transparencies. It deals with the
mythical (also traditional, such as opera references) and archetypal figures
and situations we are allowed to glimpse behind the surface. What and
who are they, and what do they tell us about Clavdia, and, more
importantly, about the female principle? It should be stated here that
Clavdia carries many themes—surely she is a representative of the East
as opposed to Settembrini's Western humanism. She is also, as we have
indicated, at least an early attempt at a synthesis of the hostile principles
that struggle for Hans' loyalty. But, in this context, I am interested mainly

[17] *The Magic Mountain*, p. 343.
[18] Weigand points this out also (pp. 79-80).

in those representations that would throw some light upon the meaning and content of the female principle.

In addition to being associated with symbolic things like doors and with symbolic qualities like transparency, Clavdia is specifically connected with two "mythical" figures—Lilith and Carmen. Lilith is mentioned only once, but very prominently—in the climactic *Walpurgis Night* chapter. If this is to be taken as a reference to the original Woman, then it is of interest to us for we are seeking the substance of the female. Why not Eve? First of all Lilith was chosen because the reference is a quotation from the *"Walpurgis Night"* scene in *Faust*, and Lilith is the one Goethe used.[19] What can we deduce from this reference to fill out our concept of the female? All we are told is that she was Adam's first wife, that she had beautiful hair, and, most importantly, that she is seductive and a danger to young men. She is associated with the night by both but Mann does not emphasize the permanence of her conquests as Goethe does.[20] Another reason why Lilith might be more appropriate than Eve for Mann is that Eve is the mother of mankind. An important aspect of Hans' attraction to Clavdia is her inability to be mother. It is the same purely erotic and infertile feeling that had bound him to Pribislav Hippe. What matters here is that, although Eve may be relevant enough to Clavdia in her connection with the temptation to eat of the tree of knowledge and her closeness to the serpent, Lilith carries the seductive qualities of the first woman. Clavdia is not man's loyal mate. What we do derive from this association, then, is an erotic attraction and a kind of demonic, somehow dangerous seduction that we may ascribe to the female. So far, motherliness, the kind of concern for others that was mentioned in the introduction, is not part of our female portrait.

Another specific and traditional figure, one that we see behind Clavdia repeatedly, is Carmen. Here, the reference, unlike that to Lilith, concerns the opera as a whole as both Hans and Joachim are at times identified

---

[19] Herman Meyer, in *Das Zitat in der Erzählkunst* (Stuttgart, 1967), comments on the ironies of this usage.

[20] Mephistopheles: Note her especially,
   'T is Lilith.
   Faust: Who?
   Mephistopheles: Adam's first wife is she.
Beware the lure within her lovely tresses,
The splendid sole adornment of her hair!
When she succeeds therewith a youth to snare,
Not soon again she frees him from her jesses.
Goethe's *Faust*, trans. by Bayard Taylor (New York, 1950), pp. 157-158.

with Don José. But for now we are interested in Clavdia only. How does the Carmen background underline certain existing qualities or add new ones to Mme Chauchat's character? Like Lilith, Carmen is a seductive woman. Indicating an association in Hans' mind between Clavdia and Carmen also emphasizes the exoticism of Mme Chauchat which is usually conveyed through that in her which is specifically Slavic—the slant eyes and high cheek bones, for instance. Like Carmen, Clavdia is a "gypsy" —she roams the spas of Europe, having no real attachment to her home in Daghestan. Her conviction that it is better to adventure in sin, to live dangerously, though more intellectualized and self-conscious, is reminiscent of the spontaneous abandon of the gypsy, an attitude more amoral than immoral. "Quant à moi, tu sais, j'aime la liberté avant tout", says Clavdia to Hans during carnival night. And liberty is what Carmen is after. ("Et surtout la chose enivrante, la liberté! la liberté!" and "Jamais Carmen ne cédera, Libre elle est née et libre elle mourra.") [21] Clavdia's refusal to be faithful to a lover is also reminiscent of Carmen. From the Carmen connection, then, confirmation comes of the seductive and erotically potent aspects of the female image that we saw in Lilith. What is added? Beauty, eroticism, the dangers of seduction—all these the two figures have in common. The obsession with liberty is the most significant new contribution, with the succession of lovers resulting from it. For Clavdia at least the attachment to freedom is not merely a justification for promiscuity. Her relation to Peeperkorn is not the wild instinctual choice of a Carmen; as we have said, it is a passive reaction, though not the passive reaction associated with sexual servility. If Clavdia is in some ways a ministering woman for Peeperkorn, and she is frequently referred to as "serving" him, and Hans calls her Peeperkorn's thrall (*Hörige*), then it follows from a feeling of the spiritual, or more accurately, emotional superiority and majesty of the man. It is the same sort of awe that Hans feels for Peeperkorn and that makes him also to some extent serve the older man. Her desire for freedom, then, is not a rationalization of hedonism. But how does it coexist with what we have earlier called passivity and attributed to the female principle? How can Clavdia flaunt her liberty and then admit to Hans that she had to stay with Peeperkorn because he chose her? Apparently freedom means to Clavdia absence of external restraints—especially valuable to her, she says, is the liberty to choose her own domicile. It is important to her

---

[21] Georges Bizet, *Carmen*, words by H. Meilhac and L. Halevy (New York, 1958), pp. 382 and 207.

not to establish personal commitments that would set up certain justified expectations. She seems afraid to commit herself in any way. Thus, from what we know, she has made no promises to Hans during carnival night, though the probability of return at some time has been mentioned. When she does return and Hans tells her that he has waited, she feels compelled not only to state but also to hear Hans admit that no such promises had been made, and that he had waited without any encouragement. Liberty, then, to Clavdia is this openness, this lack of definition in human relations. It is questionable whether this is a tenable position—whether, that is to say, lack of commitment is not already commitment of some sort. An acknowledgment that it is indeed so, another aspect of the same problem of liberty, is Clavdia's reactive nature, her passivity, which we already discussed. She senses that active commitment limits and defines one, that an active exercise of liberty inhibits future choices. Thus Clavdia's love of liberty is directly and essentially connected with the whole complex of qualities which we proposed at the outset as part of a tentative definition of the female principle—passivity, openness, and a relative lack of individuation, at least in the sense of a set of irrevocable and binding commitments that are eventually felt to be imprisoning.

Clavdia is passive because she feels that active choice sets up expectations in others and hence obligations for her that would limit what to her is liberty. She is thus more "open" and less imprisoned in a self that is walled around by slowly accruing precedent, by sets of decisions that start to imply consistency. After all, some such core of continuity is what being a self, what individuation implies. As much as possible, Clavdia wants to avoid such commitment. And the measure of her success is her very transparency. She seems highly individual physically. The author's striking description of her body and physiognomy, of her exoticism and her defects, takes care of that, though even physically she is not unique. She shares appearance and voice with Pribislav, and that sharing is, as I pointed out, an important part of her attraction. In Hans' dreams she not only merges with the boy but gradually comes to stand for a generic and symbolic human body and Life itself. Spiritually, transparency is even more easily achieved—Clavdia quickly comes to stand for disease, for the mountain, for the fascinations of death and their dialectical reversal into life. That she must do so is part of the design of the author. But that she can be made to do so with seeming naturalness and inevitability is due to Mann's skill in establishing Clavdia as a representative of the female principle and in making the latter stand for certain qualities. This is why the Body of Life in Hans' dream still retains, even in its symbolic apotheosis, some feminine characteristics.

Liberty, then, is in Clavdia's attitude consistent with passivity, with a reactive and open rather than a sharply assertive self. That this is indeed her attitude can be seen from her statements about liberty as well as from her avoidance of commitment. But she goes farther than that. Not content with guarding against further definition of her individuality, she speaks of a destruction of the already existing individuality, of self-abandonment. When Hans inquires about the subject of her conversations with the Russian guest she frequently receives, Clavdia tells him they speak of morality. What have they decided about morality, Hans, always eager to learn, asks immediately. In order to be a moralist, one needs to adventure in evil, she answers. This adventuring takes the form of loss of individuality, of a deliberate abandonment of the self.

Eh bien, il nous semble, qu'il faudrait chercher la morale non dans la vertu, c'est-à-dire dans la raison, la discipline, les bonnes mœurs, l'honnêteté — mais, plutôt dans le contraire, je veux dire: dans le péché, en s'abandonnant au danger, à ce qu'il est nuisible, à ce qui nous consume. Il nous semble qu'il est plus moral de se perdre et même de se laisser dépérir que de se conserver.[22]

And yet this self-loss, even though said to be more moral in the long run, is identified with sin. In a later conversation, Clavdia accuses Hans of lacking the capacity or the desire to give up the self.

"I am extraordinarily relieved", she said, breathing out, as she spoke, the smoke she had inhaled, "to hear that you are not a passionate man. But how should you be? You would have degenerated. Passionate—that means to live for sake of experience. Passion, that is self-forgetfulness. But what you all want is self-enrichment. C'est ça. You can't realize what revolting egoism it is, and that one day it will make you an enemy of the human race?"[23]

Weigand[24] sees an accusation of German character in the generalization that Clavdia makes when she goes from the polite "Sie" to the second person plural. It would support my thesis of the difference between male and female attitudes in relation to individuation to construe the form as referring to men as contrasted with women. Since the critique of German nature and various juxtapositions between classical Western attitudes and

[22] *The Magic Mountain*, p. 340.
[23] *The Magic Mountain*, p. 594. The German pronoun in the last sentence is second person *plural*, as is the noun, but that does not solve the problem of whether the "enemies" are men or Germans.
[24] P. 136.

Russian ones are admittedly important in the work, such an interpretation
may do violence to the text as a whole. Still, the possibility is at least
worth suggesting, especially since Hans immediately responds with a
statement about male-female polarity rather than one of national character.
What is there behind such an accusation that you are really and
specifically getting at, he asks,—you women rarely speak impersonally
and abstractly.

Whether Clavdia means to criticize Hans as a male or as a German,
however, she is speaking against self-enrichment, even in the spiritual
guise in which it appears in the book. Not only does Clavdia speak for
the forgetting of the self. There is in her very portrayal a lack of the
feeling of an individual self growing within time, as there is with Hans.
Like Gerda, Clavdia does not seem to change physically. When she
returns to Berghof, she looks exactly the same as she did when she left.
A confirmation of the privileged position of the female principle in
relation to time, this permanence is at the same time a sacrifice of the
kind of self-enrichment which Clavdia credits to Hans. Hans changes as
a result of accruing to his self the various things he learns painstakingly
and sometimes painfully, by no means only through selfish acquisition.
As he points out, there is a fluid boundary between selfishness and
abandonment, and he can grow precisely because he is willing to risk
himself when necessary, to take the road to life that leads through death.
We never really see Clavdia "abandon" herself. Her passivity, especially
in relation to Peeperkorn, seems more like a painless built-in forgetting
of the self, stemming from an initial commitment that may have been
her choice, but is more likely to derive from her femininity. If Clavdia is
the foe of the principle of individuation that she seems to be, then some
allusions in the work gain considerable significance in the argument.
I am speaking of several indirect references to the realm of Dionysus.
And, according to Nietzsche, the very essence of the Dionysian spirit is
the breakdown of the principium individuationis, the rigid boundaries
between man and man, and man and nature. We have seen references
to Nietzsche's catlike woman earlier. In the same passage of *Ecce Homo*,
Nietzsche calls women "amiable Maenads".[25] Nietzsche's conjunction of
the catlike and the maenadic, however, does not suffice to connect
kittenish Clavdia with Dionysus. Are there more specific connections
between the unselving Dionysian realm and the characterization of Mme
Chauchat?

---

[25] *Ecce Homo,* p. 65.

In addition to Clavdia's remarks about the desirability of self-loss and her association with transparency, there are aspects of her portrayal by the author that suggest such a connection. In spite of Clavdia's teasing and carping remarks about the "phlegmatic passions" that Hans ascribes to himself, Mme Chauchat herself does not appear very passionate. As we see her, those passions that she is hinted to have are controlled, seen at a detached distance, even by herself. The tone of her voice when we do "hear" it is usually ironic. She awakens passions in Hans, but neither he nor the reader can assume that she really shares them. Yet, behind her conversation and behind her acts we can sense the more vivid counterparts, the sources of her superficial and seemingly merely unmannerly vices. Hans feels the connection between her nailbiting and doorslamming and her surrender to disease in which, in turn, he can by now sense the voluntary complicity that ties it to Mme Chauchat's desire for freedom. I have tried to analyze this desire for freedom. Now I shall, like Hans, try to look beyond the seemingly cool portrayal of Clavdia to see if, beyond her capacity to waken passions, she herself might have connections with the realm of passion represented by Dionysus. We could glimpse Lilith and Carmen in her background, types of seductresses. But, in order to strengthen the important connection with abolition of individuation, it would be helpful to see more specifically Dionysian features.

Clavdia is no raging maenad. Mann knew this type well and could portray it when he needed to do so. In the Joseph-novels Eni is stylized in this way.[26] Eni, however, leaves her femininity behind and betrays the female principle when her pursuit of Joseph becomes too aggressive. Thus, the "female principle," though it is significantly related to the Dionysian one, is by no means equivalent to it. The passivity, for instance, that was singled out as a pervasive characteristic in Clavdia and proposed as an aspect of the female principle, does not mesh with the Dionysian.

Clavdia has both—passivity and Dionysian ties, not only in the general deindividuating tendency, but also more particularly. Earlier I spoke of the importance of her clothing in a different connection. Now, its color may have significance. Except for the *Walpurgis Night* scene when she wears the snakelike dress, Mme Chauchat frequently wears white on important occasions. In the first dream, when he makes the important connection of Clavdia with Hippe, Hans sees her in white. At the initial

---

[26] "... for I am presently on the point of stylizing the passion of Potiphar's wife in a Dionysian, Maenadic way," Mann writes in a letter. Thomas Mann-Karl Kerényi, *Gespräch in Briefen*, p. 66.

lecture where Krokowski speaks of the connection between suppressed eroticism and disease, Hans can watch the incarnation of the statement as Clavdia sits in front of him. Her clothing again is important, since the transparent sleeves of her blouse start Hans' rumination on the way women dress. But the blouse is white. So is the lace morning gown that Hans so loves. Later, as Hans meets Clavdia on his morning walk she is, as we saw earlier, all in white. The white sweater appears again on the day of her departure.

As the emphasis on Clavdia's bone structure connects her with the symbolic body that Hans saw in his vision as the image of life, so her white clothing links her influence on Hans with the most important vision he has—a vision that takes place in snow. It can also be taken as a Dionysian note. Karl Kerényi, in noting that dark clothing was originally worn for the Eleusinian mysteries, goes on to say: "White garments were first introduced into the festival in A.D. 168. Probably this was due to the influence of the Egyptian mysteries, the cult of Isis, of which such white linen garments were characteristic." [27]

Clavdia's association with the conjunction of sun and moon may also have implications beyond those of East against West. As I said, Hans connects her to the youthful experience when he saw day and night simultaneously while sitting in a boat. On that bright autumn morning, as Hans encounters Mme Chauchat in white, sun and moon again can be seen at the same time. A similar conjunction occurs on the night of the new moon at the celebration of the Greek Panathenaia festival when sun and moon seem to meet.[28]

The antagonism of the female principle to the principle of individuation and generally to lucid articulate expression can be seen in a contempt for words that is frequently associated with it. Women are not necessarily inarticulate—Clavdia's French seems fluent and at times elegant, though her German has a fractured charm that arouses ambivalent feelings in Hans. She never writes letters. Her negligent nature has no respect for the form and rhetoric that to Settembrini is the very discipline of life. Asked by Hans if Mme Chauchat ever writes to him, Behrens laughs:

"Lord bless you!" Behrens answered, "she'd never think of it. In the first place, she's too lazy, and in the second—how could she? I can't read Russian, though I can jabber it, after a fashion, when I have to, but I can't read a word—nor you

---

[27] Kerényi, *Eleusis*, p. 64.

[28] Karl Kerényi, *Die Jungfrau und Mutter der griechischen Religion* (Zürich, 1952), pp. 41-42.

either, I should suppose. And the puss can purr fast enough in French, or in book German, but writing—it would floor her altogether. Think of the spelling! . . . .[29]

When it comes to talk of love, Hans is the one that stammers ("lallen" is the verb used, the same one that was used to describe the archaic appeal of certain names in the essay discussed above). His speech is no more the clearly articulated, rhetorically respectable talk of Settembrini's Western man. It is no more the individual that is speaking but rather something trying to express itself through him. Love is, after all, a renunciation of the boundaries of individuation. In the Joseph-novels a vague sense that by renouncing clear articulate speech she is somehow also shedding individual responsibility for what she is saying drives Eni to bite her lip and thus give herself a lisp before she offers herself to Joseph.[30] This principle, I noted earlier, also determined Mann's choice of the name "Chauchat."

Clavdia's effect on Hans fits well into a Dionysian conception—it is intoxication that she produces in him. He has fever; he lives as in a fog which he thinks the doctors would diagnose as the chemical result of poisons set loose in his body. But, most importantly, not only does he love Clavdia, the mediator of his trance—he loves the intoxication for its own sake.

For that is an intoxication, by which one is possessed, under the influence of which one abhors nothing more than the thought of sobriety. It asserts itself against impressions that would weaken its force, it will not admit them, it wards them off . . . . But he was enraptured not so much because she looked so charming, as because her charm added strength to the sweet intoxication in his brain, the intoxication that willed to be, that cared only to be justified and nourished.[31]

And Dionysus is, after all, the god of intoxication.

These points have shown the closeness of the female principle (here seen in its partial incarnation in Clavdia) to a realm of passion which

---

[29] *The Magic Mountain,* p. 353.

[30] Kerényi identifies this with the maenadic, as he compliments Mann on the perfect touch in inventing the melting words on the painful tongue. *Gespräch in Briefen,* p. 77.

[31] *The Magic Mountain,* p. 227. Mrs. Lowe-Porter translates the first description of Hans' intoxication as that "by which one is possessed." The German phrase is "dem es um sich selber zu tun ist" or that "which is concerned with itself." In the translation the sense of love for love, of transcendence, is entirely lost. This point will gain importance later in my argument. Though it is documented elsewhere in the passage and the work, I would not want a difference in translation to obscure an explicit statement of it.

need not be seen exclusively as Dionysian, though the connection helps to clarify and dramatize it. Finally, this closeness is stated by the author explicitly during the *Walpurgis Night* episode. As he is taking the symbolically fraught step of asking Clavdia for a pencil, Hans is physically transfixed by the knowledge of what he is doing—pale as a corpse, trembling, his heart pounding, he presents a pitiful spectacle. But Clavdia has no pity for such ailments. This lack of pity and the consequent superiority in the realm of passion is, significantly, ascribed to her sex.

The sex knows no such compassion, no mercy for the pangs that passion brings; in that element the woman is far more at home than the man, to whom, by his very nature, it is foreign. Nor does she ever encounter him in it save with mocking and malignant joy . . . .[32]

This is not to say that all women have this gift and all men do not. Not all women represent the female principle, and some men do, at least partly. But let us first look at the other side of the dialectic—at a relatively pure representation of the male principle.

[32] *The Magic Mountain*, p. 332.

AN EARLY VIEW OF THE MALE REALM:
GUSTAVE ASCHENBACH

Gustave Aschenbach lives the life of the closed fist, an image that is to become an emblem of the male principle in Mann's work. "You see, Aschenbach has always lived like this," says one of his contemporaries, tightening his fingers into a fist; "never like this"—letting the fingers hang loose over the back of a chair.[1] Significantly, a gesture is used rather than words. The same gesture is invoked again and again in Mann's work to objectify his feeling about the contrasting attitudes toward living that can be focussed in the opposition of the male and female principle.

What is the significant difference between the closed fist and the open hand? One is an easy gesture, relaxed and submissive to the natural force of gravity; the other requires sustained effort and concentration, a refusal to let go. When open, the hand can give and take, expose its sensitive palm to the touch of things and people. The closed fist refuses such contact. It guards itself and whatever it may enclose—there can be no giving or taking. Yet an artist creates in response to an exchange with the outside world. The human feeling symbolized in his art is not merely his own feeling. Even if it were, feeling cannot feed on itself forever. Neither should the artist's symbolism be an exclusive and private one. Aschenbach, then, is bound to have difficulties in growing or even maintaining himself as a working artist.

When this comparison first occurs, the closed fist appears to denote Aschenbach's tension and his self-discipline more than his isolation. Yet from the description of his life it is clear that the writer is lonely. No wonder, then, that he should think of his creative powers as of a fixed reservoir that is getting depleted without replenishment and needs to be carefully husbanded. ("... with the increasing exhaustibility of his powers.") The walk that is to set the events of the novella in motion is necessitated by Aschenbach's preoccupation with his current project. The

---

[1] *Death in Venice,* transl. by H. T. Lowe-Porter (New York, 1930), pp. 16-17.

strangely mechanical image used to describe this preoccupation is telling: it is a "rotation of the productive mechanism within him." Perhaps the mechanism cannot stop because there is no friction, no real connection with the external world. The desire to travel, then, that overwhelms Aschenbach in the course of the walk is an instinctive attempt to stop the merely compulsive perpetuation of the mechanism, to escape, primarily. But behind it there may also be a half conscious further need to enrich the creative reservoir by fruitful contact with the outside. This lust for travel is a desire to get out not only from the confines of accustomed surroundings but also from those of the rigidly circumscribed self.

This breaking of individuation is a mark of the female principle. In the guise of "Wanderlust," the simple striving out with no definite goal, the revulsion at being limited and confined is especially evident. Even when Aschenbach's longing attaches itself to a locale in a vision, this locale itself confirms the wish to go beyond the self. It is a place we have already associated with the female principle—a swamp.[2] Luxuriant, crawling with tropical vegetation and exotic animal life, this graphically visualized swamp is a fitting contrast to the economy and careful preservation of creative powers, the self-imposed discipline of Aschenbach. Here fertility has run amuck and proliferates itself without heeding any apparent law of allocation or even purpose. It is the vision of a world that Aschenbach is to find realized half literally, half symbolically in Venice.

Demanding in his judgment of his own writing, Aschenbach, we are told, has suppressed and cooled feeling in the service of perfection of form. Though it is not simply an outpouring of personal emotion, art deals with feeling. The perfection that an artist seeks is the closest attunement of form to the human feeling that it symbolizes.[3] The vengeful eruption of the repressed feelings, then, is a belated and violent correction not only of a personal psychological imbalance but also of an artistic one.

We are given a detailed account of Aschenbach's work and his early life, even his ancestry. At first, only male ancestors are mentioned. Officers, judges, administrators, even a preacher are among them—a long line of respectable and honorable men. Surely there must have been women for the line continues, but they are ignored. At last, one is singled out—the writer's mother. Through her, new and different blood is added to the race. More sensual blood, quicker, Mann tells us, and, most

[2] See Chapter 1.
[3] Susanne Langer, *Feeling and Form,* esp. Chapter 4.

importantly, an infusion that could produce the artist. The recurrence of this constellation in Mann's work proves its deep-seated and constant nature. Mann's own family background, in some ways gratifyingly similar to Goethe's, has something to do with this recurrence. But this is not only or finally a comment on actual family situations or even on fundamental sex differences. Rather, it evolves into a symbolic commentary on two ways of being. Here a woman brings the relaxation and widening that we have associated with the female principle into a line of sober and conscientious clerks. The artist emerges only after this confluence.[4] Like Clavdia, Aschenbach's mother is exotic—the son has inherited some foreign facial traits from her. Women are frequently "foreign" in Mann's novels. Making them foreign to the setting in which they appear emphasizes their openness, their lack of strong and confining ties to the locale. They have a privileged position in space as well as in time.

If travel means venturing out not only of accustomed surroundings but also of the domesticated self that is in tune with these surroundings, Aschenbach's earlier view of travel is an extension of his desire to enclose. Such contact with the outside world as is absolutely necessary is confined to a world that is not only familiar but really an extension of the writer's personality, one that does not challenge his mode of existence but reinforces it at every step. Aschenbach's place in the country is described as "rough." It is also lonely and isolated. The maid and the servant who share the small house with him are seen as appurtenances rather than human beings, mere functions—"the maid who prepared his meals and the servant who served them up for him." They hold no possibility for personal relationship, no latent power to surprise. They confirm Aschenbach's isolation. Other people have the same functionally circumscribed relationship to him. They are seen either as patron or public—the readers of his books, including the schoolchildren whose curriculum eventually comes to encompass them, the nobleman who confers a title on the author. In passing, we are told that he has been briefly but happily married. He even has a daughter, now married herself. But these are mere biographical facts; the experiences have left no permanent traces on Aschenbach, at least none that we are ever shown. The emblem of the closed fist indicates isolation as well as tension. And the two are related.

---

[4] The artist's mother is already connected with art indirectly. Her father is a bandleader. We might well ask whether music is more closely associated with the female principle than other arts. In Hans Castorp, at least, an increasing dominance of the female element went along with growth in musical interest.

As a sickly boy, Aschenbach is excluded from school and taught privately at home. Thus he is denied the kind of experience that sets up a pained but fruitful tension in another Mann artist—Tonio Kröger. In that novella, the tension is seen as one between Life and Art, and Tonio's continued capacity to produce art derives from this tension. There the fist is forced open, causing much futile longing and humiliation but also enabling the kind of exchange with the outside world that an artist needs to go on. How, then, does Aschenbach succeed in being a good and productive artist for so long?

He does it by maintaining a constant tension *within* himself to replace the lacking one with the external world. The key to his work is his famous dictum that all greatness derives from its genesis as an "in spite of" (*Trotzdem*). Aschenbach's greatest barrier and hence also his most potent incentive is his physical weakness. Laboring on the edge of exhaustion and using this very possibility of exhaustion as a goad, he produces a large body of work. The sign of martyrdom stands over this work—St. Sebastian is seen as the symbol of his art. It is martyrdom because Mann tends to conceive of human productive energy as a given reservoir that, once given, cannot be replenished. Aschenbach's punctiliously proper bourgeois life style is the result of a feeling that such a manner best conserves his energy, not so much, as it is with Tonio, a compensation for the chronically bad conscience of the artist. Martyrdom consists in the knowledge of one's own weakness and exhaustibility. It is, then, inextricably bound to the solipsism of the male principle in its purest form. Aschenbach spins his work out of himself, not attempting or even conceding the possibility of attempting to replenish the dwindling source of energy until it is too late. The recurrent hero of Aschenbach's works, this St. Sebastian figure, is described as "the conception of an intellectual and boyish *masculinity*." Even though Aschenbach gives his work to his contemporaries, he is closed to the world. It can give him nothing that he might be capable of receiving. It is this incapacity to open himself and receive that necessitates economy and discipline. As a last resort he uses this very weakness as a challenge to maintain his artistic productivity. Increasingly he feels a falling off in his work, due not to lack of craftsmanship but to dearth of joyful and spontaneous inspiration. The voyage to Venice is a last desperate attempt to open himself up to enable himself to live and to write. Unlike Tonio who experienced the crisis as a boy and who thus learned to live with and to utilize artistically the intense pleasure and pain of such openness and vulnerability, Aschenbach comes to his crisis too late. Deferred so long, the experience carries him along helplessly and destroys all of the earlier discipline. The female element, the swamp of his vision, engulfs him totally. No dialectic can emerge, and, as a result, there is no new possibility for art, or, finally, even for life. Total openness without content is Death. The fist that has always been closed, has not learned to close itself even partly after being opened.

This openness is the final vengeance of feeling. Aschenbach has subjected his feelings, cooled them and enslaved them. Yet emotion is a necessary slave—it "carries" his art and "gives it wings." Once it is totally subdued, the chafing of this slave can no more provide the artificially set up internal dialectic that is vital to Aschenbach in the absence of a dynamic interchange with the external world. An artist such as Aschenbach is headed for eventual emptiness or catastrophe. No wonder, then, that at the beginning of the novella his work is described as "dangerous." Perhaps more significant yet is the image of artistic production as an internal productive *mechanism*. A Ciceronian phrase is also used—"motus animi continuus"—a self-contained process, with no apparent need for the outside, a perpetuum mobile almost where such contact would mean friction and thus cause the movement to slow down and stop.

The enslavement of feeling is one aspect of Aschenbach's substitution of art for life. Mann's heroes have complex and ambivalent views about the relationship of life and art, and their various maladjustments appear to be caused by such notions. Dominated almost entirely by the spiritually demanding yet enclosing male principle, Aschenbach cannot find new energy and hence needs to allocate his powers jealously between art and life. His face, we are told, appeared to be lined by a life full of exciting adventures, even by unruly passions and pleasures. Yet it was really art that had here undertaken the task of life. Art becomes a vicarious experience of the life which cannot be enjoyed if one has chosen art.

But Aschenbach does give his work to the world, one might argue. That surely is a communication of sorts. More than that, the work is appreciatively received—received because of a hidden compatibility between the fate of the author and that of his contemporaries, because of "sympathy." This similarity, however, does not stem from Aschenbach's awareness of the fate of those around him. It is a historical accident that his fate resembles that of many others. His own problems and concerns, his own face are what he projects in various guises in his work. Even his surroundings are an extension of his personality. The Spartan setting of the country house was mentioned already. As a symbolic landscape, one that is actually a projection of an attitude or an emotional state, it contrasts with the dominant landscape of the novella—Venice, as well as with the exotic swamp that is a symbolic evocation and foreshadowing of Venice. If Venice is to become an objectification of the female principle, the setting of Aschenbach's country house can be clearly connected with the male principle. It is in the mountains, among peaks and high walls, encouraging as well as reflecting the writer's own walled in, isolated state. A harsh scenery, difficult of access and control, it is also full of challenge. Its astringent effect discourages passive relaxation. To make it quite clear that spending summers there is a hygienic measure, the narrator wants us to know that they were rainy summers.

Perhaps the most important quality of Aschenbach's summer retreat is its utter loneliness. It reflects Aschenbach's own isolation and guarantees it. He has not travelled elsewhere because he has been too occupied with the duties set him by "his ego and the European soul." The two seem closely associated, almost identical, and the priority of the self indicates that even Aschenbach's "European soul" is a projection of his own. Preoccupied with these, the writer cannot afford to be "a lover of the colorful outside world." (Another clue that the European soul is not part of this outside world but rather of his interior one.)

The meeting with the redhaired stranger not only precipitates Aschenbach's flight from work but it also sharpens his fear of the sterility that this isolation brings. Travel, then, he must—first of all to indulge a whim but in a deeper and only vaguely sensed way perhaps also to regain artistic productivity. Where should he go? The destination is at first vague, but two significant qualities already occur to Aschenbach. These come to mind first, and thus seem to be connected with the needs that impel him to travel. He wants to go South. And he is looking for a resort of wide appeal and varied clientele—an "Allerweltsferienplatz." North against South—this is another version of the dialectic. The other demand—that it be a bustling public resort—stresses Aschenbach's desperate need to break out of his isolation.

What he sought, Mann tells us, was the alien or exotic and the unrelated. Both concepts are relative—alien to whom, unrelated to what? Surely it must be to himself, the enclosed self seeking an outlet to the other. And it turns out that there is, after all, one particular destination that best fulfills these demands. It is Venice. A visit to an

Adriatic island is seen as a false start, and when Aschenbach finally thinks of going to Venice, the decision is at the same time surprising and self evident.

Why Venice? As the novella unfolds, the events connected with the Venetian epidemic serve as an enlarged objectification of Aschenbach's emotional life. But the disease could occur in another place as well. The city itself stands for the female principle, purified and concentrated so much that it is bound to hold danger for Aschenbach. Even the plague that befalls it seems not so much an external visitation as a necessary and inevitable excretion of the very nature of the place. It is so in realistic terms. The marshes help the disease to breed. So do the stagnant canals and the sirocco. But the cholera seems to be as much an efflorescence of an inward corruption. Unlike the Ganges delta, the primeval swamp of the tiger where the disease arose, Venice is a swamp raised to a psychological level, one that makes the inherent symbolism of the dream locale more explicit. The illness intensifies and brings out into the open the evils and corruptions of the city—the greed, disloyalty, and deceit of its inhabitants as well as the communal vices of public secrecy and prostitution. It does not create those vices; it merely heightens them and makes them more apparent. In this process of dissolution the city serves as a symbol for Aschenbach's state of mind.

Venice, then, because it can serve as a reflection of Aschenbach's feelings. A swamp both realistically and symbolically, Venice is occasionally portrayed as a woman by poets. Perhaps best known is Rilke's equation of the city with a courtesan in his poem "Die Kurtisane." It is a symbolic Woman here as well, an objectification of all the aspects of the female principle. This concentration allows it not only to mirror Aschenbach's emotional life but also to precipitate it by focussing the events leading to his death into properly novellistic form. Venice is to him "the most improbable of cities." In it, Aschenbach feels dissociated in time, space, and moral responsibility from all ties of his earlier life. And the epidemic which seems at first to inhibit his enjoyment of the place, becomes more and more an enhancement of those qualities in it that Aschenbach instinctively sought. It goads him on in feverish pursuit of Tadzio by holding out the wild hope of total collapse of civilized restrictions. In this "improbable" city probabilities need not be weighed realistically. Once in it, Aschenbach is symbolically set adrift, as he is literally adrift much of the time he spends getting there and even afterwards.

The arrival, Aschenbach had felt, must be by the sea route. On earlier visits he had come by land, but this time it would not do. To arrive at the railroad station would be like entering the palace by a back door. But the sea voyage itself is significant, and one of the attractions of Venice is its proximity to the sea. Here used as a counterpoint to the mountain retreat, the sea is a recurrent locale in Mann's work. Aschenbach senses its power. When the ship starts moving he feels an "unreasonable" shock. The severance from land is felt in all its symbolic weight. Though this is by no means the only value that an artist may impute to the sea, to Mann it constantly carries the associations of the female—mystical unselving, lack of determinate structure and articulation, the impossibility to impose space and time dimensions. When Aschenbach sits by the sea, as he is to do much of the time from now on, he "lets his eyes lose themselves in the reaches of the sea, lets his gaze glide away . . . ." His love of the sea, we are told:

> . . . had profound sources: the hard worked artist's longing for rest, his yearning to seek refuge from the thronging manifold shapes of his fancy in the bosom of the simple and vast; and another yearning, opposed to his art and perhaps for that very reason a lure, for the unorganised, the immeasurable, the eternal—in short, for nothingness.[5]

It is the enmity toward articulation and individuation that characterizes the female principle. To submit to it completely is to stop being an artist for it means ceasing to articulate human feeling with precision.

On the second day of his stay on the Lido, the writer is sitting by the sea, with his portable typewriter on his knees, trying to catch up on some correspondence. But writing seems futile, an "indifferent occupation" in view of the sea. He pushes the writing materials aside and turns to the sea. He is to do this again and again until even the half-hearted attempt at articulation becomes mere pretense. Aschenbach needed to open himself to the outside world in order to remain productive as an artist. And we are indeed shown the briefly beneficial effects of this renewal of his emotional life. In the end, the deprivations turns out to have been too long and too rigid so that the swing to openness goes all the way to extinction of individual form and to Nothingness. But at first there are moments when the new wealth of feeling demands articulation, moments of achieved transcendence when thoughts of Tadzio bear fruit as art or meditation. The first appearance of the boy leads

[5] Pp. 60-61.

Aschenbach to abstract and deep thought on beauty and the problems of form and art. And it is by the sea that he writes a single last gemlike essay.

The sea is described as having a "quiet even rhythm." The same word is used to portray Aschenbach's days at the resort. The conventional divisions of time are gradually dissolved as are those of space. As Aschenbach becomes engulfed by the female principle time ceases to exist for him. Instead there is the personal time perspective of the dream, a strenuous attempt at reversing time through cosmetic rejuvenation, and the timeless vision of the myth.

Gushes of cold water over chest and back, two or three hours of intense writing, lunch, a nap—this, along with an occasional hygienic walk, had been Aschenbach's day. Conscious of the need to husband time as well as energy, he has divided his days into small, neatly separated, and regularly recurring parcels. A wider annual cycle includes the summer stay in the mountains. Venice not only breaks the long term pattern in place and time, but completely dissolves the daily rhythm as well. As he sails for Venice, Aschenbach rests on deck with a book in his lap and finds the hours slipping by unnoticed. Once at the Lido, he spends long leisurely hours on the beach, and his days are punctuated only by the appearances of Tadzio. Described in terms utterly different from Aschenbach's routine in Munich, it is now a time of "lightly ordered leisure adorned with innumerable closely packed chances of lovely coincidences." Such structuring as still exists is not predetermined but rather the result of accident, luck—a force beyond Aschenbach's control. The natural attitude to adopt, then, is one of watchful waiting or, to put it in terms that stress Aschenbach's growing involvement with the female principle, of passivity. He no longer keeps track of elapsed vacation time, no more even thinks of going home. The days are "deliciously monotonous." The linear time of practical reckoning opens up into myth.

The most prominent mythical figure is the boy Tadzio, seen at times as Phaedrus, at times as Eros, Hermes, or Hyakinthos. But Aschenbach's own existence, his surroundings, everything that happens to him becomes transfigured and mythical. Time loosens up and doubles back when within the same hour Aschenbach bids farewell to Venice while gliding through the Grand Canal, only to return along the same route, sheepishly happy and relieved that an opportune accident has made it possible for him to reverse his decision to leave. At first, the direction of time is merely reversed. In a vision, he goes back in time, seeing himself as a gently ironic Socrates courting Tadzio-Phaedrus. Then, linearity ceases altogether and all is myth. Sitting by an open window, the writer watches a sunrise that appears to him as enactment of myth. As the day goes on, white clouds seem to him flocks of gods or Poseidon's horses. He is engulfed in "a world possessed, peopled by Pan." [6]

Aschenbach would also stop time for Tadzio. Going up in the hotel elevator with him, the writer catches a close look at his idol. The boy's teeth are bad, he notices, uneven and pale, strangely transparent. From that, Aschenbach deduces that the youth is delicate and sickly. "Probably he will not get old," he thinks, refusing to analyze the feeling of satisfaction that overcomes him at the thought. He does not want Tadzio to change. He wants to take him out of time. An early death will ensure him against the disfigurement of age. This happens early in the affair. As Aschenbach himself gets beyond time consciousness, as he relinquishes any desire to control it and lets it wash over him in an unstructured flow, he need no more fear change in Tadzio. As a god the loved one is safe from time.

The qualities of the female principle all work together here. The desire for a special status in time goes along with increasing openness, the shattering of the limits of individuation. To see a mythical figure beyond an actual one is to reduce the individual value of the latter, though it may increase his stature. It is also to transpose him within or beyond time. To dream is to suspend realistic time sequences, but the dream is to Mann also the prime example of the melting of individual limits.[7] The third traceable strand in the web of the female principle was passivity. It is a condition for the achievement of the other two. For Aschenbach to relinquish his control of time or to leave the places and commitments that defined his personality, later to get out of that very personality, there has first to be a relaxation of the will.

One of the most striking objectifications of this loosening of volition is the succession of conveyances in *Death in Venice*. Aschenbach walks briskly as we first meet him. To get back home, he takes the tram. A night train brings him to Trieste, and from then on, he always travels by waterway. A ship brings him to the Adriatic island on his failed attempt to seek out a dimly sensed destination. Realizing the mistake, he boards a motorboat, touching land only long enough to board another

---

[6] *Death in Venice*, p. 99.
[7] See Chapter 6.

ship, this time for Venice, the predestined place. With that instinctive moment of fear at being adrift, Aschenbach frees himself of old associations. He has relinquished control. That capitulation is confirmed as he is transferred to a gondola, this time directly from the ship, without touching land at all. Again, a hidden fear possesses him on boarding. He shudders. No wonder, comments the narrator, for the Venetian gondola, archaic and black, evokes awesome thoughts of death. But in this context, more important than these external associations of hushed solemnity and funeral dark is the dissolution of the will that binds the sensations of the passenger to the experience of dying. The seat, Aschenbach finds, is the softest, most luxurious, most relaxing seat in the world. He closes his eyes and enjoys an uncommon moment of "sweet passivity." (The word used here is again *Lässigkeit,* one whose wide and significant implications were discussed earlier.) The gondolier's rude and determined insistence to take Aschenbach all the way to the Lido rather than to the steamer station where he wants to go has a briefly astringent effect, as Aschenbach pulls himself together in a last effort to preserve the semblance of self-assertion and self-determination.

But it is mere atavistic ritual, dutiful satisfaction of remembered conventions. A hypnotic spell seems to emanate from the soft cushions, and even the thought that the gondolier might be a criminal stealthily waiting to beat his passenger to death to get his money fails to penetrate the trance. The insouciance of the hired man sweeps away the vestiges of active determination and even resistance within Aschenbach. It seals his passivity by showing his shameless acquiescence and positive enjoyment of this impudent and tyrannical oarsman. A last attempt to show initiative by sudden departure from the stifling city peters out in sad regret and indecision, until the luckily misdirected luggage allows him to stay with some little face saving. Again, it is the incursion of chance, guidance from the outside that Aschenbach most happily and passively accepts. His posture reflects this increasing relaxation—when he is not sitting in a gondola, he lounges in his beach chair, hands folded in lap, watching Tadzio or waiting for the boy's appearance. There are no more actively brisk walks for Aschenbach. On his visits from Lido to city he either wanders the streets in a daze or slavishly follows Tadzio as though drawn by a magnet.

A more concentrated sign of the change in Aschenbach is the gesture he performs on his return to the hotel after the aborted departure. He is sitting by his open window watching Tadzio. Love for the boy held him back, he is now ready to admit. And a symbolic gesture summarizes and seals his acceptance and final submission to whatever is to come. It is a slowly turning, lifting movement, performed with arms hanging loosely over the arms of the chair, palms outward—an expansion, an opening as well as an embracing. This is the kind of gesture Aschenbach's acquaintance used to illustrate the qualities the artist lacked, contrasting it with the closed fist. Aschenbach's change is thus made dramatically apparent. Even the words used to describe the motion are words that we see again and again in connection with the female principle. The gesture is willing and welcoming; it is relaxed (*gelassen* is used again).

Accepting the finality of Venice, Aschenbach now finds that he can enjoy his stay. Enjoyment is a new sensation. To fit him for it, the faculty of volition needs to be virtually abolished. Now that the process is almost accomplished, Aschenbach feels its necessity. Only this place, he senses, "bewitched him, relaxed his will, made him happy." Note that the three phrases are similar, not set up as equal but rather cumulative and intensifying. Though no conjunctions or other words clarify the relationship, the order itself suggests a crescendo, a groping and growing clarification of what Venice means to Aschenbach. At first, he feels merely enchanted; then he tries to grasp the precise meaning of this enchantment and sees that it consists in a loosening of volition. This freedom then becomes a condition of the final phrase, the ultimate revelation of the nature of his state, one new to him and one that, for him, requires the other two—happiness.

From now on, Aschenbach either sits by the sea or in a gondola. Like Hans, he invites intoxication for its own sake. On two occasions he has a chance to establish a conventional, casually social relationship with the boy. He lets both slip by. As Hans painstakingly avoids such sobering contact, so does Aschenbach. The conversation, as it was between Hans and Clavdia, is a conversation of eyes. This eye contact, as it does elsewhere in Mann's work, creates a state of intense interest, a "hysteria" of suppressed attraction and desire. Lack of opportunity for closer acquaintance guarantees continuity for the enchantment.

The first occasion for civilized contact presents itself one morning when Aschenbach notices Tadzio walking ahead and thinks of adressing the boy in a bantering way. He suppresses the desire, realizing that the trance is dear to him. This trance is ascribed to Aschenbach the artist. The connection between Aschenbach's love for Tadzio as the love of a man for a boy and his artistic longing for Tadzio as a symbol is problematic. It will have to be faced eventually.

To deal with the second chance of Aschenbach to have a conventional relationship with Tadzio, one must go forward in that time which no more exists for the artist. His suspicions of the epidemic, fed by the slyly evasive answers of tourist-greedy Venetians, have been confirmed by an English travel agent. The knowledge excites him, but it also horrifies him. Excitedly he contemplates warning Tadzio's mother to leave the city and thus "flee the swamp" himself. Escape, however, is only a momentary phantasy. It would, he feels "lead him back," "give him back to himself." The words used to show Aschenbach's feelings at this decisive moment are all of this sort, dealing with the self/world relationship. He who is outside (beside) himself has no desire to return within himself, Aschenbach thinks. And here he clearly connects his desire to travel with the desire for psychological extension and openness. Returning home means not only a change in location but also, and to Aschenbach necessarily, emotional sobriety, responsibility, labor. The symbolic function of places is here quite evident. We should remember that Aschenbach's first impulse to travel was accompanied by a feeling of inward expansion.

Venice is the right and necessary place for what was to happen to Aschenbach. If he had any doubt of it, his attempt at departure and the happiness at its defeat removed that. Tadzio is the right and necessary agent of these events. What are the significant qualities that Mann ascribes to Tadzio to make him that?

Aschenbach first sees Tadzio in one of the common rooms of the resort hotel, in midst of a satisfyingly cosmopolitan bustle. Guests, politely ignoring each other, share the pleasant anticipation of dinner. Both the international character of the society and the ritual of a lengthy public meal recall another encounter. Hans Castorp met Clavdia Chauchat in the Berghof dining hall at similarly solemn and plentiful repasts among a similarly international crowd. It is striking and significant that the agents of the female principle should be associated with such recurrent situations. The public nature of the events, Mann's pains to widen the horizons as much as possible, derive from the openness of the female principle. Not only must individual barriers be surmounted—better yet if those of nationality are exploded also. One of the shortcomings of Aschenbach's first try to find the place of his vision was the lack of just this worldliness. The Adriatic island was lovely and exotic, but there were two disappointments. Both have to do with the female principle. There was no free access to the sea. Instead of a smoothly sloping open beach the island sported ragged cliffs, perhaps reminiscent of the rocky

peaks of Aschenbach's usual summer retreat. And the society there
seemed to him depressingly chauvinistic. It was Austrian, and, significantly, "closed." Now, in Venice, all this is righted. Varied in composition,
sophisticated and tolerant, the Lido tourists form a "wide, indulgent
all-embracing horizon."

This search for the widest possible horizon is easily seen as part of
the struggle to break out of the self. Perhaps the association of Clavdia
and Tadzio with meals is not as evident. And yet it is part of the same
striving. The meal (and that may explain its importance not only in these
two but also in many other works of Mann where eating is frequent
and lovingly dwelt upon) is a communal event. Eating is sharing. One
becomes what one eats, and in partaking of the same fare all tend to
become one.[8] In *Death in Venice* the sacramental nature of the meals
is not as clear as it is in *The Magic Mountain,* but the association helps
a reader see the import of a first meeting at dinner.

Tadzio is a boy. Would it not be simpler to have Aschenbach fall
in love with a woman, a young girl perhaps?[9] Making the artist's passion
homosexual renders it, first of all, less common. Also, it makes it less
likely to be consummated and thus better suited to an aesthetic function.
Consummated passion cannot be sublimated into art. The artist wants
to render his love object transparent and use it as a vehicle for personal
transcendence.[10] He might be tempted to think that choosing a lover
who is not easily accessible would ease this transcendence. Even if the
wooing is successful, homosexual love, like incest, stresses the illusory
nature of self-loss in blending with the other. When the other is much
like you—a sister, a brother, even a member of the same sex, Narcissism
and defeat are inevitable.

What makes the choice of the boy as an incarnation of the female
principle even more striking is the exclusive femininity surrounding him.
Three sisters, a lady companion, a mother spoil and pamper the boy
because he is the youngest and beautiful, neither his merit. The severity
of the girls' upbringing is evident in their soberly colorless grooming and
deliberately disfiguring dress. Against the sexlessness of the girls, the
boy appears to be strikingly feminine. His hair is soft and long. Like
that of the Spinnario it falls in soft curls around his face. The delicate

---

[8] Norman Brown, in *Love's Body* (New York, 1966), has in the Chapter "Food"
collected a good array of sources to document such conventional uses of food
symbolism.

[9] Mann originally meant to do that.

[10] See Chapters 2 and 6.

limbs, the grace of movement, the pretty mouth, the fanciful and flattering apparel—all are things usually associated with a girl. Tadzio does not share the rigid stance of his sisters; rather his posture is one of relaxed grace (the word is "lässig" again, tying his appearance to the female realm). Beauty itself can be seen as part of the female principle. It is a state of Being rather than a result of Doing.

Beginning with the first meeting, Tadzio is related to art. Aschenbach approves of the partiality in the children's upbringing: an unfairness, he feels, that produces beauty. He approves of it in his capacity as artist. At the outset it is generally in this role that he contemplates the boy. The perfection of his beauty as yet strikes no desire, only wonder. He counts the beauties of Tadzio's body; they remind him of Greek statues. The dinner table meditations the boy has inspired are vaguely aesthetic. From pondering the precise and mysterious combination of universal and individual ingredients in the beautiful human form he proceeds to "general problems of form and art."

Tadzio's mother, a bejewelled Polish matron, stately and aloof, rounds out the all female entourage. There is no sign or mention of a father. The boy's preferential treatment is seen as a sign of the rule of the mother. She is an imposing matriarch—a woman of large stature, dignity and simplicity governing her appearance and gesture. A small but impressive scene is enacted before the eyes of Aschenbach. Having waited for the mother's appearance before going in to dinner, the children take turns kissing her hand while she restrains herself to a reserved smile and speaks briefly to the governess. A processional ensues as she walks to the dining hall and the girls, in order of their age, follow, in turn followed by the governess and Tadzio. Indeed, a quiet but solemn ritual, centered around the grandiose matriarch, one that glorifies the female aspect of her realm and is to be repeated.

The following morning Aschenbach sees the boy at breakfast. The rest of the family have almost finished eating, and the lenience that lets Tadzio sleep late again inspires Aschenbach to find aesthetic and mythical parallels. This time, he notices the boy's movement, the way he walks, smiles, gestures, and the sheer beauty of feature overwhelms him anew. The mythical transformation deepens, as the beauty somehow seems godlike. And shortly the god is named—Eros, not surprisingly. As yet, the admiration has a cool and detached cast. It is the craftsmanlike tribute of an artist for a masterful work of art.

Tadzio, then, has so far been associated with the realm of the mother, with the communal meal, and with art. Another connection emerges on that same morning. As Aschenbach is meditating on the sea as perfection in nothingness, his lost gaze is brought into focus by a figure crossing the horizon. It is Tadzio, and from now on the beach is inextricably linked with the boy in Aschenbach's mind. Tadzio is at ease in it; it appears to be his element. By association with it, he partakes of the "female," unindividuating and dissolving aspects of the element. Later, Tadzio swims far out into the sea. Called back by anxious women, he runs toward shore, looking to Aschenbach like a god "approaching from the depths of sky and sea." It is a mythical moment, he feels—"like a poetic myth of beginnings, of the origin of form and the birth of gods." The two meet in many places, but it is on the beach that Aschenbach is most assured of seeing Tadzio, and it is there that he most enjoys seeing him. The sea is the foil and background for the leisurely and childish occupations of the boy. When news of the cholera has finally reached Tadzio's family and Aschenbach finds out they are leaving, he walks to the shore to take leave. He watches Tadzio slowly (*lässig* is again the adjective used, as it is too many times to be cited) walk into the sea, along a sandbank in its midst and turn around toward the watcher. It seems to him that Tadzio in motioning to him and, in "following" he dies. This is now the only possible consummation of his love, with death aiding in the final attempt to relinquish the self. And it is fitting that it should happen by the sea.

Tadzio and the sea form a constant visual association. There is another world of sense that Tadzio's presence evokes for Aschenbach—that of sound. Tadzio is Polish. Much of the Eastern European exoticism that adhered to Clavdia by virtue of her Russian origin also clings to the Pole Tadzio. And perhaps it is the even less known sounds of the language that induced Mann to make the boy Polish. It is at breakfast that Aschenbach first hears those sounds. Sitting down belatedly at the family table, Tadzio speaks in a low voice, and Aschenbach hears the language as "softly blurred" (the German term is "verschwommen"—a word whose association with the sea should not be ignored). It is this aspect of it that is constantly emphasized. The melodic calling of the boy's nickname is so indistinctly articulated that it takes Aschenbach some time to piece it together and then to trace it to the full Thaddeus. From there on the novella is punctuated by the calling of Tadzio's name—by playmates who compete for the boy's attention and by the women who constantly hover over him. The beach resounds with the refrain of the name. Its identifying mark is the long drawn-out final "u"-sound. Aschenbach finds the name appropriate for the boy. The euphony seems to suit his beauty; the consonants are "soft," and the name has a quality at the same time sweet and wild. The refrain grows until it sparks a musical response within Aschenbach. While he listens to Tadzio's name he hears an incipient singing within himself. Like he sea and like the increasingly dissolving time, this kind of unarticulated music is a measure of disorganization, of an increasing loss of finite divisions and limits. Later, when Aschenbach overhears Tadzio's childishly eager tales of beach adventures to the women it is again the incomprehensibility of the speech that elevates it. Not a word did the writer understand, we are told, but it is precisely this alienation that transforms language into music.[11] How different this is from Aschenbach's earlier conception of language can be seen from the image he used then to describe it. Not an unarticulated euphonious flow, it was then a massive piece of granite out of which the artist must form the semblance of his vision. But the passion that rules Aschenbach now is a very different passion from that which empowered him to create. That productive feeling was a "sober passion."

Along with the crescendo of Aschenbach's inner music, there is an intensification in awareness of external sounds. From the musicians who try to regale him from a neighboring boat on his first gondola trip, to the performance of a band of streetsingers in the hotel garden, music (and sound generally) permeates the story. The hotel performance is a culmination of the external music at the same time that it marks a high point in Aschenbach's passion. He listens to the concert, sitting not far from Tadzio. The leader of the small troupe, one of the incarnations of the recurring red-haired stranger, carries the atmosphere of disease with him. He assures Aschenbach that all is well in Venice, a lie for which the writer pays him well. The final number he sings is an objectification of the dissolution and total disintegration of the city and of Aschenbach. Again, the words cannot be understood. Mann wants to make sure of that—he tells us that the text was not only in a foreign language, but also in an incomprehensible dialect. A refrain of laughter, one that eventually drowns out the rest of the song and involves the rest of the audience marks the climax of the entertainment. It turns into a wild and uncontrollable paroxysm of communal laughter with only Aschenbach and Tadzio abstaining. Laughter of this sort [12] takes one out of

---

[11] Again the word "verschwommen" is used in an attempt to fix this quality.

[12] *In Doctor Faustus*, Mann develops the theme of laughter, its association with the devil and its use in music, more, consistently and fully.

oneself. Aschenbach feels the hypnotizing and bewitching effect of the laughter in conjunction with the nearness of Tadzio and the carbolic acid smell that reminds him of the cholera. As yet, he retains some individual reserve—he does not join in the laughter.

To say, on this evidence, that music is always an accessory of the female principle would be wrong. The use of music in *The Magic Mountain* and especially the complex problem of the literary usage of music in *Doctor Faustus* would have to be examined first. Still, some kinds of sounds and certain aspects of music seem to go along with the dominance of the female element. Music is also the art most intimately related to time. The female principle has a special association with time too. While articulating experienced, felt time, music tends to facilitate a breakdown of linear, practical time. It should, then, not be surprising that the final dissolution of Aschenbach's sense of time occurs precisely at the end of this performance. After the singers and the other guests have gone, Aschenbach remains seated at his table, over the remains of his grenadine and soda, much to the discomfiture of the waiters:

Time passed, the night went on. Long ago, in his parental home, he had watched the sand filter through an hourglass—he could still see, as though it stood before him, the fragile, pregnant little toy. Soundless and fine the rust-red little stream ran through the narrow neck, and made, as it declined in the upper cavity, an exquisite little vortex.[13]

This is a foreshadowing of the waning of Aschenbach's life. But even more importantly it is an indication of the disappearance of his sense of measured time itself. And it happens in the aftermath of the strolling musicians' performance.

Once Aschenbach's sense of time is undermined, events move swiftly to the destined end. Disease and passion rise to fever pitch. On the following day Aschenbach irrevocably confirms his suspicions about the danger of the epidemic. That night he has a dream. This dream too is a culmination. At home in Munich Aschenbach had employed sleep for revitalizing creative energies; now he expends them in dreaming. What had gone into art is now diverted into the private and self-serving medium of the dream. Starting with the vision of the swamp, Aschenbach indulges in many dreams, visions, and daydreams. Often, in

---

[13] *Death in Venice*, pp. 126-127. Here I must insist on a more stringent translation of "Die Zeit zerfiel"—"time fell apart." "Time passed" is too vague and fails to convey the disintegration of time sense itself, inherent in the German and essential to my argument.

twilight moments between waking and sleeping, he sees grotesque variations of people he has encountered earlier. His dreams become more frequent after he meets Tadzio. The night after he first sees Tadzio he sleeps well and has varied dreams, but we are not told their content. Increasingly, the artist sits by an open window, daydreaming. The contemplation of Tadzio's body leads to another vision, based on tradition but articulated in imaginative detail. The vision of Socrates and Phaedrus comes again at the end of the novella. It is an attempt to understand the dissolution and to see the cause for the chaos that has engulfed Aschenbach.

Most often, however, dreams serve to further the unselving process itself. They display the extent of the breakdown of Aschenbach's earlier self and finally of all boundaries of the self in the burning desire to merge with the Other. On the night after confirming the gravity of the epidemic, Aschenbach dreams a dream that incorporates virtually all the themes of chaos and dissolution that have been sounded separately. It is a climax of the interior chaos of Aschenbach. It occurs just after he has decided against warning Tadzio's mother against continued residence in Venice, thus rejecting a last chance of civilized social intercourse and human responsibility.

The dream begins with a sense of fear. It is felt as a violation of his soul from without. After this, there is no more privacy or individuality. Aschenbach's self is completely torn open, invaded and laid waste. The dream is a concentration of all the disorganizing influences of which we have spoken. The coming of the "stranger God" is heralded by an odd mixture of sounds: some are decribed in terms reminiscent of the indefinitely articulated sounds of tropical and diseased Venice. A howl can be heard, a drawn out "u"-sound which is clearly associated with Tadzio. Even the flute music is not pure and distinct but rather shapeless and shamelessly visceral (it "bewitches the intestines"). The terrain reminds Aschenbach of that surrounding his summer home in the mountains. This place is said to be his soul, confirming the symbolism of places. An orgy occurs there—a Dionysian rite. We have seen traces of Dionysus in *The Magic Mountain* in his most important aspect as enemy of individuation. This is also his role here. While the celebrants howl their "soft consonants" with the final "u"-sound, Aschenbach is drawn into the frenzy. It is a temptation to "supreme sacrifice." What is this supreme sacrifice? It is the final triumph of the female principle—the yielding of the self. At the beginning of the dream Dionysus is described as "the alien God." Even while Aschenbach slowly succumbs he still

feels fearful disgust, and this resistance takes the form of "protecting
his own against the alien." His senses are finally overwhelmed by the
growing sound and the smells, among them some of the scents (stagnant
water and rampant disease) and even sounds (the laughter of the song)
of Venice. As the rite becomes a sacrament of communion, the participants
lick blood from each other's limbs, blood they have themselves shed.
In the bullfight in *The Confessions of Felix Krull* we are to see another
version of this final sacrifice of selfhood. Here, the Dionysian connection
is explicit. His last reserve overcome, Aschenbach is now passively
immersed in the will of the mob; he is outside of time doubly through
the act of dreaming and through partaking in a mythical and an ancient
rite; he is no more an individual. The words used and especially the
sequence of phrases makes this progressive immersion clear:—the dreamer,
we are told, was *"with* them, *in* them . . . they *were* he himself."* No
more prepositions are needed in the final transformation; there is complete
identification.

To accept Tadzio as the agent of this transformation we need to
associate him more closely yet with the female principle. One of its
attributes is transparency. In Clavdia's figure this symbolic quality was
painstakingly articulated on various levels, starting with her clothing
and skin. Tadzio is also made physically transparent. When Aschenbach
first notices the apparent ill health of Tadzio, the quality of transparency
is ascribed to the boy's teeth. They seem to lack the gloss of health and
are so pale they seem transparent. Watching Tadzio play on the beach,
Aschenbach again notices the youth's transparency. In *The Magic
Mountain* x-ray and fluoroscope were used to give the virtual quality
an actual basis. In *Death in Venice* penetration of the surface is more
clearly symbolic. It can be so because Aschenbach, unlike Hans, is an
artist and naturally given to dealing with symbolic forms. Yet even
here transparency is at first a bodily attribute. It is not only Tadzio's
teeth that are transparent. As he stands near Aschenbach, the sun clearly
marks his backbone. His ribs and breast cage are outlined. The bluish
veins in back of the knee show and make the whole body appear to be
made of translucent, clear matter. We recognize this dwelling on bone
structure and blood vessels, this penetration into anonymities of shared
body features where any individuality is lost to the eye. The same preoccupation was evident in *The Magic Mountain,* as it is in other works
(*Tristan,* for one).

By making the body of the beloved transparent Hans transcended
the particular attachment and derived more general benefits in the

ambitious project of educating himself. For the artist Aschenbach transparency is even more essential. The essence of art, its symbolic nature, has repeatedly been described as transparency. José Ortega y Gasset writes in *The Dehumanization of Art*:

The majority of people are unable to adjust their attention to the glass and the transparency which is the work of art; instead they penetrate through it to passionately wallow in the human reality which the work of art refers to. If they are invited to loose their prey and fix their attention upon the work of art itself, they will say they see nothing in it, because, indeed, they see no human realities there, but only artistic transparencies, pure essences.[14]

It is in being "a glass and a transparency" that a work of art differs from other beautiful objects. As an artist, Mann wants to impart the quality of transparency to the entities portrayed in his work. More han that, he makes his heroes share in this desire.

If transparency is important for art, we can understand Aschenbach's preoccupation with it. But why would Mann make Hans share in that desire? Hans is no artist. At most, he is an amateur philosopher. Perhaps it is in this role that Hans seeks to make Clavdia transparent—to have her yield the metaphysical secrets that he is trying to unlock. But more significantly it is in his role as lover. For lovers when they try to achieve perfection as lovers also seek to make the loved object transparent. This is why, as we will see later,[15] both art and love are associated with the female principle. As Aschenbach is both artist and lover, it is difficult to determine at any time which desire impels him more. In the quest for transparency, the longing for artistic rejuvenation converges with the hope for personal renewal.

The closest the novella comes to examining the meaning of this quest is in the identification of Aschenbach with Socrates, ironically wooing Phaedrus/Tadzio near the walls of Athens. Twice are Socrates and Phaedrus explicitly invoked. But even when the context of the Platonic dialog is not mentioned, its central concern—the longing for transcendence and the inquiry into the meaning of love—are felt hovering over Aschenbach's acts and feelings.

The first explicit allusion is a vision that comes to Aschenbach as he admires Tadzio by the sea. At the outset, as he idolizes the boy as a work of art, he seems capable of transcendence. Beauty itself, the divine

---

[14] Quoted in *Feeling and Form*, p. 54.
[15] See Chapters 2 and 6 especially.

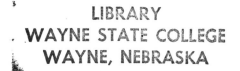

intention, is what he sees. A reflection of Beauty has assumed bodily
form to be comprehensible to man. He thinks at first of that part of
the dialog where Socrates speaks of love as a power for the good. Only
briefly does he mention those who cannot rise above the beautiful object
to Beauty itself. The focus is on transcendence achieved—the detailing
of the lover's progress from first shock at the sight of the beloved, through
a sense of warmth, to the desire to sacrifice to him as to a god. In all
this, the text follows the dialog closely in sequence and wording. One
reaction is attributed to Aschenbach that has no antecedent in Plato's
list—the lover described by Mann is "beside himself." The soul of Plato's
lover sprouts wings in recollection of her earlier winged state. Rather
than adopt this metaphor of transcendence, Mann follows his own recurrent image of unselving, one that stresses the negative (the resentment
at being imprisoned in the self) instead of the positive aspiration of
transcendence. Perhaps this difference explains Aschenbach's eventual
failure as lover and artist.

For the moment, however, love appears to bear fruit in art. The
Socrates of Aschenbach's vision, even more strongly than Plato's Socrates, assures Phaedrus that physical beauty is an essential and unique
mediation but no more than that—a means, a way. And this awareness
helps the writer to fashion that single lucid page-and-a-half of prose
exposition which arouses much posthumous admiration. The productivity
is shortlived. Still, it is a transcendence, no matter how momentary. The
way in which it is described testifies to that. Aschenbach wanted to
"snatch up this [Tadzio's] beauty into the realms of the mind, as the eagle
once bore the Trojan shepherd aloft."[16]

Why, then, can the transcendence not be more lasting? That it fails is
clear. Instead of inspiring Aschenbach to write, his love for Tadzio
eventually makes him forget art completely. As an artist Aschenbach
does not turn his infatuation to profit. Neither does he succeed as lover.
He never touches Tadzio, never exchanges a word with him. Perhaps
transcendence requires a deep and real involvement with the loved one
to begin with. Lacking such solidity, the mediation does not work. Like
the would-be artist Spinell in *Tristan*, Aschenbach fears a real encounter
with the beautiful human being. He elevates Tadzio into myth without
knowing the actual Tadzio first. He sees the boy, among other mythical
figures, as Narcissus. Yet even the Narcissism is his own. What he finds

---

[16] *Death in Venice*, p. 93.

in Tadzio is what he himself has first imputed to the boy. Transparency comes too easily; it is ready made.

For Socrates, on the other hand, there is a mutuality in the striving of the lover and the beloved. They want to reinforce those qualities in each other that remind them of the god they both serve. There is real interaction between the two, physical affection as well as intellectual exchange. The molding of the beloved is not done in daydream but in actual guidance and education. The beloved "has received every true and loyal service from his lover, *not in pretence but in reality.*" [17] Much as he likes to fancy himself as Socrates, Aschenbach has not given such service. Any ennobling of Tadzio is performed in Aschenbach's mind only, symbolically rather than in actuality.

Plato's lovers continue to "live in light always" as long as they exercise self-control and subdue the vicious elements of the soul. They can err if they are unable to see true beauty beyond its temporal incarnation. Then the lover becomes mere object, a source of sense pleasure, enjoyed without perception of its mediating power. To Socrates, it is a danger against which one should guard. To Aschenbach, the failure seems inevitable. Sitting in a dilapidated Venetian square, frustrated in his shameless tailing of Tadzio through the streets, Aschenbach envisions himself as Socrates again. Now, he speaks to Phaedrus of the impossibility of transcendence. Earlier, Aschenbach was sympathetic to Socrates, but outside him, referring to the philosopher in the third person. Now, Aschenbach himself mutters the words of the Greek. Or, more correctly, he speaks the words he *attributes* to Socrates for what follows, though based on the concepts of the dialog and similarly centering on the mediating power of beauty, is a rejection of the Socratic argument. The artist can only attain to the spiritual through beauty and this necessity makes a lover of him. Rhetorically, his Socrates asks Phaedrus whether the sensually mediated way can ever lead to true wisdom. The words "necessity" and "necessarily" recur throughout the passage. The pull to the abyss is inborn to the artist—"an incorrigible and natural direction." The poet's longing must remain love and thus attached to a specific object. Longing would shed that object. This is an assertion of the impossibility of transcendence. [18]

---

[17] *Phaedrus,* in *A Plato Reader* (Boston, 1953), p. 179. My emphasis.

[18] In his role of new husband and father Mann assigns values to love and longing differently. Longing suits the boy who romantically desires what is not his; love belongs to the man who protects and blesses his own. "Gesang vom Kindchen," *Gesammelte* Werke VIII, 1072.

Has Aschenbach failed completely? Death comes to him as he sits by the sea watching Tadzio; it comes in the guise of fulfillment in a deep and satisfying slumber. Has Tadzio mediated something after all? In dying Aschenbach feels that Tadzio hovers before him, waving to him to follow. Yet such transcendence as death may offer is not a succes for artist or lover. Unlike Hans, who finds the way back from an infatuation with death into an enriched sense of life, Aschenbach can find no road back. As an artist, he must find one in order to derive any benefit from his new insights. From a false spirituality that owes its elevation to deliberate ignorance and suppression of the sensual, he has leapt into an orgy of eroticism that is almost entirely intellectual. There is no confession of love except to himself, no contact except that of the eyes. Hans possesses Clavdia's body and perhaps that enables him to base a series of progressive abstractions upon it. Aschenbach's eroticism is as baseless as was his original spirituality. His choice of a beloved may be an early indication of the selfishness of his love and its inevitable defeat. The boy's physical weaknesses attract him. Socrates, in his ironic presentation of the lover as "the victim of his passions and the slave of pleasure" [19] describes the principles that govern such a lover's choice:

Will he not choose a beloved who is delicate rather than sturdy and strong? One brought up in shady bowers and not in the bright sun, a stranger to manly exercises and the sweat of toil, accustomed only to soft and luxurious diet, instead of the hues of health having the colours of paint and ornament, and the rest of a piece? [20]

Before we can call Aschenbach's quest a failure, we must once more ask whether we have understood that quest. In the final indictment of the poet, Aschenbach says he is unable to soar (*aufzuschwingen*); he can only succumb to excesses (*auszuschweifen*). The failed transcendence is clear in this, especially if one notes the German prefixes. Not upward has he moved but only outward. Throughout the novella we have traced this outward movement, this opening up of the self; and we have associated it with the female principle. Has Aschenbach, then, been successful in his effort to come nearer that pole of existence? He has become more and more passive. Sitting in his chair by the sea, ready to die, accepting it all, he is totally relaxed. The closed fist has opened. But it is empty. Or almost empty—one essay, modelled on Tadzio's body, is to delight the world. Sense of time has increasingly dissolved for Aschenbach. His

[19] *Phaedrus*, p. 165.
[20] *Phaedrus*, p. 166.

old personality has been left behind and the very sense of an individual and enduring core of self has disappeared. He has come so close to a realization of the essential qualities of the female principle that the fertile dialectical tension is lost. Is death, at least, a final confirmation of his escape from individuation? Even in this sense, death is a false solution. Instead of freeing man from the bonds of the self, it is the final seal of his individuation. Only individuated beings die.

CHAPTER IV

DOCTOR FAUSTUS: CULMINATION OF THE MALE WORLD

Like Gustave von Aschenbach, Adrian Leverkühn is an artist. Like the writer conceived 35 years before, he struggles with the problems of his art and of his own productivity and tries to separate them from the problems of his life. He also lives in a closed world, carefully structured to accommodate the work which is brought forth with pain and difficulty. This difficulty is compounded here by a sense of art's late state which renders many devices impossible. If the aesthetic task is more complex, private existence has become more impoverished, more isolated, more rigid. When Adrian goes to Italy—not to Venice to be sure, but to Rome and Palestrina—he is inaccessible to any release of a hidden emotional life. All is channeled into art, including the effects of disease. Yet the world represented in the earlier work by Venice is also present in *Doctor Faustus*. The "eternal feminine" aspect of Frau von Tolna was mentioned in the Introduction, and so were the "ministering women" surrounding Adrian. The two worlds do not really touch. In this chapter, I will deal with Adrian's realm. The other, the world outside him, will appear as a contrast, as a stage necessary for his activity, and as an object of attraction or repulsion.

As Mann does often with his heroes, he takes pains to attribute Adrian's physical appearance and gestus to his parental heritage. Strangely enough, for one who is to represent the psychological aspect of the male principle so exclusively, Adrian looks much like his mother. He has the mother's dark skin tone, a feature moreover which is frequently used by Mann to characterize the chthonic, earthy aspect of the female, or the exotic, artistic, Southern blood brought into a union by the mother. Her dark coloring, Zeitblom tells us, was inexplicable in terms of genealogy. The shape of the eyes, that of the mouth—neither sensuous nor harsh, even the slightly pointed chin—all are traced to the maternal line. And it is worth noting that it takes a beard, a dramatically and conventionally masculine attribute, to minimize the resemblance. Adrian grows this beard, a striking Vandyke beard, in the later years of his life, in times of worsening illness and intermittently soaring and waning productivity, at the height of what Zeitblom is to describe (in the postscript) as "the proud flight of his manliness," or "the Icarus-flight of the hero-son, the bold masculine adventure of him who has outgrown her [the mother's] guardianship."[1] It may be a part of his attempt to get away from the mother whom, as we will see, he both seeks and flees.

Another important physical characteristic of the mother, one which Adrian does not inherit but that nevertheless exercises an incalculable and lasting influence upon his life, is Elsbeth Leverkühn's voice. A "warm mezzosoprano," it testifies to a natural, totally unselfconscious musicality, never developed but filling Adrian's childhood with a beauty of sound that, Zeitblom believes, fosters the composer's later "incredible" sense for sonority. The voice is, for Mann, an important category in the description of female characters (Clavdia, for instance, as we saw in Chapter 2). The association seems to lead to an intimate link of "music," at least in this general sense of beautiful, more or less articulated sound, with the female principle. We witnessed, in *The Magic Mountain,* Hans' reaction to music as a relaxation of the bounds of time, space, and individuality, a letting go and an immersion in an element whose power is sensed but not really understood. Adrian is a composer and his approach to music is incomparably more rigorous; his temperament is also very different from Hans'. It remains to be seen whether, even in this stricter definition, music may be connected with the female realm.

From the father, Adrian seems to have little, yet the inheritance here is also carefully chosen. In the son's eyes, the hues of the parental eye colors are mixed, the maternal pitch-black producing with the father's azure a mixture of "shadowy blue-grey-green that showed small metallic sprinklings and a rust-colored ring around the pupils."[2] Mann's use of eye color is clearly schematic. It indicates one's allegiance to father or mother, North or South, one's belonging to one or the other of the worlds carved out by the Mann dialectic. Adrian appears to have some claim, then, to both worlds. Later, he is to vacillate between the attractions of the dark-eyed and the blue-eyed (always the extreme, Zeitblom notes),

---

[1] *Doktor Faustus, Gesammelte Werke,* VI, 671. I have translated very brief quotations, those that appear within the text, myself. For longer quotations, I have used the Lowe-Porter translation. In chapter 6, we will see that Joachim, another representative of the male principle, also grows a beard during his final illness and the accompanying male apotheosis.

[2] *Doktor Faustus,* p. 34.

and a scene set in an excursion train elaborately sets up tensions between the blue eyes of Rudi Schwerdtfeger, the black ones of Marie Godeau, and the same-colored ones of Adrian and Rüdiger Schildknapp. But the tarry glitter is still associated with the feminine character, while the charms of blue are connected with Rudi's lovely steel-blue or even with the skyblue of the boy Echo.

A propensity for migraine is the other, very ambivalent and highly significant gift of the father. In the latter, it is a regular but slight discomfort, indicated by a veiled and strained gaze, but in Adrian it is to become physically excruciating and to grow into myriad symbolic associations—with the sensation of cold and nausea which in turn is connected with boredom and despair at the worn convention of art; with the disease whose organisms lodge in the brain and make possible his hothouse creativity as well as his eventual madness; even with the knife-like pains of Hans Christian Andersen's mermaid who exchanges her comfortable tail for a pair of beautiful but aching legs. In the migraine, then, an indication can be seen, a potentiality for disease and the kind of spiritual and emotional heightening that disease can bring in Mann's world. Adrian starts to experiment on the piano at his uncle's house at age 14, and it is also at this time, at the onset of pubescence, as Zeitblom points out, that the migraine begins to trouble him. It is significant that here this "decadent" influence comes through the father. Neither should that be surprising. It is the German heritage that is under attack in *Doctor Faustus*, the decadent and dangerous possibilities hidden under imposing and seemingly benign movements of the German spirit. And it is Jonathan Leverkühn who is "altdeutsch," who is described as "a man of the best German type, a type one rarely encounters in our cities any more and one you will surely not find among those who today represent our kind in the world, with frequently rather depressing gusto—a physiognomy as though graven by past ages, rurally conserved and brought over from German days before the Thirty-Years War." [3] Jonathan is dissociated from contemporary Germany, but, as we find out in the novel, there is an ominous continuity in German history nonetheless.

In the father's "speculation of the elements" there is also a fore-shadowing of Adrian's later activities. Specific leitmotifs connect the two—the "devouring drop", for instance, which is part of Jonathan's experiments and later recurs not only as a theme of Adrian's composition

---

[3] *Doktor Faustus*, p. 20.

of Klopstock's "Frühlingsfeyer" [4] but also starts him on a train of thought which leads him into long and ambitious speculations about the cosmos, not unlike the amateur attempts of his father. The osmotic plants that the father cultivates are likened by the Devil to the syphilis organisms in Adrian's brain, and generally the frequency of references to the father in Adrian's interview with the devil are striking. In his dealing with the marginal, the "night side of science," Jonathan prefigures his son's darker and deeper involvement with the outrightly satanic. In any case, the world of the father is at least as important as that of the mother and perhaps more so since its influences tend to be intellectual and spiritual, and since they are a link in the chain of associations that bind Adrian's career to German history. Significantly, both mother and father are associated with music and not surprisingly it is the mother who represents its warmly corporeal qualities while the father conducts experiments such as that of "visible music," a demonstration where sand grains arrange themselves into intricate and precise patterns determined by the vibration of a cello bow.

Once his appearance and nature are given by this heritage, Adrian does not change much. In his physical appearance, Zeitblom never detects changes but rather an intensification, a heightening of what was already there. While Zeitblom is in military service, the friends have not met for a year. In the meantime, Adrian has decided to devote himself entirely to music, and has contracted syphilis. Consequently, upon their reunion, Zeitblom carefully watches Adrian for signs in face or manner that would document these events. Instead, he finds that the friend is unchanged, or rather, as he determines after a probing second look, he had become "more distinctively himself." [5] The only physical changes noted by Zeitblom have to do with the ravages of disease, and even most of those constitute an intensification of existing features and gestures. This is true, for instance, of the veiled look of Adrian's eyes which later becomes more distant, almost hostile. When, during the composition of "The Lament of Doctor Faustus," Adrian grows his beard, the effect is "alienating," since the similarity of his face to that of his mother is now hidden. In this escape from the motherly element, he now resembles Christ who is frequently used by Mann as an epitome of the male principle. [6] The

---

[4] Gunilla Bergsten in her excellent book *Thomas Mann's Doctor Faustus. The Sources and Structure of the Novel* (Chicago, 1969) comments on the recurrence of this motif, among others. Pp. 170-171, especially.

[5] *Doktor Faustus*, p. 211.

[6] See Chapter 5, for instance, on Schiller's resemblance to Jesus.

suffering in his face becomes increasingly spiritualized; and the male realm is the domain of the spirit. When Zeitblom sees him in 1935, the next to the last time, he again comments on Leverkühn's "Ecce-homo face."[7] He seems smaller and his face thinner. Again, four years later, at their last meeting, Adrian's face has become thinner and longer, the beard has greyed, the eyes are more deepset, and the brows bushier. It is once more an impression of progression and intensification rather than change that Zeitblom carries away. He comments on the irony of nature in producing the appearance of "the highest spiritualization" in a body now devoid of spirit.[8]

If Adrian does not change,[9] neither does he seem to believe in changes in the material or the intellectual world. Both are modelled on the sphere. As one can only progress on a sphere, or a circle which is also often invoked, by retreating to origins, so the revolutionary aspects of political as well as musical development are fraught with reactionarism and even archaism.[10] This is, on the one hand, a rigidly determined view of life, placing the only hope in the difficult and dangerous act of "breaking through." Yet, it can also be seen as the relaxed and accepting posture of the artist, and at least on one occasion Zeitblom sees it thus.

...I should have patterned myself—and tried to do so—on Adrian, who was no schoolman but an artist and took things as they came, apparently without thought of their proneness to change. In other words, he gave to impermanent becoming the character of being; he believed in the image: a tranquillizing belief, so at least it seemed to me, which, adjusted to the image, would not let its composure be disturbed no matter how unearthly that image might be.[11]

To impute into the flux of Becoming the character of Being—that, to Zeitblom, is the nature of the artist. And, in its resemblance to the dialectic of Being and Doing, it may tempt one to see Adrian as at least tending in the direction of the female principle, as a number of artists do in Mann's world.[12] There is indeed a desire to ignore if not to obliterate the passage of time, to reduce the sequence to the moment. At school

[7] *Doktor Faustus*, p. 674
[8] *Doktor Faustus*, p. 675.
[9] Of course we have to remember throughout that we see everything through Zeitblom's eyes, but he tells us later that, unlike Adrian, he is usually quite sensitive in his perception of change.
[10] This is a summary and an oversimplification. For a thorough discussion of the historical and the historico-philosophical implications of the novel, see Gunilla Bergsten, Chapter 4.
[11] *Doctor Faustus*, transl. H. T. Lowe-Porter (New York, 1948), p. 467.
[12] Tolstoy and Goethe, for instance, of the actual artists he portrays.

already, during an intermission between a Greek and a trigonometry lesson, Adrian confides to Zeitblom his thoughts about the conversion of the interval into the chord. It is, to him, the transformation of the horizontal into the vertical, of the successive into the simultaneous. Simultaneity, he claims, is prior to sequence.

If this is a movement toward Being, it is to be achieved by the most strenuous Doing. Zeitblom's envy at Adrian's contentment in the contemplation of the image is misplaced because Adrian's attitude is never the effortlessly relaxed, open one associated with the female principle. The recurrences in his art—the ambivalences, relationships, the circular and dialectical patterns of his compositions—are consciously worked out; they are highly sophisticated devices. To arrest the flux and arrive at this Being, Adrian must use much intelligence and will power. Surely it is not the naive state of, say, the mothers. It is perhaps rather a third state, a female realm spiritualized throughout, an objectivity not pre- but post-conscious, one that has gone through the minutest individuation as, Adrian thinks, Beethoven's music has moved from objectivity through total subjectivity, to a new combination of subjectivity and convention related to death, a mythical and collective transcendence.[13] One could see it perhaps also as a Hegelian movement from being-in-itself, to being-for-itself, to being-in-and-for-itself.

If the recurrent patterns in Adrian's compositions are not surprising —an artist is expected to structure his work—those in his life seem more jarring.[14] They consist mainly of a deliberate repetition of location, thus a spatial recurrence, which may be related to the closed-in nature of the male principle. Like Schiller, in *A Weary Hour* and like Aschenbach before his departure for Venice, Adrian needs the enclosure and security of the same place. Or, if not the same, then one that could pass for it. Like Schiller who (according to Mann) had no desire to see the places he portrayed in his work, Adrian thinks little of travelling for the sake of seeing, of new impressions, change or recreation. He was, he told Zeitblom, not a man of the eyes but rather one of the ear, and though Serenus protests that his sense for "the magic of the eye" belies this categorization, he must agree that not only did Adrian not care to see anything—he "wanted to know nothing ... actually to experience nothing, at least not in the manifest, external sense of the word ..."[15]

---

[13] *Doktor Faustus*, pp. 73-74.
[14] Most commentators take note of the recurrences, Bergsten among them.
[15] *Doktor Faustus*, pp. 235-236.

This attitude of Adrian makes Zeitblom uncomfortable. It frightens and depresses him. He sees it as conservative and occasionally even rigid. Early in his account, as he describes Adrian's birthplace and childhood home, he warns the reader that he will later encounter an imitation of this location. And indeed he does—down to the smallest detail. Though the farmhouse is different, the farm itself and its surroundings follow the same pattern. A tree—though in one case it is a linden, in the other an elm—grows impractically in the middle of the yard; there is a hill (Zionsberg as against Rohmbühel) in comparable distances from the two farms, both with rest benches erected at public expense; and, perhaps most importantly, again at a comparable remove, there are the two ponds —Kuhmulde and Klammerweiher—known for their extremely cold water. Not only is there a recurrence of location with a variation of regional accent (or "transposed into another but not remote key," as Zeitblom likes to put it, in musical terms); the farm is similarly populated, from the clearly parallel mother, father, and older son figures, through the barefooted stable maids, even down to the scarred watch dogs. Max Schweigestill smokes a pipe much like Jonathan Leverkühn and dies almost at exactly the same time as the latter. And it is this sameness within apparent variety, not the possibilities of variation within sameness that Adrian seeks. He even changes the name of the second watchdog to conform to that of the first.

Even in between these two identical stations, the conservatism or rigidity of Adrian's life style is apparent. He never changes apartments while in the same city, looks for simplicity, functionalism, and "the familiar." Even when he goes to Italy, it is not for change or expansion. Palestrina, the village where he has the crucial dialog (or monolog) with the Devil, does not constitute a widening of the self, a sensuous or even intellectual opening up to the outside world, as Venice does for Aschenbach. It is instead merely the setting for a "dialog with *my* life, *my* fate,[16]"—with himself. The village is also a repetition of the patterning of living arrangements that precede and follow it,[17] especially in the presence of "Mother" Manardi whose hair is parted and pulled back in a way reminiscent of Adrian's own mother and of Else Schweigestill, and who, like them, has well formed but competent hands. During his winter stay in Rome, Adrian manages to find the Villa Doria Panfili which is to play "the role of the monastery garden of Palestrina." There, as in

---

[16] *Doktor Faustus*, p. 280. My underlining.
[17] Bergsten, pp. 150-152, discusses this in some detail.

the country, he lives a life almost totally isolated socially, avoiding natives and tourists. Adrian's retreats are, in a humble way, also reminiscent of the castles of Louis II of Bavaria which he visits with Zeitblom and a group of friends later in the novel, those monuments to loneliness.

These are not only attempts to repeat spatial arrangements and to seek the security and enclosure of a known pattern. In a sense, they are also manipulations of time, endeavors to repeat the same situation again and again, at widely separated times of one's life. And such manipulations evince the forced and uneasy response of one who is not at home within the flux of time, who cannot trust it as the female characters do. The final evidence for this violent activism is the need for "breaking through" (*Durchbruch*) which occupies Adrian especially on the level of art (Zeitblom is perhaps more concerned with the *Durchbruch* of Germany) —an act born of frustration and despair. When Adrian tries to expand spatially, it is a purely intellectual act and yet full of the extremism of the breakthrough. Like Hans, he develops a sudden interest, disquieting to the humanist Zeitblom as Hans' was to the humanist Settembrini, in the cosmos, in the ages and spatial relations of planets in space where common quantification loses any meaning. Usually he shows no interest in place, but in this abstract guise, disconnected from sense immediacy, it suddenly becomes an object of fascination for him, further proof of his "extravagent existence," the vacillation between extremes, such as heat and cold. And heat and cold (which I will discuss presently) perhaps play a part here. The euphoria fanned by sweeping statements about the cosmos is safely removed from any human excitement engendered by emotions—it is a spiritual, mathematical, cold enthusiasm.

An essential category in determining the male or female affiliation of Mann's characters is their relationship to others and the outside world generally. With Adrian that aspect is nearly circumscribed by the theme of cold so prominent in the novel.[18] In the very first section of his memoir, Zeitblom mentions the atmosphere of cold around Adrian. And

---

[18] This too has been noted by many critics. Mann remarks on it himself in *The Story of a Novel. The Genesis of "Doctor Faustus"*. (New York, 1961): "The laughter!" he said. "What are you getting at there? Oh, I know, I know ... We will see." With insight and foresight, he thus picked out one of the small motifs of the book, the kind I most enjoy working with—like, say the erotic motif of the blue and black eyes; the mother motif; the parallelism of the landscapes; or, more significant and essential, ranging through the whole book and appearing in many variations, the motif of cold, which is related to the motif of laughter." p. 71. In turn, both laughter and cold are connected with the devil.

immediately it is associated with his loneliness and lack of love, an association that is fundamental and lasting. The statement about cold culminates a rumination by Zeitblom about Adrian's relationships to the narrator himself and to others, punctuated by rhetorical questions. Leverkühn respected and honored the friend, the latter admits. But loving? Whom might this man have loved? he asks. "In whom had he even confided, to whom had he opened his heart?" The answer is the statement about cold. It is the cold of isolation and of a realm of rarefied spirituality and intellectual calculation, and we are to see it even in Adrian's relationship to music. In his letter to Kretzschmar, Adrian connects his "Weltscheu" with his lack of warmth, sympathy, and love. It is, thus, also associated with Adrian's pride, another frequent indicator of male allegiance which is an affirmation of individuation, a glorying in the particular self.[19] About this pride, Zeitblom is more ambivalent than he is about Leverkühn's frigidity. "I believed in his pride," he tells us, "and was for my part proud of it . . ."[20] Yet it is part of the same complex as the friend's coldness which never fails to shock and sadden Serenus. The director of Adrian's school, however, recognizes the dangers of pride very well, and immediately connects them with the Devil: God's antagonist, he tells his pupil at a farewell interview, came to fall through pride, and Adrian is one of those who should especially watch against his tricks. It is in its aspect of pride that cold is associated with boredom, the nausea of the latecomer in art who knows "how it is made" and sees through all devices—boredom is cold,[21] it is "the coldest thing in the world."[22] It is here also that the inherited migraine joins this cluster of themes, as a result of cold boredom. And, appropriately enough, this cold crystallizes into objective existence in the Chapter 25 interview with the Devil. The first inkling Adrian has of the Devil's presence is a wave of cold, and this cold continues as background to the conversation. He cannot turn it off, the guest tells Adrian. Kerényi sees Mann's devil as being essentially an emanation of "the human, or more correctly, the inhuman coldness, the 'life-coldness' of Adrian himself."[23] At the height of the dialog cold is again characterized as lack of love: "Love is

---

[19] For a discussion of pride, see especially Chapter 6, the section on *The Holy Sinner.*

[20] *Doktor Faustus*, p. 111.

[21] *Doktor Faustus*, p. 175.

[22] *Doktor Faustus*, p. 175.

[23] Karl Kerényi, "Thomas Mann und der Teufel in Palestrina," *Neue Rundschau,* 73 (1962, p. 343.

forbidden you, in so far as it warms. Thy life shall be cold, therefore thou shalt love no human being." [24] And pride is connected with that alternation between extreme heat and icy cold, and "extravagant existence": ... "that extravagant living, the only one that suffices a proud soul. Your arrogance will probably never want to exchange with a lukewarm one." [25]

In *Story of a Novel* Mann writes that he was "infatuated with his [Adrian's] 'coldness,' his lack of 'soul'—that mediator and conciliator between spirit and instinct." [26] In Mann's psychological scheme, the soul is a mixed entity in a trinity of "Geist," "Seele," and "Trieb" (spirit, soul, and instinct), which partakes of both the extremes and is the seat of sentiment. Zeitblom calls it, similarly, "a middle, mediating, and heavily practically inspired instance in which spirit and instinct permeate each other and conciliate each other in a certain illusory way." It is, he admits, a sentimental medium in which he feels quite comfortable but that cannot satisfy the pure and strict tastes of Adrian. In this sentimental aspect, however, it guards one against the seductions of naked instinct, the undisguised and crude lure of sex, for instance. Mann's female figures are mostly at home in this mediating area rather than in that of animal drive, and thus they can become mediators themselves.

What are the moments of warmth in Adrian's life? They usually result from initiatives of others rather than representing any attempt by him to reach out from his isolation. This is certainly true of his relationship to Zeitblom who admits loving Adrian onesidedly. Leverkühn accepted the devotion of others without really noticing it, Zeitblom claims; it was swallowed up without a trace by the abyss of his loneliness. Serenus' own relationship to the friend is touched with pain and bitterness and complicated by his jealousy of those who come close to Adrian. Among them, he enumerates the boy Echo, Rudi Schwerdtfeger, and Marie Godeau to whom Adrian is to propose in a rather bizarre and self defeating way, through the mediation of Rudi. We might add Zeitblom himself. All of these could be said to move in the female realm. The episode of Nepomuk Schneidewein, Adrian's nephew, is complex and not pertinent to this enquiry in its entirety, but as the "divine child" [27] he is above individuality

---

[24] *Doktor Faustus*, p. 332.
[25] *Doktor Faustus*, p. 333.
[26] *Story of a Novel*, p. 89.
[27] Karl Kerényi has written on the phenomenon of the "divine child."

and clearly beyond time. And he does manage to reach into Adrian's loneliness and to touch him deeply. Zeitblom, the self-styled representative of the "soul", has professed loyalty to the female principle in this very allegation. He lacks many of the advantages and attractions of the more complete embodiments of this realm, but even his Catholicism tends to put him on that side, as compared to Adrian's sober and masculine Lutheranism.[28]

Rudi is "female" is many and more explicit ways. His physical attractiveness is described in feminine terms; the relationship of flirt and insistent (rather crude, Zeitblom finds) seductiveness in which he sets himself toward Adrian conforms to conventional notions of feminine wiles; and, finally, he enters into a homosexual affair with the clearly male Adrian. "Erotic irony", that sole link between the male and the female realms,[29] is said to characterize the relationship between Adrian and Rudi.[30] Though Leverkühn's motives for seeking Rudi's mediation are at the least ambivalent, he does make a convincing case for the violinist's suitability as a mediator. Also, Rudi whose sentimentality often seems cloying even to that acknowledged man of sentiment, might well be associated with the "soul". And Rudi's sexual role is ambivalent in other relationships as well. In his fatal adulterous affair with Inez Rodde, Rudi complains to Adrian, the usual sexual roles are reversed by the preponderance of love on Inez' side and her consequent aggressivity; she treats his body as a man would a woman's. Rudi remains passive throughout the affair, drifting into it half willingly, not being able to get out of it—reacting rather than initiating.

We come closer to the fully and explicitly female when we deal with Marie Godeau. She is a woman of sophistication, an artist, a working girl. Not, then, a creature of instinct or an obviously elemental, "telluric"[31] being. Yet she is associated with all those aspects of the female principle that would most attract Adrian and that hold out most promise to him of escaping from his rigid isolation—she holds much physical attraction for him, yet she can also serve as an intellectual complement.

---

[28] This is a simplification, but one could make a case for such a distinction on the basis of *Doctor Faustus*.

[29] See the brief discussion of erotic irony in the concluding chapter.

[30] *Doktor Faustus*, p. 551.

[31] See the discussion of Bachofen's theories in the Conclusion.

Did not "the world" come near to him in her, the world from which he shrank
—and, in an artistic and musical sense, that part of the world which was outside
Germany? And it came in the most serious, friendly guise, awakening confidence,
promising fulfillment, encouraging him to abandon his recluse state.[32]

She might, then, grant him an outlet to the world in the widest possible
sense. Her power is enhanced by an association with the mother's
sphere. Marie's eyes are black, pitch-black like those of Elsbeth Leverkühn. Knowing the effect of such eyes on Adrian, Zeitblom thinks
lovingly of "the night of her gaze." Her warm, winning voice (surely
material for a singer, Zeitblom finds, as he did with Elsbeth) is like
that of the mother not only in its pitch and tone color—at times, we
are told, in listening to her one would believe to be hearing Elsbeth.
This ties Marie closer to the senses, the maternal instinctual world;
it tends to infuse her with the animal warmth of this realm from which
her urbanity might at first remove her.

To connect Marie with the most positive attributes of the female
principle, I might mention some words that are attached repeatedly
to her or to her relationship with Adrian. One of them is "sympatisch"—
and, to Mann, "sympathy" stands for a desirable and intimate link with
all of the physical world as well as with the world of culture.[33] Another
is "human" ("menschlich"), a term we have encountered often in
connection with Clavdia Chauchat. When Adrian asks Rudi to be the
mediator "between him and life", his "advocate with happiness," he
uses the word "human" in various grammatical forms with a frequency
that prompts Rudi to chide him for it. He longs, Adrian says for "a
more human atmosphere"; he hopes that a union with Marie will
increase the "human content" of his future work; he asks Rudi to look
at the matter in a "human" way, and he speaks of "human warmth." [34]
Warmth appears again, reminiscent of the imagery and wording surrounding Clavdia and contrasting both with the coldness around Adrian
and with the extreme and inhuman heat of his devil-inspired genius.
He speaks of the desire for a "warmer home," suggesting the middle
domain of the "soul."

This quality of sentiment appears even in the crassest relationship
that Adrian enters—the seemingly only sexual encounter with the
prostitute Esmeralda. In any case, Zeitblom would impute some soul

[32] *Doctor Faustus,* p. 423.
[33] See Chapter 7 on love.
[34] *Doktor Faustus,* p. 579.

to the fatal meeting through its element of choice and consideration—Adrian has gone a long way to sleep with the woman whom he originally met in a Halle brothel; and she warns him of her disease. Yet, this woman remains mainly the representative of the darker side of the female principle—unless Victor Oswald is correct,[35] and she and Frau von Tolna are identical. It would not injure my argument to accept this identity and to see the prostitute Esmeralda and this socially and spiritually noble woman as contrasting aspects of the female, in the same body. In her night side, Esmeralda is an incarnation of Privat-dozent Eberhard Schleppfuss' statements about the female sex. Woman, he claims in one of his lectures, singly represents the whole realm of sexuality on earth. The "curse of the flesh" goes on her account through the attribution of man's lusts to her seductions, since she is thought of as the object of his desire. She is, thus, the instrument of the devil, associated also with other unsavory spirits such as incubi and succubi and often rightly accused of witchcraft.

Esmeralda fits this description of woman. She brings about the pact with the devil by infecting Adrian with syphilis. In the conversation with Adrian, the devil refers to the disease organisms as "my little ones," and he speaks of Adrian as "the far-travelled customer of my little one."[36] She is, then, literally a tool of the devil, though the latter points out the customer's own eagerness for the disease, his complicity. Like Clavdia, Esmeralda [37] is also associated with transparency. As Adrian describes the bordello scene in his letter to Zeitblom, he refers to the women as Nietzsche's "daughters of the desert," and as "Esme-ralden"—in the plural—making the prostitute less individuated, part of a sensual, undifferentiated, feminine realm. They are transparent in this symbolic sense. They are also transparent literally since Mann dresses them in gauze and tulle, giving a realistic dimension to this symbolic quality, as he did in the case of Clavdia. A connection is also established with Jonathan Leverkühn's benignly demonic researches into

---

[35] See "Thomas Mann's *Doktor Faustus*: The Enigma of Frau von Tolna," *Germanic Review*, XXIII (1948), 249-253.

[36] The statement could be construed as referring either to the organisms or to the prostitute herself: "Der weitgereiste Kunde *meiner Kleinen*..."

[37] Her Spanish name and the Spanish jacket she wears may connect her with the Spanish abandon of Carmen, associated with Clavdia in *The Magic Mountain*, and perhaps also with the elemental realm of the bullfight and Maria Pia in *Felix Krull*.

the night side of natural science and his shade-loving transparent Hetaera Esmeralda butterfly.

If this attraction is demonic, in this instance it is also productive. Even in its dark aspect, the female element facilitates, enriches, makes fruitful. Zeitblom, who claims to have no personal understanding of such things, admits that genius has more of a share in the demonic, the irrational, the nether world than he would like. The world of the spirit, he fears, cannot be divorced from the lower realm and may indeed need the "fruitful contact" with that realm.[38] And the most dramatic manner of contact is through love. Perhaps a feeling of discomfort at that realization is partly what prevents Zeitblom from ever discussing "love, sex, or the flesh" with Adrian in an intimate way. (There are other reasons, having to do with the ambiguous and complex relationship between the two, an alter-ego relation of which Mann speaks in *Story of a Novel*.) They only talk of it in its purified manifestations in art. With one exception. After his sister's marriage, Adrian comments to Zeitblom on the words of the service that man and wife are one flesh. In a monolog much like one of Felix Krull,[39] with a more subdued and skeptical tone, he marvels at the "exceptional phenomenon" of love. A man of distance, disliking the physical closeness of others ("noli me tangere," as the humanist puts it), Adrian for once admits the miraculous nature not only of love but of desire also. The relation of I and Thou, he says, is so much altered even in mere lust that separating the merely sexual from the more inclusive concept of love is meaningless.[40] The flesh will normally not want anything to do with the Other, feeling only disgust at this closeness. The essential wonder is the overcoming of this obstacle, and that is achieved in desire as well as in a love replete with emotional and spiritual overtones. Unusual ruminations, coming from Adrian. And Zeitblom is properly embarrassed. The terms in which he couches his confusion are telling—never, he claims, "had he [Adrian] gone so far *out of himself*." [41]

It is this occasional, albeit half hearted, desire to get out of himself that propels Adrian into such contacts with "the world" as he exper-

---

[38] *Doctor Faustus,* p. 9.

[39] See the discussion of Felix in Chapter 7, on love.

[40] Compare similar passages on the fortunate vagueness of the concept of love— in *The Magic Mountain,* for instance.

[41] My underlining.

iences.[42] If they are all finally unsuccessful it is because he cannot change his own nature. He defeats himself by sending Rudi to Marie to woo for him; he blames himself for the death of Echo which he sees as punishment imposed by the devil for the infringement of his prohibition against love; he will not court audiences through the mediation of the impresario Saul Fitelberg. For a nature like his, there is no easy and natural outlet to the outside world. Perhaps the only way would be the one he finds in his art—that of "breaking through," a violent and forceful action. Without the mediating aspect of personality—soul or sentiment—he is reduced to such alternatives, or to the use of other people as mediators. In some ways, his relationship to Rudi, Marie, Echo, even to Esmeralda, can be seen as "breakthroughs." They are clumsy, as clumsy as the attempt of Germany to break through her isolation and loneliness. (She started the war, Zeitblom feels, to "convince all and to win everybody," and would "beat the world over its head until it changes its mind about us and not only admire but also love us.") Adrian's more refined efforts are reserved for art.

Perhaps no union is possible for Adrian with the human world because, in terms of his "extravagant existence," it has to be achieved on the terms of one extreme or the other. And, on those terms, the female element finally engulfs him. As he collapses, a group of protective women gathers around Adrian, and Frau Else takes charge of him. Later, his real mother is to bring him home like the helpless child that he has become, with the "proud flight of his manhood" all but forgotten. And the mother receives him back into her care with some satisfaction.

Anything more fearfully touching or lamentable cannot be imagined than to see a free spirit, once bold and defiant, once soaring in a giddy arc above an astonished world, now creeping broken back to his mother's arms. But my conviction, resting on unequivocal evidence, is that the maternal experiences from so tragic and wretched a return, in all its grief, some appeasement as well. The Icarus-flight of the hero son, the steep ascent of the male escaped from her outgrown care, is to a mother an error both sinful and incomprehensible; in her heart, with secret anger she hears the austere, estranging words: "Woman, what have I to do with thee?" And when he falls and is shattered she takes him back, the "poor, dear child," to her bosom, thinking nothing else than that he would have done better never to have gone away.[43]

---

[42] Zeitblom sees, for instance, the relationship with Frau von Tolna and the very different meeting with the impresario, though they are treated in different chapters, as belonging under the same heading —"the world"—and his friend's relation or lack of relation to it.

[43] *Doctor Faustus,* p. 506.

Adrian is also aware of this humbling of his manly pride, even in his mental darkness. Zeitblom feels that it is in response to that humiliation, out of a desire to escape the mother, that he attempts suicide by trying to drown himself in the Klammerweiher, his cold element. He is said to have repeatedly commented on the coldness of the pond while being led away.

The imagery of heat and cold also explains the relationship between Adrian's art and his life. With Mann's assumption of a fixed fund of psychic energy, the peaks in Adrian's artistic production go along with a cooling off in his personal relationships. When he tries to infuse some warmth into his life through love or friendship, the white heat of creative inspiration not only lets up but often passes into icy sterility. His reluctance to change his external situation can also be explained in this way. He must simplify his private life to save energy for art. His real life goes on in music while his practical existence is reduced to the most basic level.

Given such an allocation of powers, it should not be surprising that, as I indicated above, Adrian's efforts at breakthrough in music are more skilled and successful than those he half heartedly makes in life. One might also expect that the fundamental dialectic of male and female would be evident in Adrian's compositions and in general conceptions about music as they appear in *Doctor Faustus.*

The dialectic does appear quite explicitly on this level of the novel. In one aspect, music here represents the female realm, as it does in many of Mann's earlier novellas. In the latter, *Tristan* and *The Blood of the Walsungs* most prominently, it does so at least partly because the art in question is the sensuously saturated music of Wagner which, to Mann, always remained an ambiguous mixture of the sublime and the boldly profane in an erotic guise. Other composers make their appearance in *The Magic Mountain,* but music there is still used for the sake of its literary allusion. Hans plays *Carmen,* for instance, to feel the presence not only of the roving gypsy Clavdia but also of Joachim, the brave soldier. When the music does not have such direct allusion to his problems, it merely affects Hans by bringing him out of himself. It is, in this sense, the unindividuating effect of the female principle. In listening to concerts or recordings, Hans relaxes whatever posture he may have shown before. His head hangs to one side (as it does in the contemplation of the deep past and of death), and his mouth is open. It seems a rather stultifying effect, a letting go of inhibitions and a surrender to the engulfing element. Strangley enough, music, the highly articulate art, is here connected with the erasing of clear boundaries, with oblivion, contempt for words, and, finally, with silence.[44]

It is, at least, a domain where the usual distinctions do not apply, as they do not in Hans' speaking French. This is the effect of "music" as mere sound distinguished from the clearly understood sounds of one's native speech. And it is worth noting that Adrian indulges in a similar experiment with speech. When the disease affects him badly, a speech impediment appears. His words lack articulation; they are slurred due to an inertia of the lips. This, Zeitblom explains, did not hinder Adrian's communication. Rather, he exploited the condition to say things that were themselves only partly articulated in his thought and only partly intended to be understood by the hearers.

This kind of direct, only half understood expression of strong emotion is often associated with music by a layman. It can perhaps be applied more to the appreciation of music than to its production, and in Mann's earlier work music is usually heard by the characters, not composed by them. When we encounter performers, their playing tends to be the acting out of some personal crisis, and the repertoire is chosen accordingly. It may not be fair to invite the reader to speculate on the unselving, chaotic, and often dangerous effects of music on the basis of such evidence. Yet Mann is not alone in doing so. Hermann Hesse, in a speculation of his own about the relationship of his hero and of the German spirit to music, also connects the latter with the female realm, as a representation of the "matriarchal link with nature" and thus suspect.

In the German spirit the matriarchal link with nature rules in the form of the hegemony of music to an extent unknown in any other people. We intellectuals, instead of fighting against this tendency like men, and rendering obedience to the spirit, the Logos, the Word, and gaining a hearing for it, are all dreaming of a speech without words that utters the inexpressible and gives form to the formless. Instead of playing his part as truly and honestly as he could, the German intellectual has constantly rebelled against the word and spirit, carousing in music, in wonderful creations of sound, and wonderful beauties of feeling and mood that were never pressed home to reality; has left the greater part of its practical gifts to decay.[45]

---

[44] See the discussion of repetitive and infantile sounds in Chapter 2, in connection with Clavdia's name.

[45] *Steppenwolf,* transl. Basil Creighton (New York, 1963), pp. 154-155. Käte Nadler, in *Hermann Hesse. Naturliebe, Menschenliebe, Gottesliebe* (Leipzig, 1956)

At best, this is a one-sided evaluation of music, and Adrian, as an accomplished composer could hardly subscribe to it. We will see that he does not. Yet to deny to music the function and the power of expressing human feeling would be to deprive it of meaning. And Adrian also realizes that. In *Doctor Faustus,* a work dealing so intimately with music, the problem becomes much more complex and music, rather than being vaguely connected with the female principle, comes to serve as a supreme embodiment of the dialectical tension itself.

It is the warm, female side of music to which Adrian is exposed first. Zeitblom believed, we saw, that hearing his mother's lovely voice gave the composer his lifelong sense of the bodily aspect of music. And his initiation into the more formal mysteries of music—canon-singing—is presided over by the stable maid Hanne, an embodiment of earthy natural womanliness, complete with wobbly bosom and manure-encrusted feet. She is connected with animal existence, exuding an animal smell, and in the enthusiasm of singing her face contorts into a laughing grimace similar to that of the dog Suso at feeding time. The other contacts that Adrian has with music at an early age are also concrete and tangible:— his father demonstrates "visible music" to him; at his uncle's warehouse he learns all about the technical and physical properties of musical instruments. By setting Adrian's rudimentary first attempts at composition at the beginning of pubescence, Mann deepens the sensual associations of music.

But, in the meantime, Adrian has become interested in mathematics —"Order is everything," he announces—and now he is ready to see the other side of music. It is at one of Kretzschmar's lectures that he is introduced to a form of the dialectic: the opposition of polyphonic objectivity and harmonic subjectivity.[46] The former tends to be connected

correctly points out that there is another side to Hesse's views on music, manifesting itself in the same work, but especially in *The Glass Bead Game* where the Music Master becomes a polar opposite to Adrian in his attitude to and use of music. See especially page 115 and 136. Mark Boulby (*Hermann Hesse,* Ithaca, 1967) comments that this is a "passage reading a good deal more like Mann than Hesse and fitting none too well into the general conspectus of Harry's views on music." (p. 204) It is true that Harry Haller at times sees music as a paradigm of discipline and ascetic control, often associated with religious sources. This view of music as representing order and the spirit prevails especially in the later works.

[46] See Bergsten on the sources for this chapter. It is interesting to note that in the main source, Theodor W. Adorno's *Philosophie der Neuen Musik* (Tübingen, 1949) the author connects "negative objectivity" with schizophrenia and depersonalization. P. 115.

with convention, the latter with personal expression. In another lecture by Kretzschmar, Adrian encounters another kind of visible music— the great care composers can devote at times to the optical patterning of their music on the page nad to intricate devices that are apparent to the eye but lost to the ear of most of the audience. This, the lecturer feels, is proof of the spirituality of music, of its tendency to the abstract and away from the sensual.

These insights are communicated to Adrian by Kretzschmar, a male, and through the intellectual medium of the lecture. Inspired by his teacher's disclosures, Adrian offers a statement of the musical dialectic in terms familiar to him—those of cold and heat. Lawfulness, rational order, the aspects connected with the category of polyphonic objectivity, he labels cold; the body warmth, "stable-" or "cow-"warmth of music, on the other hand, is the quality of imagination, related to harmonic subjectivity. It is evident how closely the musical dialectic corresponds to the sexual one, both in scope and content.

There is still another kind of objectivity, the one Adrian attributes to twelve tone music, which is not conventional but rather has merged with the subjective element and transcended it, one that is determined and yet free, that leaves no room for contingency and yet remains spontaneous. This is a third kingdom of sorts, a higher synthesis of the opposites, something to which Adrian himself is to aspire in his art, though not in his life. And we are given to believe that in " The Lament of Doctor Faustus" he may just possibly have attained at least a momentary semblance of such a synthesis. Composed by the twelve tone method, it was, Zeitblom insists, rigorously calculated and yet fully expressive. He can explain it only as an artistic paradox, this birth of expression out of a totally determined construction.[47] Elsewhere, it is seen as a dialectical reverse. A synthesis may be possible in music because it is, by its very nature, an art of relationship, of ambivalence and circularity, encompassing within its techniques the "unity, exchange-ability, identity" of opposites, such as horizontal and vertical, cold and hot, and, finally, even male and female. In his composition Adrian can hope to approximate such a synthesis through concentrating his intellectual

---

[47] Such a coincidence of opposites is always a paradox. C. G. Jung writes: "Naturally the conjunction can only be understood as a paradox, since a union of opposites can be thought of only as their annihilation. Paradox is a characteristic of all transcendental situations" ... Aion. Researches into the Phenomenology of the Self (New York, 1959), p. 70.

power and vital energy upon it; in his life, he cannot do so because he has decided to spend himself in music, and because he is incapable of love. As man, Adrian is exclusively linked to the male principle. As artist, he is early exposed to a generous infusion of the female aspect, and his later reaction against its stable warmth merely ensures that a lasting dialectical tension will be maintained.

CHAPTER V

MALE AND FEMALE IN ACTUAL ARTISTS:
MANN ON GOETHE AND SCHILLER

In *Death in Venice*, Aschenbach's greatest work "Spirit and Art" is likened in scope and theme to Schiller's *Naive and Sentimental Poetry*. Naive and sentimental ways, when seen as modes of being and not merely as varying ways of artistic creation, form a dialectic similar to the male-female one. The sentimental nature with its highly articulated self-consciousness comes close to aspects of the male principle. The naive one in its effortless attunement to its own state as well as to the outside world shares in the female principle. For the purpose of examining Mann's views of Goethe and Schiller in terms of broadly inclusive and intuitive categories, these similarities are important, but we should not forget that, as I pointed out in the Introduction, the typologies are not identical.

In Mann's consideration of Goethe and Schiller, the female-male polarity is one of the central themes. My concern is not with the actual Goethe and Schiller as they can be known from historical tradition. Neither is it with their works nor yet with Mann's commentary on their works. It is rather with Mann's view of the two as personalities, as different, opposed, and perhaps complementary modes of being.[1] With

---

* This chapter has already been published in a shortened and modified form in *Mosaic*, VI/2, pp. 37-53 (Winter 1973), The University of Manitoba Press.

[1] A criticism I would like to make of some of the studies on Mann's literary relationship to either Goethe or Schiller is that by concentrating on one side of the polarity, the authors lose the essential sense of tension and fruitful interactions. They recognize the impact of Goethe especially as a personality (Bernhard Blume. *Thomas Mann und Goethe*, for one), but do not separate it from the more professional "imitatio." Most of the articles on the Mann-Goethe connection work along the lines of the "unio mystica" suggested by Mann himself. (Grete Schaeder, "Thomas Mann's Goethe-Bild," *Sammlung*, IV, Aug./Oct. 1959, for instance, who chafes at the ironic Goethe-image in *Lotte in Weimar* but sees a true meeting in *The Magic Mountain*; Wolfgang Leppmann, "Thomas Mann" in his *The German Image of*

Goethe, it is clear that in spite of abiding interest in the work it is the person that fascinates Mann. In *The Beloved Returns* (Lotte in Weimar) the personality in its relationship to itself and others is in the center. Even in the essays this focus is noticeable. With Schiller, the work appears at first to be central. Though Aschenbach might be likened to Schiller as a person too, it is Schiller's work that is mentioned in *Death in Venice,* not the man himself. As a representative of the male principle, Schiller may indeed be more important for what he does than for what he is. This is not to say that his influence on Mann is the lesser one; it may well be dominant, especially since Mann sees himself as belonging to Schiller's side of the Dialectic.[2] And though Mann's typology is not that of Schiller, he never questions the validity of Schiller's categories.

Since I am not concerned with Goethe and Schiller as Mann's literary models, a look at his more striking references to the two men will suffice.

Goethe, who realizes that Mann's Goethe concentrates on problems important to Mann but still credits Mann's extreme familiarity with Goethe; Edith Braemer, "Aspekte der Goethe-Rezeption Thomas Manns," in Georg Wenzel, ed. *Vollendung und Grösse Thomas Manns,* who sees Goethe mainly as an ethical and political example.) The strongest dissenter is John Alexander Asher, "Thomas Mann's Unio Mystica with Goethe," PEGS, XXV, who sees unremitting irony (which he too readily identifies with lack of seriousness) in Mann's reatment of Goethe, along with serious inaccuracies and frivolous overemphasis of negative elements, especially in *Phantasie über Goethe.*

On Mann's attitude to Schiller there is considerable agreement; this is often seen as a less spectacular but more lasting influence. Richard Täufel, "Zu Thomas Manns Schillerbild," *Spektrum,* XI, recognizes the importance of Schiller as man as well as artist. Fritz Strich, "Schiller und Thomas Mann," *Neue Rundschau,* LXVIII, would stress Mann's "Schillernähe" over the usually stressed Goethe-relationship. Horst Daemmrich, "Friedrich Schiller and Thomas Mann: Parallels in Aesthetics," *The Journal of Aesthetics and Art Criticism,* XXIV, folows through Mann's artist characters and his essayistic comments on artists the deep and persistent influence of Schiller's aesthetics. Herbert Lehnert, "Thomas Mann und Schiller" (*Rice Inst. Pamphlet,* XLVII), emphasizes the "respectful reserve" and the permanent ambivalence in Mann's attitude to Schiller. He believes that it derives from repulsion by the official German Schiller-figure inculcated in the Gymnasium and aggravated by Schiller as "Menschheits-patriot" and engagé artist. See also Lehnert's *Thomas Mann: Fiktion, Mythos, Religion* (Stuttgart, 1965).

[2] Self-analysis is always implicit in Mann's dealings with other writers, a search for his own artistic temperament and place, for the pattern of his own life. See T. J. Reed, "Thomas Mann, Heine, Schiller: the Mechanics of Self-Interpretation," *Neophilologus,* XLVII (January 1963): 41-50, who refers to Mann's "creative memory" —his free hand in crediting influences and assessing them.

The more important essays on Schiller and Goethe will be examined
first. Then, to see how these insights appear in Mann's art, I will in-
vestigate the portrayal of Goethe and Schiller in a novel and a short
novella. In *Lotte in Weimar* Goethe alone appears. Schiller has been
dead for 10 years, and we see him through the survivor's eyes. In
A Weary Hour he shows us Schiller at work, thinking of the absent
Goethe with envy and longing.

In the essays, not only does Mann describe Goethe and Schiller in
terms we have come to associate with the male and female principles;
he also frequently uses the terms "male" and "female." In "Phantasie
über Goethe"[3] Mann speaks of Goethe's heroes. They tend to be
weaklings, he believes, to lack masculinity. This is not to say that
Goethe's own association with the female principle is a sign of weakness.
The heroes are male, but their male nature is poorly articulated. In any
case, Mann considers Goethe's work confessional only in a special—
"radical" or "penitent"—sense, so that the heroes are autobiographical
only in this limited way. Goethe's art, Mann feels, is human rather
than masculine. That of Schiller is "much more masculine." Schiller is
surrounded by an atmosphere of "manly ideality, of ideal manhood."[4]
As the most inclusive quality of Schiller, his association with the male
principle frequently caps Mann's lists of the attributes of Schiller's
greatness.[5] His masculinity is "excessive, anti-natural, this espousal of
will, freedom, awareness."[6] Finding reasons for Schiller's attitude in his
early life, Mann reminds us of the barracks masculinity of the military
school.

When the male-female polarity is mentioned, it often occurs in the
company of other dialectics—life set over against thought, conscious
morality over against innocence, saint over against God, spirit over
against nature.[7] Some of the other polarities are also expressly associated
with Goethe and Schiller. Thus, Schiller is presented, like Dostoevski, as
a saint whose high status results from conscious and heroic struggle
whereas Goethe, along with Tolstoy, is divine. The male-female dialectic

---

[3] In *Gesammelte Werke*, (Oldenburg, 1960), IX, 744, for instance. The translation
"Fantasy on Goethe" is by Richard and Clara Winston.

[4] *Versuch über Schiller*, in *Gesammelte Werke*, IX, 872. I have used the Winstons'
translation "On Schiller" (p. 6).

[5] *On Schiller*, p. 11, for instance.

[6] *On Schiller*, p. 11.

[7] See *Goethe and Tolstoy*, p. 122.

is again a culmination and a summation of these qualities.[8] It is given this power and privilege because it alone among the dialectics clearly possesses a force that Mann imputes to them all—mutual attraction, the drive for synthesis, an inherent dynamic. And for Mann this attraction of the Other, of the unlike, is the province of Eros, "the ironic God."[9] Because he thinks of spirit and nature not merely as a polarity but a dialectic, Mann sees their attraction as being erotic and determined by the polarity of the sexes.

Goethe's roots in the female principle are stressed by a constant association with the sphere of the mother. At times this is achieved by reference to Goethe's life. Again and again Mann reminds us of the strong influence of Goethe's mother. Though he incorporated some of his father's interests in his own life (the collector's impulse, for instance, of which Mann speaks in *Lotte in Weimar*), Goethe was, to Mann, not a "Vater-Mensch." He is rather the son of the mother, the joyful Frau Aja. Often, Mann pursues this blood line of the mother and its influence on the son farther back into the past—on its female side only. The continuity of the female principle asserts itself again as the maternal line flows into the Great Mother, the Universal Mother.[10] Goethe's artistic creativity is compared to childbirth.[11] The pleasure that Goethe found in the patient execution and in the frequently lengthy dormancy of his artistic plans Mann likens to the mother's patience in carrying a child.

This feminine patience is connected with attributes of the female realm—passivity and a privileged relationship to time. Goethe, Mann tells us, was at home in the past as well as in the future. His "joy in the future was comprehensive."[12] On another occasion, he blames Goethe's complex nature that makes it so difficult to capture him unambiguously. The example that Mann chooses to illustrate this difficulty

---

[8] For Goethe himself, also, the male-female opposition constitutes the epitome and consummation of all other polarities. In his introduction to the *Theory of Colors* he uses it to cap a series of five other contrasting pairs that cluster, predominantly, around the active-passive distinction.

[9] *Goethe and Tolstoy,* p. 123.

[10] *Fantasy on Goethe,* p. 120.

[11] See Chapter 6 for a discussion of this conjunction.

[12] *Goethe as Representative of the Bourgeois Age,* in *Essays of Three Decades,* p. 91. Mann forms a compound "Zukunftsfreudigkeit" (future-happiness) to stress the special nature of the quality.

is Goethe's relationship to time. Though he could occasionally indulge in a veritable cult of time, more often he would leave himself time, procrastinate and wait on a grand scale. He "passively and vegetatively left things to take their course." [13] Schiller, on the other hand, never rests. Neither is he ever described as passive. His life is, rather, one of "always pushing forward, upward." [14] In another context, we will encounter these contrasting attitudes later.

In the essays, Mann uses the same vocabulary to describe that aspect of the female principle which I have summarized as "passivity" as he does in his fiction. At times, Goethe is said to be "passive;" at others, kindred words appear, words that evoke memories of Clavdia and other representatives of the female principle. Along with forbearance and kindliness, Goethe possesses indulgence—"Lässlichkeit." [15] Schiller, the creature of spirit, moves in the sphere of will and freedom; nature, Goethe's maternal element, is instead mildly tolerant—"lässlich" again. [16] Children of God in whom the divine as well as the animal force is alive— Goethe and Tolstoy—also contain "the folk, being, peace, woman . . . ." [17]

Goethe is Antaeus-like; strong when he is close to the earth. Sometimes, these roots are expressed in other terms. Mann's own composites, they often repeat or resemble words one encounters in *The Magic Mountain* or the Joseph stories. "Lebensbürgerlichkeit" is one,[18] emphasizing commitment to life in the guise of citizenship. Another term that stresses if not passivity then at least receptivity is "Schicksalsfähigkeit"—the capacity for opening oneself up to and accepting whatever may turn out to be one's destiny. This capacity ensures that passivity is not empty, that it lets powers unfold.

The passivity connected with the female principle is related to the

---

[13] *Fantasy on Goethe*, p. 128.

[14] *On Schiller*, p. 68.

[15] *Fantasy on Goethe*, p. 121.

[16] *Goethe und Tolstoy*, in *Gesammelte Werke*, IX, p. 97.

[17] *Goethe und Tolstoy*, p. 173.

[18] *Goethe als Repräsentant des bürgerlichen Zeitalters, Gesammelte Werke*, IX, 321. Mrs. Lowe-Porter understandably has difficulty in translating the term. She renders it as "the bourgeois attitude towards life" (In *Essays of Three Decades*, p. 83) which misses the implication of allegiance to life itself, but then, realizing the insufficiency of the phrase, puts the German term in parentheses. Knowing Mann's antithesis of burgher and artist, one might construe the term as an opposition to "Lebenskunst."

dialectic of Being and Doing.[19] The female is; the male does. Mann implies that talent has more to do with what one is than with what one can do.[20] This is true of life as well as of literature. Both Goethe and Tolstoy are exact and sensual in their art. The plasticity of their imagination endows their characters with "the reality of being," whereas the "sentimental" writers Schiller and Dostoevski need actions to give the density of real existence to their heroes.[21] The other two are immersed in the sensual immediacy of physical life—they possess this density themselves. That quality rates another composite epithet—"Seinswirklichkeit" or reality of being.[22]

Being and Doing are behind Schiller's distinction between talent and merit. Merit is a personal achievement, carved out with conscious will power in the awareness of individual freedom. Talent, being a gift of nature, is sometimes seen by him as superior and enviable in its effortless grace. At other times he claims equal rank for effort and struggle. E. M. Wilkinson and L. A. Willoughby in the introduction to their edition of Schiller's *On the Aesthetic Education of Man*[23] comment on the persistent concern of Schiller with this matter and on his ambivalence toward it. Ambivalence is also inherent in Goethe's thinking about the problem of talent and merit—his famous phrase "angeborene Verdienste" indicates a desire to give credit to both sides, to synthesize, at least through language. Mann's own mixed feelings, then, though they derive partly from his own complex attitude toward Goethe and Schiller, are also founded on an ambivalence and ambiguity inherent in their statements.

Yet another version of the active-passive, or Doing-Being dialectic emerges in Mann's essay on Schiller. There the antipode of Being is "the beholder" ("der Schauende"). The word implies the contemplative existence with its inherent self-consciousness, but it also preserves the

---

[19] E. M. Wilkinson and L. A. Willoughby in "Having and Being, or Bourgeois Versus Nobility," GLL v. XXII, 1968-69 point to Doing/Being among other Goethe-Schiller antitheses such as Having/Being; Bürger/Adel; Seeming/Being. The authors suggest that these oppositions, as they appeared in the third chapter of the Fifth Book of *Wilhelm Meisters Lehrjahre* and in a number of Goethe-Schiller distichs, influenced Coleridge and through him other English thinkers as well. Mann here is dealing with a commonplace.

[20] *Goethe and Tolstoy*, p. 103.

[21] *Goethe and Tolstoy*, p. 118.

[22] *Goethe and Tolstoy*, p. 118. The translator insufficiently renders the terms as "life-likeness," thus missing the emphasis on Being as opposed to Doing.

[23] Oxford, 1967, pp. xli-xlii.

literal meaning of seeing. The persistent theme of eye color and eye contact in Mann's art may gain depth if it is examined in this context. Another theme that appears frequently in the work and that emerges here in connection with this fundamental dialectic is that of the skin. Mann cites Goethe contentedly musing on how well he felt in his own skin.[24] Those that share in the female principle feel no desperate striving to penetrate the skin. Their Self is not a prison but a source of comfort. Open as they are to the world, the skin to them is not a symbol of painful separation but rather a permeable and natural boundary.

This sense of wellbeing is one's own skin, this pleasure in the self, is elsewhere described as a "magnificent narcissism."[25] Those who knew both man and work (Mann cites Humboldt) speak of the great impact Goethe had merely through his being, his personality, apart from the greatness of his work. But even in the work the uncommon force of the personality makes itself felt. The love for oneself that Goethe shares with Tolstoy is deeper and more productive than mere vanity. To Mann, it is not narcissistic in the narrow sense; rather, love of self and love of world are so closely interwoven in this feeling that they cannot be distinguished. Egoism and altruism merge in love.[26] In the work, the result is autobiography, either explicit or implied. The reader's empathy with the author can be assumed because of this intimate association of self and world. Out of such sef-concern, comes preoccupation with themes of education and a preference for the genre of the *Bildungsroman*. In the novel of education the self becomes a project, and the author can separate himself sufficiently from this other self to serve as his guide. He can even treat the hero with considerable irony. In view of Mann's own contributions to the genre, it is not surprising that he should be charmed by Goethe's reference to his Wilhelm Meister as "a poor dog," all of course in the spirit of paternal tenderness.[27] Mann believes that, in order to bring to life the mysterious bonds of sympathy between the writer and his public, it is enough for the artist to express *himself*. No need even for a pretense of universality. Whatever in the portrayal emerges as representative may well be unintentional and work its charm

---

[24] *Goethe and Tolstoy*, p. 126. The translator uses the idiomatic English phrase: "felt so much at ease....," but preserves the metaphor by showing the original parenthetically.

[25] *Fantasy on Goethe*, p. 99.

[26] *Goethe and Tolstoy*, p. 103.

[27] *Goethe and Tolstoy*, p. 159.

without any need for a real or felt correspondence between the nature and fate of the artist and his public.[28]

It may well seem odd that Gustave Aschenbach, male as he is, should benefit from these mysterious bonds that make for the public's involvement in an artist's work no matter how aloof he is himself. Yet it is this ineffable "sympathy" that renders Aschenbach's work popular and famous. Any artist, we will see, needs some share in the female principle to remain productive, but for a limited time he can spin the work out of himself, through sacrifice and discipline. The male principle held almost exclusive sway over Aschenbach before he went to Venice. The overwhelmingly "male" artist must take special measures to keep writing. Schiller's maleness is further enchanced by associating him with this fictional artist.

At the outset, I remarked that Aschenbach's most ambitious work is compared to Schiller's essay, the work that, to Mann, contains and makes superfluous all other German essays.[29] Aschenbach's obsession with the "impurity" of the artist's perception of truth presents a negative aspect of a problem that Schiller resolves in seeing art as the reconciliation of spirit and senses. Aschenbach, too, at his happier moments recognizes the fullness of this "middle ground" and its special privilege. Amor, he muses, works like some mathematicians who make simple models of pure forms to show to backward children. In the same way, he uses the beautiful forms of a boy to make the spiritual attract us. Mann is ascribing to Aschenbach a thought whose supreme expression he himself admires in a Schiller poem. Its title is, significantly, "Verkindlichung" ("becoming a child again," perhaps; the term focusses on the "making childlike"). Urania whose fiery sight we cannot endure, helps us by changing her aspect:

And with her flaming chaplet laid aside,
Upon her sun-illumined throne appears
Beauty personified—our light and guide.
With every attribute of grace endued,
Her childlike innocence appeals to youth,
And that which is today as Beauty viewed
Anon will prove to be the very Truth.[30]

---

[28] *Goethe's Career as a Man of Letters*, in *Essays of Three Decades*, p. 49.
[29] *Goethe and Tolstoy*, p. 95.
[30] *On Schiller*, p. 9.

Other bridges connecting Aschenbach to Schiller are personal. Their work is a result of struggle against their own nature, against external obstacles, finally against time. No less than Aschenbach's, Schiller's work is a "Trotzdem," a possession wrested from adversity and perhaps owing its very existence to the goad of that adversity. Disease is the foremost of the obstacles, and it demonstrates this ambivalence well. Schiller's illness, as well as Dostoevski's, is to Mann an inherent and necessary part of their personality and their artistry. It is a symbolical quality. Nature has not made them divine, as it has Goethe and Tolstoy: the greatness they achieve ("nobility" is the word Mann uses) is conferred upon them through spirit by disease. Disease is not equated with spirituality, though it seems that occasionally it can work for the same ends (one only need think of Hans Castorp to corroborate this). Like spirituality, illness alienates one from nature. The more alienated one is from nature the more human, until this painful process of humanization ends in the saint. The saint is totally unlike the god, the pinnacle of an opposed development. As naiveté is associated with nature, along with objectivity and health, so sentimentality encompasses the realm of the spirit, subjectivity, and the pathological. Plasticity is the artistic hallmark of the former, while that of the latter is its critical acumen.[31] It should be clear from this that Gustave Aschenbach belongs with Dostoevski and Schiller (as does Mann himself). The strength of their critical faculty which is evident in their art as well as in their discursive writing adds yet more credibility to that grouping. Goethe, Mann believes, did not bother about the didactic effect of his work. Unlike Schiller, who is concerned with moral questions, he does not see art as a means to an end.

These parallels between the imagined artist Aschenbach and Schiller, "real" but also seen through Mann's imagination and recreated by him, strengthen the association of Schiller with the male principle. They also stress the remarkable persistence and the permanent content of Mann's vision. This continuity can be seen even in the similar ways in which Schiller and Aschenbach are said to accomodate themselves to disease. Mann actually uses the same phrase to characterize the strenuous mental life that results from physical weakness and that the two share—*motus animi continuus*.[32]

Schiller partakes of another of Aschenbach's attitudes, one that deserves mention because it is closely and significantly connected with the male

---

[31] See *Goethe and Tolstoy*, pp. 113-114.
[32] *On Schiller*, p. 68 and *Death in Venice*, pp. 3-4.

principle and its active striving. That is his sense of place. Aschenbach, as long as he remains faithful to the male principle, seeks out enclosed places. He has no desire to travel, no yearning for physical expansion or adventuring in unknown locations. When he strives to escape from the confines of his life, the struggle is intellectual and spiritual rather than physical. The attitude toward places, to Mann, apparently is an important category to be considered in revealing a personality. No wonder, then, that in essays on Goethe and Schiller their feeling for places should be mentioned. Schiller, Mann tells us, never had a desire to see and feel the places which served as settings for his plays. For *Wilhelm Tell*, Goethe gave his friend information about Switzerland, and the latter used it well, though he did not want to go and see the country for himself. Never having been near the sea, let alone on it, Schiller was planning stories of adventure upon the high seas.[33] Goethe, on the other hand, felt drawn by distant places. It is with approval that Mann cites Goethe on the necessity for the German to "take the world into himself in order to influence the world" rather than to close in upon himself.[34] Along with Goethe's free movement in time, Mann names his enviable spatial freedom. Goethe writes world literature; he is a citizen of the world; his concern always encompasses all. His is an "imperialism of love." [35]

Mann's essays on Goethe and Schiller are not strictly biographical. Neither do most of them deal with the work of the two. They are rather investigations of personality in its fundamental relationship to art, to itself, to the external world, and to existence. The aspects under which Mann sees these relationships and the categories he chooses under which to discuss them betray his own attitudes. We have just observed one persistent concern—sense of place. Time, a more prominent theme, was discussed earlier. Another obligatory category is the relationship of Goethe and Schiller to women. It is surely pertinent to a dialectic cast in terms of sex, and it also points toward the necessity of an examination of the role of love, to be undertaken later. A theme in both *A Weary Hour* and *Lotte in Weimar,* this relationship is constantly dealt with in the essays as well.

Noting Goethe's rich and varied love life Mann marvels at the creative role of Eros in the writer's career. Love's close association with the

---

[33] *On Schiller,* p. 70.

[34] *Goethe as Representative of the Bourgeois Age,* p. 87.

[35] See *Goethe as Representative,* p. 91, where Mrs. Lowe-Porter translates it as "benevolent imperialism."

artistic process in Mann's scheme becomes clear here. Women inspire works, by proffering warmth of life to be built into the foundation of fictional characters and by quickening the emotions of the author. Mann does not speak of love affairs for their own sake; they are always seen in their relationship to the work of art. And it is not only an undifferentiated creative force that is engendered in these affairs. The intensity of love determines the scope of the work produced, if not its quality. Out of an uncommitting lighthearted affair might come "a Venetian epigram ticked out in hexameters on a maiden's back," [36] but the great work is stimulated by other kinds of relationships. Renunciation is always necessary for them. Love and art appear to be alternate ways, and when the artistic process is totally successful, when the work is great and good, love has been a mediation. Even if this is painful, the object must be left behind. It may be that such renunciation is what an artist thrives on—is a requirement of artistic creation, and that Norman Brown is correct in suggesting that: "Freedom in the use of symbolism comes from the capacity to experience loss." [37] Art, as a supreme symbolic expression, would necessitate much loss.

Thus, Goethe's elusiveness in love affairs receives a higher endorsement. All those who have basked in his love must needs accept this elusiveness and pay the price. In a sense, *Lotte in Weimar* is a testimonial and a compensation for those who suffer from this necessity, who cannot quite understand it and fail to cope with it.

If Goethe's loving is to Mann "a means to an end, a means to the work," [38] so is Schiller's. As Mann mentions each love affair, he consistently follows the account with an assessment of its yield in art. Lottchen von Wolzogen helped *Kabale und Liebe* along; Charlotte von Kalb facilitated the creation of *Don Carlos.* Yet, as we saw earlier, Mann admits that Schiller's nature in which the male principle predominates so heavily prevents him from creating convincing female characters. Why? There is transcendence of the object here as well. The two affairs are not consummated in life. One might expect that circumstance to result in an immediate transcendence. Yet it seems to be this very lack of vitality in the relationships that prevents their bearing fruit in art. Again, Schiller

---

[36] *Goethe and Tolstoy*, p. 139. It is Roman rather than Venetian. The reference is to Goethe's *Römische Elegien*. In the fifth, the poet speaks of composing poetry in his love's arms.

[37] *Love's Body* (New York, 1966), p. 260.

[38] *Fantasy on Goethe*, p. 130.

here is reminiscent of Aschenbach.[39] For transcendence to be meaningful, something must be transcended. For renunciation to be costly one must have a lively and real appreciation of what is given up. His early love affairs bring only slight familiarity with women to Schiller. His dealings with women remain "relationess relationships."[40] For Schiller, the fruitful erotic tension resides rather in his friendship with Goethe. In another assertion of the male-female polarity Mann confirms my impression of his assessment:

> In him the polarity of the sexes was transformed into intellectual terms, as was everything else. The great adventure of his life, his experience with passionate attraction and repulsion, with deep hostility, deep yearning and admiration, with giving and taking, with jealousy, downcast envy and proud self-assertiveness, with long-lasting emotional tension—was an affair between man and man, between himself, who was so essentially masculine, and that other poet to whom he was inclined to attribute a feminine disposition . . . .[41]

In this relationship Schiller conformed to his usual role. He was the active one, the one who sought contact, while Goethe attracted by his mere being. Schiller wooed. Mann quotes him as speaking of Goethe "as if he were some coy an self-willed beauty who must be 'knocked up' if she is to be held."[42] Yet in spite of the seeming onesidedness of the longing, the female principle is not the only goal of striving. For one, its adherents are by no means unquestioningly happy. Mann's typology is not simplistic, at least in this respect. On the contrary, their single minded dedication to spiritual values and their conviction that those values are good gives the children of the spirit a clarity and harmony that nature's favorites lack. These frequently suffer from their own "negativism" and torture themselves and others with their Mephistophelian spirit of constant contradiction. Nature, they know, is "evil," or rather morally indifferent. The icy neutrality of Goethe, summed up so well in the judgment—"he is tolerant without being mild," derives from that elemental indifference.

What makes the relationship a dialectic is tension on both sides. Though envy and resentment occur, mostly the tension manifests itself in attraction that is felt by both poles. The children of nature strive toward the spirit, and their striving is as "sentimental" as the striving of the *sons* of the spirit (note the masculine gender, another indication of

---

[39] See Chapter 3.
[40] *Versuch*, p. 877. *On Schiller* (p. 11), the translator omits the phrase.
[41] *On Schiller*, pp. 74-75.
[42] *On Schiller*, p. 75.

their male affiliation) toward nature.[43] Thus, both Goethe and Tolstoy strain away from "mere" nature.[44] Feeling their own lack, they praise the other kind, but spirit tends to humble itself more in front of nature. Irony is part of the admiration on both sides. In the essays, Mann appears to find it more frequently on the "male," spiritual side. Repeatedly, he cites Schiller's warning Goethe against Kant's philosophy of freedom. Immersion in it would destroy his Spinozist friend's "beautiful naive nature." [45] As in Tonio Kröger's refusal to make his beloved and different friend like himself, Mann sees in this a gentle contempt along with love. Yet it is another testimonial of this love, one that does not contain irony, that evokes ecstatic praise from Mann for Schiller's love-hate struggle, his heroic altruism and sublimation. It is a poem *Fortune* ("Das Glück"). Mann calls it a "love song of the mind" and would gladly give volumes of erotic lyrics for it.[46]

The goal is in the middle, and the terms in which Mann describes that middle are telling. It is "difficult"; it is also "fruitful." [47] The fruitlessness of exclusive association with either pole emerges from this. It is demonstrated in many ways throughout this discussion, especially in terms of artistic production. The middle ground gives rise to irony—irony is said to be its pathos, its morality, its ethos. The synthesis or the "higher unity" is not described precisely or concretely, but we are pointed in an approximate direction: This goal carries the name of "humanitas." [48] Perhaps our closest encounter with it so far has been in the examination of *The Magic Mountain* where Clavdia's identifying tag was her peculiarly Slavic version of the word "human."

Mann strives for this middle ground, emotionally and politically, for himself and for Germany. Our concern is with manifestations of the male and female principles in his work, not with fixing Mann's own coordinates in this range. Yet his empathy with the troubles and felicities of representatives of the male principle indicates his position. Since his own stance colors and even determines the presentation of the polarity in the work, it needs at the very least to be pointed out. Since it may also explain the placement of Goethe and Schiller in this scheme, one

[43] *Goethe and Tolstoy*, p. 141.

[44] *Goethe and Tolstoy*, p. 104.

[45] *On Schiller*, also *Goethe and Tolstoy*, p. 122.

[46] *On Schiller*, p. 78. It is also described as a homage of the one who beholds to the one who exists.

[47] *Goethe and Tolstoy*, p. 174.

[48] *Goethe and Tolstoy*, p. 174.

should examine not only what he says about the two authors but also how he says it and what he implies. It is in his treatment of the two personalities that Mann most often uses the terms "male" and "female" to describe the contrast. This, then, might well be seen as a pattern for the dialectic throughout Mann's work. It deserves a closer look.

Reading one of Mann's essays on Schiller just after finishing one on Goethe, one is struck by a difference in tone. It is a matter of entering a totally new world of feeling. Frequently, the author mentions his love for each, but this love finds expression in widely varying ways. An analysis of Mann's discursive rhetoric may well be worth while, but here I can only point the particular contrast with which I am concerned by a few examples.

The extensive essay "On Schiller" and the shorter Goethe-essay on "Goethe as Representative of the Bourgeois Age" are sufficiently similar in intent to yield some instances of the kind of comparison that might be carried through Mann's entire discursive writing on these two authors. His love for Goethe molds his rhetoric into admiring but gently ironic tones. That for Schiller, no less intense, is inhibited in its expression by a feeling of embarassment. Sensing himself akin, Mann cannot find it in himself to praise with such simple warmth. Instead, there is a violent wrench of detachment that occasionally rushes forth in high pathos. Pity, love, respect—all shine through Mann's essays on Schiler—but there is no humor, no irony. His affinity with Schiller renders his love awkward to express. When the expression is not so directly a pronouncement of the author as it is in the essay, that is, when Schiller is seen through the imaginative and detaching transparency of a work of art, the pathos is reduced. The tone is quite different in *A Weary Hour*. In the essays, however, that "erotic" quality which results from the attraction of an opposed force, that gentle, loving irony is reserved for Goethe.

An imaginative reconstruction of Schiller's funeral introduces the Schiller-essay. This prelude culminates in a vision of Schiller resurrected, which illustrates one of the pinnacles of Mann's Schiller-rhetoric.

Set loose from matter's corruption, surrounded by manly ideality, ideal manliness, bold, fiery and tender, with its Redeemer-gaze, baring its royal visage to the stars —thus it [the figure of Schiller] was already in this hour of burial—and for always— erected in purity for the intimate love of its people and the sympathy of humanity, this immortal figure, branded with all the marks of unique life, and on its forehead, ennobled by the dignity of thought, shines, as on that of the high Uranide in the poem, the combined luster of "sense happiness and soul's peace," the artist's notion that *Beauty* relieves us of the frightening choice between them, that it gives rise to a human unity between sensuality and virtue, that it reconciles our earthly and our higher nature, building a bridge between ideal and life; that the varying idea of "the good" belongs in praise to both worlds, the aesthetic and the moral, and that beauty and truth fuse in art, that tutor of the human race.[49]

Some of the inspiration for the rhetoric of this sentence comes from Schiller's own style, so different from Goethe's, but it is predominantly the result of Mann's emotional involvement. By comparison, the syntax and level of discourse is much more restrained and common sense in the Goethe essay. Both essays begin similarly. Both have prefatory elements that set the mood and deal with Mann's own reactions to Goethe and Schiller. The Schiller essay begins with poetry and proceeds to the reconstruction of the funeral. A formula of humility follows: 'Who am I that I should praise him. . . .' Finding, nonetheless, a mystical "fraternity" with Schiller, based on their common artistry, he goes on to discuss the man and his work at some length. Similar elements introduce the Goethe essay. There is no verse, but instead a concrete experience is evoked. More concrete, to Mann, than Schiller's funeral, it is his own first visit to Goethe's ancestral house on the Hirschgraben in Frankfurt. Instead of a poem, we are presented with a house; we are breathing the atmosphere where genius existed for a while—Being as against Doing. Again, a homily forms the high point of the introduction, and again it immediately precedes an expression of humility. It even sports an exclamation point, something that is frequent in the Schiller essay but much rarer in the Goethe one. Yet, its tone is quite different from that of the comparable passage I just cited from "On Schiller."

The bourgeois and the patrician have become the resort of the Muses, where the foot falls with reverence, as at the cradle of a hero; here reign dignity and respectability, preserved and held sacred for the sake of universality. I looked at it, I breathed it in, and the conflict between familiarity and awe was resolved in my heart in a feeling wherein humility and self-assertion are one: in smiling love.[50]

It is "smiling love" that Mann feels. And one can sense the smile hovering over the words even before it is mentioned. Mann's erotic irony is at work here as it cannot be with Schiller. Even the disavowal of special

---

[49] *Versuch*, pp. 872-873. The Winstons in *On Schiller*, pp. 6-7, make a much preferable translation, but I did my own to try to give a sense of the complexity and the sustained cadence of the original. The translators understandably make four sentences out of the one in the original.

[50] *Goethe as Representative*, p. 66.

qualification on his part to speak of genius so great, similarly placed and similarly phrased, is resolved differently. The legitimacy he seeks for speaking on Schiller, Mann finds in "the kinship of experience, the brotherhood, the intimacy which exists among all creative artists irrespective of differences of rank, time, and kind."[51] With Goethe, such kinship, far reaching as it is said to be, is not invoked. Instead, Mann claims affinity and justification for his comments "in the human and natural."[52] It is in Mann's own substance, in his own being—specifically in being, like Goethe, German and "bourgeois" (with all the associations of humanism, middle ground and the other overtones that the word carries for Mann) that Mann finds his legitimacy here, not, as with Schiller, in the creative *act*.

A heightening and an imaginative structuring of these insights occurs in Mann's fiction, where his empathy impels him to look inside the two minds and hearts. We witness the thoughts of both—Schiller's briefly, Goethe's more expansively. *A Weary Hour* introduces Schiller in his bare hexagonal study on a cruel December night long past midnight. Like Aschenbach in the later novella, he first appears in flight from his work. But he is even more enclosed physically than was Aschenbach. The doctor's well meaning regimen keeps him in a "narrow imprisonment," a virtual house arrest. This limits his flight sadly—he walks to the opposite corner of the room. He is cold. One suspects that here as elsewhere in Mann's work (most prominently in *Doctor Faustus*) coldness is more than physical. It is a metaphor for lack of human contact, for loneliness and isolation. It plagues representatives of the male principle (Adrian Leverkühn in *Doctor Faustus* surely is one of them). Here, Mann clothes his typology well with the fabric of art. Schiller's chill is concrete. As he places his hands against the tiled stove only to be disappointed in the expectation of a remnant of warmth, the typology is lost, and we participate in the pattern of Schiller's feeling. It is damp and chilly in the room; he has a cold. Warmth to him is a physical necessity. But it also points to his yearning for human affection and happiness. The gathered red curtains on the upper panes of the windows, tiny as they are, seem to him warm. They bring in a note of luxury and sensuality. If Schiller standing by the cool stove, vainly hoping for a vestige of its benefit, makes for pathos, it is pathos of a different sort than that in the high flown rhetoric of the essays.

[51] *On Schiller*, p. 7.
[52] *Goethe as Representative*, p. 66.

Mann's view of Schiller, I have indicated, stresses those aspects which he articulates as the characteristics of his own creation Aschenbach. Caught first in flight, they share this chafing at the burden of their proud but draining work. In terms similar to those used by Aschenbach, Schiller thinks of his study as a place of wrestling and struggle. His striving for recognition and fame from his public, the desire to be loved by all in return for his suffering is also reminiscent of Aschenbach's eager acceptance of public honors. The "male" attitude toward individuation is evident. To want to be loved by all the people of the earth—known and loved—may seem egoistic, he admits, to those who know nothing of the sweetness and power of this kind of egoism. It shows, on the one hand, the compulsion to break out of individuation. The wider the aspiration the more telling it is of the suffocating sense of confinement which gives rise to it. It is not akin to Goethe's love of travel and his spiritual cosmopolitanism; it is not a true opening of oneself to the external world, not effortlessly receptive. Straining and compelling, it is rather the will to yoke the world to oneself in an obligation to admire one's own supreme self as manifested in the work. Out of his travail this work is spun, and for it reward is his due. Anyone extraordinary who suffers, Schiller thinks, is egoistical. The extremity of Schiller's pain pushes his sense of self to extremes. Thus, in the final analysis, though he claims to want to be loved by all, he does not really long to break his solipsistic self-concern. A "passion for his self" burns forever in the recesses of his soul. It is also termed love and "secret intoxication." [53] Occasionally, even a glance at his own hand would fill him with "tender enthusiasm."

Anticipating Aschenbach's vocabulary Mann's Schiller speaks of his victory (and the language of struggle that Mann attributes to his hero is prominent in Schiller's own work) as a "bleeding 'despite,'" the famous "Trotzdem" of *Death in Venice*. His is the heroism of weakness that Aschenbach's works are said to celebrate. He uses his own suffering as a goad to writing because, like Aschenbach, he lacks the tension of a fruitful intercourse with the outside world. No wonder, then, that he should feel superior because he creates "out of nothing, out of his own breast." [54] If Aschenbach thinks of the duties set him by "his own self and the European soul" Schiller ascribes his fatigue to a wrestling with the mission set him by his Self. Standing in his study, his nostrils aflare,

---

[53] *A Weary Hour*, p. 294.
[54] *A Weary Hour*, p. 295.

his gaze imperious, Schiller pushes his right hand under the lapel of his robe, Napoleon-like. The left hand performs a gesture that we know well by now. It forms something that has become a virtual symbol for the male principle—the fist. While his mind is preoccupied with thoughts about artistic egoism, his left hand hangs down, clenched into a fist.

Yet Schiller is not wholly isolated. He has close ties with two human beings—his wife and Goethe. Tempted to reach for a cup of strong coffee, he hesitates for a moment remembering the doctor's prohibition. But it is the warning of his friend that finally gives him the strength to resist. Goethe is never mentioned by name. He is always "the other one," the one in Weimar. Twice he is identified as the one "whom he [Schiller] loved with a yearning enmity." On second mention, the formula has grown longer. It is now "the other man, that radiant being, so sense-endowed, so divinely unconscious, that man over there in Weimar, whom he loved and hated." [55] Love is there, and so is hostility, but they are both qualified by yearning. In *Death in Venice* Aschenbach is made to say that the artist's love must remain longing. Transcendence of the loved one gives impetus to the work of art without binding the artist to a demanding human relationship. Schiller's work is "a marvel of yearning after form, shape, line, body; of yearning after the sunlit world of that other man. . . ." [56] This is the source of creative tension in Schiller's life. One does not long for what one has. Schiller's strong feeling for himself is egoism, tenderness, love. It may spur him to work at times, as Aschenbach is spurred by self-generated tensions, but it cannot ensure continued productivity. Neither is his relationship to his wife creative artistically. There is a rueful tenderness in it, a regret perhaps at his fundamental inability to love. He senses that the possession implicit in marriage is something apart from those feelings which generate his art. His final interpretation of freedom, he claims, must also include that from the "silken fetter" of such contentment. Helped by the coldness of his nature, he knows how to restrain himself in relationships where the danger of commitment exists. "I must not be too utterly thine, never utterly happy in thee, for the sake of my mission." [57] This is Schiller's confession to his sleeping wife. He has a similar restraint against too much melancholy musing and too deep a descent into himself. The difficult hour we witness is temporary indulgence of his tendency toward

[55] *A Weary Hour*, p. 294.
[56] *A Weary Hour*, p. 295.
[57] *A Weary Hour*, p. 296.

these, but at its end he pulls himself together and goes back to work. Aschenbach has lost the wish and the capacity for such an act of will. Schiller recognizes both the inspiring wealth and the danger of chaos, here seen primarily as a subconscious force. Inchoate shapes lie there, ripening and waiting their turn to be lifted up into the light and receive final form. But it is best not to go down there, and if one must, at least not to stay long. Schiller retains this saving insight and with it his strength to keep working.

Some of the differences in Mann's treatment of Goethe as compared with that of Schiller derive, in this juxtaposition, from the more leisurely novel scope devoted to the former as against the compression necessary in a novella like *A Weary Hour*. Thus, well over half of Lotte in Weimar goes by before we meet Goethe. Yet there is no doubt about his importance in spite of this late appearance. Lotte is the heroine only insofar as he has made her one. All the talk has been of him. Lotte's thoughts have been of him. We see nothing but traces of the fascination and the destruction exercised by his personality upon the persons and lives of those whose existence has touched his. Lotte's nervous tic, secretary Riemer's shaking hands, August von Goethe's pathetic dependence—all are scars from dealings with the genius. They shyly exhibit their wounds to each other, recoil in horror at their depth, pity each other, and finally put a good front on it all. Goethe's force seems immense; to hurt so much and yet to keep the love of the injured, one must be very special. Suddenly, in the seventh chapter we meet him. No direct description of his appearance or even his activity has preceded this confrontation.

After the long introduction we are plunged suddenly into the middle of the aged Goethe's thoughts. He has just awakened from a sensual and concrete vision of a Venus and Adonis in the gallery in Dresden. As a contrast to the sight of Schiller in desperate flight from his work, this first glimpse of Goethe, tantalizingly prepared, conveys Mann's polarity well. Goethe is at first disappointed at the loss of the charming apparition; then he lovingly recalls its detail, thinks about the inadequacy of those who would restore works of art, and finally comes to long-delayed projects. But, unlike Schiller, he is not tortured by his own bent for postponement. Here there is no guilt feeling, no frustration, no desperate goading of oneself to get done. Goethe knows, even now, that he has time. To postpone is good, he feels. Mann, we saw, compared him to a woman carrying a child. Like the unborn infant the work gets better with time; to wrench it forth before its hour would be to kill or deform it. Presumably it will insist itself when its time has come. Neither is there in Goethe any pressing sense of the need for greatness (he is, now, *the* genius already, but, in any case, he would know that that would come in its own time). There is no feeling of compulsion to compete with another against whose work one must constantly delimit and measure one's own. It is unnecessary, Goethe muses, to fear another's taking his material away —even should he use the same substance, he could not take anything from Goethe. This is sovereign assurance, indeed. To acquire it one must be secure in the sense of one's unique qualities.

Mann displays the negative side of such uniqueness also, one of which he speaks in the essays: its nagging doubts, its irritations, its loneliness. Schiller has been dead ten years. He was the one who consoled, praised, and spurred, the one who understood the work before it existed and whose approval meant something. This is active encouragement; it is described in energetic terms: "Were he but here ... to spur me on, to challenge and stimulate!" [58] Goethe, it seemed in *A Weary Hour,* served as an encouragement for Schiller as well. But he did it passively—merely by being there and by being different. This was enough for his friend who struggled endlessly to document and describe that difference and to show his own nature in his work.

From thoughts about a projected "Amor and Psyche" Goethe progresses to consider his planned Reformation cantata. For an old pagan, he muses, he is not a bad Christian after all. For the choruses, he intends to draw on "Pandora." But in the center there must remain "Himself and the higher teaching, mind, ever misunderstood by the mob; isolation, soul's utter anguish—yet ever consoling and giving strength." [59] Knowing that Goethe is thinking of the cantata, one may yet have the impression on a first reading that "he Himself" is Schiller. On rereading, it seems more reasonable to assume it is Jesus. Yet the double sense remains and is probably intended. Only a few lines later, the same capitalized pronoun "Er" is used to refer clearly to Schiller.

Even if this earlier association of Schiller with Christ is subliminal, it persists and soon receives explicit formulation. The thought returns in a roundabout way. Among the ironies of popular appreciation is the public's misunderstanding of the attitude of Goethe and Schiller to the "folk." Mann's Goethe marvels at the absurdity of the popular perception. Schiller, to them, was the man of the people because he spoke of freedom. In *A Weary Hour* Mann tried to demonstrate how

[58] *The Beloved Returns,* p. 283.
[59] *The Beloved Returns,* p. 283.

metaphysical this conception of freedom was and how different from the general understanding of it. It is he, Goethe, branded as servant of the aristocracy, who understands the strength of the folk and draws upon it. To him, it is the natural element, a "nurturing valley of the unconscious and of rejuvenation." The folk is a concrete manifestation of the female principle. It is collective, anonymous, elemental, and timeless. Schiller does not trust this element. Pulling himself together by effort of will to end his difficult hour, he tells himself that he is too deep to ponder. "One should not climb down into chaos, at least one should not remain there for any length of time," he believes. Goethe, in a similar musing, tells himself just the opposite. "Man cannot tarry long in his conscious mind," he feels, "must take from time to time refuge in his unconscious, there his being has its roots." [60] This descent holds no danger for him. Yet what he emphasizes about Schiller's relationship to the unconscious is not fear but what he believes to be an impossibility to commune with it. The friend is "incapable of submerging" in it. Instead, he elevates the lowly to himself and to the realm of the spirit. This is where we arrive back at the association of Schiller with Jesus. The former's elevating effect is seen as being Christlike. Descent into the subconscious is descent into the female element, descent to the Mothers; one's own transcendence and especially the compassionate effort to lift one's fellow creatures is the stance of the Saviour. In the essays, Mann mentioned Schiller's "Redeemer-face." Here, he has Goethe think of Schiller's "Redeemer-arms" gently lifting his fellow men. Immediately after that, he thinks of Schiller's maleness. Too much man, the friend was close to being unnatural, and that is why his female characters were, in Goethe's eyes, just plain laughable.

Other themes from the essays and from *A Weary Hour* recur. Goethe realizes that Schiller has given himself the mission of helping the other understand himself by pointing out their differences; he also understands and humorously accepts the drive for equal rank that is behind this constant differentiation. In *Lotte in Weimar* Goethe admits he did not like much about Schiller. The qualities he then lists are mostly associated with his friend's illness—his ravaged cheeks, his bent back, the nose disfigured by the chronic cold. Other infelicities of the body are not spared. The red hair and the freckles that go with it do not please the luckier Goethe; neither does the storklike walk. A climber he calls Schiller and feels gentle contempt for the other's hustling for success,

[60] *The Beloved Returns*, p. 285.

not realizing that this is merely another aspect of his striving for elevation and, finally, of his masculinity. Only one aspect of Schiller's outward appearance finds enthusiastic endorsement from Goethe—the friend's eyes. In one of the essays, Mann decribed Schiller as the seeing or beholding one, contrasting his self-conscious nature with Goethe's pure Being. Here he portrays Goethe as remembering those eyes with praise and affection: "But never, long as I live, shall I forget his eyes, so deep a blue, so mild, so piercing, eyes of a Redeemer, Christ-eyes." [61]

Time, a constant preoccupation of both Goethe and Schiller, as seen by Mann, emerges again. Schiller, Goethe feels, was always behind him, urging on, not realizing that only time ripens the work. In retrospect, Goethe finds this irritating. Schiller felt the urgency of accomplishment because he knew he had no time. But he, Goethe, only needed to stay still and wait while time "circled" around him. [62] Time, however, does not always work to his advantage. He, too, sacrifices, as the aged Goethe explains to Lotte at the end of *Lotte in Weimar*. He, too, is a victim—not only the luring flame but also the moth that dies in it and the candle being consumed. Things not only ripen in time; they constantly change. Metamorphosis is Goethe's abiding interest.[63]

The Aschenbach side of Schiller appears again. Goethe remembers the friend's subtle understanding of Helena's first appearance in *Faust*. His only objection had been to Goethe's assertion that beauty and modesty never go together. Beauty, Schiller had objected, must shame itself in the realization that it gives rise to desire. This, to Schiller as to Aschenbach, is a problem. To Aschenbach this humiliating but necessary embodiment of beauty meant the artist's inferiority to the philosopher. Finally of course philosophy shares the "dilemma" (and the Plato of Aschenbach's vision realizes this) for it, like literature, works with language, itself a concrete symbolic form. Aschenbach is correct in sensing that the symbols of art tend to be more closely tied to the vital rhythms of human feeling than those of discursive writing. Instead of glorying in this difference or at least realizing that it suits the special purposes of art, Mann's artists frequently take it as cause for doubt

---

[61] *The Beloved Returns*, p. 286.

[62] The Sibyl Manto (Faust, part 2) uses the phrase "Mich umkreist die Zeit." Bayard Taylor translates "I wait, and time around me wheels," Act II, p. 99.

[63] The image of the self-immolating butterfly appears in the poem "Selige Sehnsucht" (No. 18 in *West-östlicher Diwan*) which deals with the necessity of metamorphosis for the continuation of life. One must be ready for sacrifice, willing to give up the self ("Stirb und werde!")

and despair. Goethe, the supreme one, probably has the right solution. He does not try to belittle or to rationalize art. In his sovereign manner, he refuses to recognize the existence of the problem. "Then desire ought to be ashamed," he says "but she is not, perhaps because she is aware that she herself represents longing for the spiritual." [64] He simply dismisses the problem, implying slyly that shame is out of place in this context and that, in any case, guilt and shame could be assigned in myriad ways. There is no need for the artist to rush headlong to assume the burden. And Schiller understands for a moment. Instead of pursuing the discussion, he laughs. A tender moment, this memory of shared laughter. It is the climax of Goethe's musings on the friendship since it shows their ability for an understanding beyond words. And it conveys, simply and economically, the sad loneliness of the aged Goethe. Remembered laughter fading, he adds an afterthought; "There is no laughing with anyone [for me] any more." [65] Knowing that the communion cannot be surpassed, Mann makes Goethe presently turn to thoughts of daily chores.

Whatever enlightenment Mann's commentaries provide on Goethe and Schiller, they reflect light back on Mann's own thinking, especially on his central dialectic which is quite explicit in his portrayal of these two artists who, in many ways, resemble the characters of Mann's fiction.

---

[64] *The Beloved Returns*, p. 288.

[65] *The Beloved Returns* (p. 288), the phrase is translated as: "Now there's no one to laugh with." The reflexive construction used in the German original ("Es lacht sich mit niemandem mehr") underscores the ease and the transcendence of such a rare instant. It is no longer two individuals laughing about a particular matter but a serene union in relaxed understanding.

CHAPTER VI

DOUBLE IMAGE AS A DIALECTICAL DEVICE

The double image is perhaps the best exposition of the fundamentally dialectical cast of Mann's mind. It shows his tendency to think in terms of polar oppositions as well as the artist's desire to see these oppositions not abstractly, but embodied. Neither is the result a mere static antithesis —this kind of presentation emphasizes the dynamism of the dialectical process since interaction and relationship of some sort naturally emerge when the poles are human. The dialectic of male and female principles is the essence of many of Mann's pairs. Yet the double is not exclusively a representation of this dialectic. Even when discussion is limited to that one aspect, ambiguity remains. Though one member of the double tends to be predominantly "male", the other "female", the distinction is often rather fluid, never rigid. Male and female principles transcend individual boundaries to show that the limits of individuation are accidental. Whether men or women, the characters tend to contain some aspect that is already a synthesis of male and female. The pair or the double image is a vivid device for the portrayal of this varied and complex interplay. It may also point the way to a possible synthesis.

Doubles of various kinds abound in Mann's work. Even Clavdia, though she incorporates the female principle, derives her charm also from a double aspect—her connection with Pribislav. At times the sexual duplicity is merely implied, as in Jacob, who after Rachel's death becomes father and mother to Joseph. He absorbs part of Rachel's personality. Joseph, also, carries an identity with his mother that is more direct and continuous than the mere inheritance of physical traits. At other times, a continuity of male and female is indicated through realistic terms of portrayal. A woman often has some physical trait usually associated with masculinity. Hans needs the female qualities of openness and passivity in order to be the malleable hero of a novel of education.

To speak of a double image, however, is to deal not only with the ambivalence, sexual or other, of a single person, but also and mainly with the frequent appearance of pairs in Mann's work. These pairs are not schematized in any obvious or even easily deducible way. An exhaustive study of pairs might be fruitful, but here I can only choose a few to help clarify my theme. The argument is clearest if one takes examples that are unmistakeably identified by the author as double images, though even those not explicitly marked demonstrate the same concern. Five pairs will be examined—two from *Confessions of Felix Krull*, one in *The Holy Sinner*, one from an early novella (*The Blood of the Walsungs*), and one from *The Magic Mountain*. They differ in ways that are significant for purposes of this investigation.

Most prominent of those clearly identified are the pairs in *Felix Krull*. There are two striking pairs—one consisting of a sister and brother and another one of mother and daughter. Both are based on blood relationship. In both cases there is a sense of theme and variation. Brother and sister are close in age and look alike—they are the same thing, more or less simultaneous in time, varied in sex. Mother and daughter do not look alike at all. The beauty of one is of an entirely different type from the beauty of the other—they complement each other. Yet they are also, as mother and daughter, a variation within time.

As variations, these pairs are extensions of individuality and palliatives for the sense of isolation that awareness of rigid individual boundaries produces. At least so they are felt by the beholder, in this instance Krull. Whether the relief is shared by the members of the pair themselves we do not know. There is some indication that the daughter resents being thought of as part of a double image. Indeed there is evidence to show that a pair may reinforce and increase the loneliness of its members. This can happen when the resemblance becomes very close, as it does in the pair of twins in *The Holy Sinner*. When the proximity is so evident that the pair are constantly aware of it, they turn inward and ignore the rest of the world. If the brother and sister in *Felix Krull* are not seen as examples of the sweet temptations of inversion, it is partly because we never get to know them well, but also because they are more fully individuated. They are never definitely identified as twins. In any case, there may be something deceptive about the freedom that seems to result from the double image. We need to distinguish between the effect the duplication has on an onlooker and that on the pair themselves. In *Krull*, Mann is mainly interested in the appeal that these pairs have for Felix and in how they add to his evolving conception of life. But in *The Holy Sinner* the reader is allowed to look inside to see the effect that doubleness has on the feelings and the lives of the couple.

Krull's first experience of a double image is to become a pattern for later ones, always to be recalled on similar occasions. It appears to him in Frankfurt. After his father's death the family has separated, with his sister making a name for herself in operetta, while Felix lives for the moment in the newly founded boarding house of his mother. He is poor and appropriates the desirable world through eyes only. Later on in his career, he is to attract many and varied people, but as yet the world ignores him. The glass of the shop windows that separates him from the luxuries which he devours with his eyes forms a similar boundary between him and the life they represent that he so desires. On a walk past the hotel "Zum Frankfurter Hof" he sees two young people walk out on a balcony, look down into the street, converse laughingly, and then, shuddering from the wintry cold of the afternoon, retreat into their room. It all lasts, Krull tells us, at the most two minutes.

Yet it means a lot to Krull. We should not be fooled by his apologies about mentioning such a trifle at all. He does apologize profusely, before telling of the incident and after. It is an indulgence on his part to bother the readers of the memoirs by describing an event of which nothing comes, Mann has Krull say. The plot, the action is in no way furthered by it. But, for some strange reason, the unimportant episode is deeply embedded in his memory, and he will follow his heart and share the experience. What the preambles and apologies achieve, and what Mann must have wanted to accomplish, is a special alertness on our part. Felix protests too much, we feel, and the episode should be quite significant. And, brief as it is, it throws much light on all double images in Mann's work, whether they were created before or after this one. What, then, are the components of the image, and what is its meaning?

The two are well dressed, extremely handsome, and possibly of South American background. But what matters more is that they are brother and sister, a relationship which must be evident from their appearance. Felix thinks they might be twins. After they retire to their room, Felix stands rooted to the spot for a long time. That night and on many following ones, he dreams of them. Why should this pair have made such a lasting impression on him? First of all, there is their evident wealth and luxury. These infallibly attract him at this stage of his development. But those he can and does find everywhere on the streets of Frankfurt, and their effect on him, though great at the time, is not as lasting. Then there is physical beauty to which Krull is also greatly susceptible. They are both beautiful, but Felix tells us that neither of the two alone would have had this special effect upon him. The beauty he perceives resides in the doubleness. Yet the pervasive impression is not one of joy in a mere multiplication of beauty. It is precisely the unity within the multiplicity or doubleness that enchants him. One of them would not do. Yet it is oneness that he seeks to find in the duplication. He does not see them as two when they appear in his dreams. In them, the sister and brother form a unit, a "double being." The dreams that result from the encounter, are "dreams of love, dreams of delight and a longing for union." [1] It might seem paradoxical that an apparition whose charm depends on its twoness is seen in Felix's dreams as one. But this requirement can be understood if we realize that unification can only result if the entities that are to be united are separate first. Still, they need to be sufficiently similar so that their resemblance impels the observer to make the effort necessary to see them as one. That is the significance of this double image. Later, Krull is to become more informed and refined; he develops the capacity to recognize the fundamental unity of less obviously similar phenomena.

As Mann gives Krull an early hint of the unity of all life in this pedagogically calculated, guiding way, so he shows the reader doubles, instances of two as one or one as two that may lead to an appreciation of the subtler unities and connections in his work. Not all the doubles are of this type; not all carry the same implications. Though they tend to point toward the same concerns, they may well lead to varying conclusions about them. In order to show the diversity, other doubles have to be examined. It should be noted, however, that this early experience in Felix's career leads him to dreams rather than actions or thoughts. And the dreams, at this point, are described as vague and as dealing with "primal indivisibility" [2] rather than with a conscious effort of unifying the separate. He is not concerned with the two people; they are chiefly important as precipitators of his growing artistic consciousness. He is not certain about the nature of the unification and has some doubt about the attempted identification of doubleness and wholeness and about their precise relationship. This uncertainty is apparent in the phrasing of Krull's reminiscence.

Dreams of love, dreams that I loved precisely because—I firmly believe—they were of primal indivisibility and indeterminateness, double; which really means that only

---

[1] *Confessions of Felix Krull, Confidence Man,* trans. by Denver Lindley (New York, 1955), p. 80. Hereafter cited as *Krull.*

[2] *Krull,* p. 81.

then is there is significant whole blessedly embracing what is beguilingly human in both sexes.[3]

A hovering ambivalence pervades the statement, not perhaps unintentionally, for Felix tells us shortly afterwards that delicate matters need to be stated thus. Nonetheless, it teases our expectations for later treatments of the same theme.

The other clearly marked double image comes much later in the novel —at its other extreme—and after much has happened to Krull. It is different mainly because Krull is now different. There are also other variations, but Felix perceives a significant relationship between the two pairs. An examination of the later one may, then, show whether there is any change in his understanding of what the phenomenon implies.

After Felix has become a stand-in for the Marquis de Venosta and feels so much at home in the new personality that he *is* Venosta, he encounters Mme Kuckuck and her daughter Susanna in Lisbon. He knows of them from Professor Kuckuck whom he has met on the train journey to Portugal. Yet, instead of being introduced to the ladies by him, Krull accidentally runs into them when, tired from a first sightseeing trip in the city, he sits at a table next to theirs in a sidewalk café. He perceives them as a pair even before he recognizes them as the wife and daughter of his travel acquaintance. Krull does not wait for us to connect this double image with the earlier one. He reminds the reader of the other experience and of the requirement of doubleness that made it significant. It is the same capacity for "double enthusiasm," for enchantment by what he calls "the dissimilarly twofold" that attracts him to the pair immediately. Again, Felix is, at least on first meeting them, not precise about how the two are united in his mind. The vocabulary he uses in describing the effect is, like that in the earlier instance, deliberately vague. The differing charms of the two women, he says, "melted together," fused, coalesced in his imagination.

What, then, are these charms, and in what way can this pair be said to be, like the brother-sister one, dissimilarly twofold? It is not the kind of mother-daughter pair that clearly represents a victory over time, the daughter looking as the mother must have looked years ago. This mother is so different from her daughter that it would be difficult to imagine that she ever might have looked as the daughter now does. Rather, as a demonstration of the possibilities of female beauty and attraction it poses

[3] *Krull,* p. 81.

another problem for Felix's developing consciousness. Two different types are involved.

To complicate matters still further, yet another double image is invoked. Zouzou, who in combination with her mother represents one twosome, forms another with the "real" Venosta's mistress Zaza. The similarity of the names is evident. The Zaza-Zouzou double is a deliberate adaptation of elements of Venosta's life by Krull. Felix's desire for a Zaza of his own can be seen as part of his appropriation of his new identity. He comes to admit this much to himself when he tries to analyze the similarity when he sensed at the first meeting. Felix feels that he must have absorbed the romantic attraction to his friend's mistress by adopting his personality, and hence was subconsciously ready to meet another version, especially one whose name is so similar.

Yet Zouzou's similarity to Zaza leads to a strange episode in the novel. Felix has told Zouzou that he had drawn her, and the transfer of drawings is to serve as pretext for a rare secret and unchaperoned meeting. The drawings turn out to be of a nude figure. Zouzou, in an uncontrolled outburst, showing the ambivalence typical of her attitude to Krull, kisses him while pummeling his shoulder with her fist. What she does not know is that the drawings have been made by the "real" Marquis in Paris, and that the model is not she but Zaza. The only change that Felix has made is to add long cheek curls, a prominent feature of Zouzou's Spanish hairstyle. Yet the girl does not doubt that the sketches represent her. To be sure, she has no reason to question Felix's word; also the drawings are not very good, and her inspection is not cool and careful. Yet Krull himself is quite satisfied and never seems to fear being exposed in this hoax. The face in the drawings, he admits, bore slight resemblance to Zouzou's, but of what importance could the face be here, he asks.

By the small role that a face plays "here" Krull might have meant to say that it is a small matter considering the precarious and promising situation. Perhaps "here" might be construed even more broadly—when dealing with pure femininity as symbolized by the female figure. I showed earlier, in the discussion of Clavdia, that Mann frequently employs the body of the woman as an image of Life itself or, in Krull's talks with Kuckuck, as a sign for the continuity of the forms and structures of the organism. The sketches Felix shows to Zozou bear some resemblance to Zaza, but the importance of any recognizable features of Loulou's friend has by now faded. There is just sufficient residue left of an individuality to lend piquancy to the pictures and to keep them from becoming abstract —the cheek curls of Zouzou.

There is a striking similarity between the wider implications of the female image that are indicated in this scene with those of Hans' dream. The sketches are even more closely related to Behrens' portrait of Clavdia. The body was important and well rendered there, especially the skin. Again, the face was a bad likeness, but it did not seem to matter. Woman does not appear to be primarily significant as an individual, but as a representative of the female principle she has the special capacity to be a symbol which stands for things beyond herself. If the function of women is to serve as media for higher insights, Krull's cavalier attitude toward their physical distinctions is understandable. Likeness resides in the mind of the beholder, in any case. If Felix were not to insist on seeing Zouzou and her mother as one entity, the reader would not necessarily perceive the potential synthesis. Their differences would be felt as variety, not as complementary parts of a more inclusive whole. Similarity is, after all, an idea, and, like all ideas, exists in the mind. "Similarity?", Krull asks, "eighteen years and black eyes constitute a similarity, if you like." [4] Thus, there is an important subjective element. This becomes even more essential when the relationship is one not of vague resemblance but of polar contrast, such as that between Zouzou and her mother.

In that double image the governing principle is contrast. Without compiling a typology of women in Mann's works, one could suggest that there are overall resemblances and recurrence of clusters of characteristics. There are common elements that cohere to a type which one might call the motherly woman. She appeared in the introductory chapter. Mrs. Kuckuck's appeal derives from her association with this group (her first name is Maria), but she is identified also with primitive racial (Iberian) symbolism. Senhora Kuckuck carries symbolic value; she stands for something. One of her representations is an ethnic association, the sense of a national type that has through centuries reached great refinement and purification.

When Felix first sees her, and even more strongly later, Maria Pia seems a combination of polite middle-class matron and forbidding distillation of purebred Iberian. There is always some element in her otherwise stylishly contemporary costume that is ancient, traditionally Iberian. On first encounter, she wears a black silver-decorated neckband and dangling jet errings. Pride, dignity, and an air of somberness strike Krull the first time he sees her. He thinks her hard—the hardness of the

---

[4] Krull, p. 188. [My emphasis.]

South, Felix calls it, as he explains that the conventional equation of the soft and mild South and the hard North is wrong. Immediately, the racial identification is established. Recalling information from his train conversation with the Senhora's husband, he assesses her ancestry. "Old Iberian blood, probably," he muses, "and all sorts of Phoenician, Carthaginian, Roman, and Arabic influence may also be at work." Thus, the wider spatial and temporal connection is dominant from the start.

Henceforth, the presence of the proud, archetypically Iberian [5] mother is necessary for him to appreciate the different charms of the daughter. As they walk with Kuckuck's assistant, a man who turns out to be the intended husband of Zouzou, Krull prefers to walk with the latter so he can observe the mother-daughter pair together. The appeal is clearly an aesthetic one. Unlike Hans, who, even though Clavdia was primarily an educative experience for him, rises to fever pitch in physical desire, Felix is serenely aware that a kiss from Zouzou is the most committing involvement he can afford. Yet even the contemplation of the lovely double makes Felix slightly feverish. No doubt the excitement comes also from a tour of the museum of natural history that he has just completed. The two appeals are related. In any case, Felix thanks the Professor for the tour—and for the pair.

Mother and daughter—there is something thrilling about that, too. Very often great charm is to be found in brother and sister. But mother and daughter, I feel free to say, even though I may sound a trifle feverish, mother and daughter represent the most enchanting double image on this star. [6]

Blood came to Felix's mind on first meeting Maria Pia. Blood, in the same sense of racial heritage, continues to be mentioned in his appreciations of her. Her majesty and somberness, he muses, could hardly be justified by her social standing as wife of a scholar; rather it seems to be based on something in the blood, a racial pride which to him as an animalistic quality. In a conversation with the Senhora at the end of their walk, Felix widens the associations of her figure still further—not only to the past of her race but to that of all mankind. Cleverly working in a compliment to the lady while seeming to express gratitude for her husband's lecture on archaeology, he weaves a long

---

[5] The German prefix "ur" conveys a truly archaic meaning, and in the Joseph-novels Mann dwells on its suggestive powers at some length.

[6] *Krull,* pp. 307-308.

winding sentence that manages to allocate gratitude to her beauty and the Professor's wisdom about equally. He could not have appreciated her charms without the prior intellectual enlightenment:

... without, if I may say so, the paleontological loosening-up his discourse produced in the soil of my mind, making it a ready seed-bed for new impressions, racial impressions, for example, such as the experience of seeing the primordial race to which such interesting admixtures have been added at various periods, and which offers eye and heart a majestic image of racial dignity. . . .[7]

The culmination and clearest expression of the representative character of Maria Pia comes at the bullfight. Like the woman, the institution is described as "ur-Iberisch." Felix has been paying more attention to the daughter, though he still sees her as part of a double. The mother, he tells Zouzou, lacks her own light elegant grace. It would help to tone down the harshness of her beauty. Yet at the bullfight Maria Pia comes into her own. Her costume now, though she still wears a contemporary gown (she does not need the affectation of the complete costume-ball ethnic dress that foreign ladies wear to the corrida) is finished off by a high Spanish comb and a black mantilla. As the elegant sacrificial ritual goes on, it becomes identified in Krull's mind with Maria Pia. A brilliant move by the great Ribeiro (who is described as a combination of power and elegance, incorporating in this aspect at least the desired qualities of both mother and daughter) makes the public applaud.

I did so myself and so did the regal Iberian beside me. Back and forth I glanced, from her surging breast to the living statue of man and animal, now rapidly dissolving, for more and more the stern and elemental person of this woman seemed to me one with the game of blood below.[8]

It is still the metaphor of the corrida that governs the passionate embrace between Senhora Kuckuck and Felix at the end of the novel. The union is a fusion of Krull not so much with Maria Pia as with all the things that she has by now come to represent to him—things Iberian and more generally human—the primal mother, the continuity of all life, and, importantly for our concern, a way out of the self and to other people, other times and places. If there is any doubt about the loosening of individuation that is accomplished in the ritual, let us listen to the expert testimony of Professor Kuckuck. He is speaking of the roots of the bullfight, of the cult of a divinity whose followers

[7] *Krull*, p. 320.
[8] *Krull*, p. 377.

were christened with the blood of a steer. What he stresses about it is
the superpersonal mystery, the breaking down of individual boundaries.

> Its converts had been baptized not with water, but with the blood of a bull, who
> was perhaps the god himself, though the god lived too in the one who spilled his
> blood. For his teaching contained something that united its believers irrevocably,
> joining them in life and in death; and its mystery consisted in the equality and
> identity of slayer and slain, axe and victim, arrow and target....[9]

If Maria Pia represents the majestic side of the double image, the
daughter is a fitting contrast. The mother might, in terms of a distinction
made by Mann in *Lotte in Weimar*, be called Junonian. Zouzou, then,
would properly fit into the contrasting category. The attitude to resemblance emerging from the following passage may also explain the
cavalier handling of portraits in *The Magic Mountain* and *Felix Krull*.

> What is resemblance! I do not assert any similarity of individual features but a
> sisterliness of the whole, the identity of type, this quality that is far from anything
> Junonian, this lightness, charm, gracefulness, gentleness—it is that which I call the
> sisterly, the daughterly quality.[10]

Felix recognizes Zouzou as a member of this category immediately.
Sitting at his table in the café, he compares her to Zaza and to her
mother at the same time. Unlike her mother who is beautiful without
being pretty, Zouzou is prettiness personified. Though her features
and her body are gracefully feminine, Krull sees boyish qualities in her.
They pertain to aspects not strictly tangible and crystallized in
physiognomy—gaze and voice. Her eyes, though black like Zaza's,
do not flirt but fix one with an expression that is so direct as to seem
insolent. This gaze is reminiscent of Clavdia's. So is Zouzou's voice
—slightly harsh, Krull finds it—direct and unaffected like the gaze,
which to him again seems boyish. Soon he finds that these are matched
by the relentlessly aggressive conversation of Zouzou who believes that
it is healthy to say what one thinks. Often, in her provocative lashing
at Felix she says more than she means, and then she will admit her
regret in a painful mastering of her temper and pride, elicited not by
manners but by a feeling of sportsmanship.

It may be the girl's boyish aspect, her participation in the male
element, that makes her approve of individual boundaries and resent

[9] *Krull*, p. 379.

[10] See *Lotte in Weimar*, pp. 274-275. The above is my own translation, more
ponderous and literal than that of Mrs. Lowe-Porter, to preserve all the implications
of the original that are important to my argument.

intrusion. She is very self-assertive. She ridicules Felix's vanity, his gallantry, and especially his talk of love. She tries to shut herself off from any closeness to others, but Felix is correct in his suspicion that her cruel irony protests too much, that she is actually fighting herself. Eventually Felix penetrates the walls and vindicates his suspicion that Zouzou does want to get out of herself after all. At the rendez-vous in the garden, the insolent eyes overflow, she embraces Felix and responds to his kiss. Zouzou seems converted to love; not completely perhaps, but that is a small matter. And, fittingly, the symbol of a residual resistance is her left fist hammering against his shoulder while the right arm embraces him. A final dramatic gesture of her persistent ambivalence, well summed up in a way that keeps recurring in Mann's work—the fist clenched in upon itself as against the arm that reaches out to the world.

The image has been prepared earlier by drawing attention to Zouzou's arms. They are lovely, like Clavdia's. Felix refers to them as "sweet arms" and "delicious arms." As Hans associated Clavdia's body with the representative body of his vision, so Felix associates prehistoric bone structures with Zouzou's arm. Instead of diminishing its beauty, that association heightens it. In embracing Maria Pia, Krull was appropriating more than just an idividual. Similarly, in kissing her daughter, he communes with the charms of a person who is unique in some respects, but he also holds in his arms an embodiment of mysterious things, inaccessible to him directly because of remoteness in time or space, or because they are ideas, associations with which he has gradually enriched the physical presence of Zouzou. As with her mother, these associations point beyond the individual, but whereas the bullfight showed Maria Pia as a symbol of obliteration of distinctions, Zouzou's arm is significant for its preservation of a distinctive form. The predecessors of the human arm, back to the earliest ones, can be glimpsed in it. The structural continuity is recognizable. Zouzou as an individual is transparent, but she stands for the preservation of form, even though that form is a shared one. Felix has given these meanings to Zouzou as gifts and now expects her to yield them back to him, enhanced by the piquancy of the individual. This quality is necessary for Krull because his appreciation of life is more that of the artist than of the philosopher.[11]

[11] Thomas Mann, [Einführung in ein Kapitel der "Bekenntnisse des Hochstaplers Felix Krull"], *Gesammelte Werke*, XI, p. 704.

If Felix has succeeded in awakening Zouzou, her resistance makes her not less of a woman but more of one. In *The Magic Mountain* Peeperkorn stipulated it as a fundamental quality of femininity that the woman be passive in love. Zouzou's resistance may be seen as an aggressive version of this refusal to choose, an absolute insistence on being courted and, in Peeperkorn's terms, being aroused and carried away. With the exception of Potiphar's wife, who is explicitly described as unfeminine in her active pursuit, Mann's female characters react in this way. Men, on the contary, are often ready for love first and then only seek an object.[12]

Like Felix, I have looked at mother and daughter from an aesthetic point of view, from the outside, and thus ignored how the two felt. Any insight the reader gets into their minds derives from Krull the narrator. This double image represents the kind of pair that is important for the aesthetic and philosophical synthesis it embodies rather than for the members' own reactions. Mother and daughter do not seem much aware of forming a symbolic pair. When their attention is forcibly drawn to it, each appears to resent being thought of as half of a larger phenomenon and to be jealous of the other. Maria Pia rebukes Felix for his uninformed preference of childish charms over fullblown ones. Zouzou, to whom Krull speaks of the double phenomenon, is harsher in her ridicule for such strange preferences and in her resentment at the slight to her beauty. The pairing, then, occurs only in Krull's mind. Is the purpose and meaning of the double image still the same when the author presents it more directly, without the intervention of an aesthetically inclined narrator?

There is a narrator in *The Holy Sinner,* a ubiquitous "spirit of the narrative" who turns out to be a Benedictine monk. Regardless of some monkish prejudice against their doings, he lets us look inside his characters. In the traditional setting of the Gregorius legend, what matters to us is the double image. There are two pairs, a threesome with Sibylla committing incest with both brother and son. This time brother and sister are definitely identified as twins. There is no protective vagueness about them or about their relationship. The joys and pains of their love are presented with sympathy but also with cutting clarity.

They are aware of being a pair from birth. Identical, differing only

---

[12] Thomas Mann, in *A Sketch of My Life* (New York, 1960), p. 35, applies this rule to himself, and later we will see that it is true of the characters he creates as well as of his analysis of those of other authors.

in Wiligis' being an epitome of physical manhood and possessing the psychological attributes that go with it, and Sibylla being a comparably perfect incarnation of femininity, they are constantly together as children and adolescents. They even have a name in common—"Joidelacourt" they are called when their companions want to flatter them and refer to them as one entity. An attack of smallpox leaves a mark of the identical spot on the two foreheads. "My feminine counterpart," Wiligis calls his sister. (In *Lotte in Weimar* Goethe uses a similar phrase to refer to his sister.) Beginning with the earliest conversations of the pair, they constantly tell each other that nobody else is good enough for them. Others are strangers and, more importantly, they can never be their equals. Aristocratic birth is part of the reason for this conceit, but it is by no means the only one. The exceptional beauty of face and figure is another. And this is not the only occasion in Mann's work when beauty is considered not merely an undeserved supererogatory grace but the result of the individual's merit. Krull, for instance, comes to feel similarly about his physical attractiveness. At first, the compliments he receives seem irrelevant and undeserved, but then it occurs to him that beauty is the result of its possessor's active desire to please the world and hence to model himself according to the world's desires. Thus, pride in one's beauty becomes justifiable.

The twins, however, feel no humility about their natural endowments at any time, and they have no need to justify their pride to themselves. This pride is total and unashamed. At times, it seems that they are even proud of their own pride. They are proud of the marks in their foreheads and of having been born out of death, as their mother dies at birth. When Sibylla becomes pregnant from their incestuous affair, the pair marvel at the surprising fertility of sin. It is especially surprising, they feel, that their particular sin should bear fruit so readily. And they see this sin not primarily as incest, as an affront to religious and social norms, though they are aware of that aspect, but as pride. All through the aftermath of the first incest and in the wake of discovering the second, that with her son and her brother's Sibylla knows that pride is at the core of these events. Yet she makes no attempt to control it until very late and even then one senses the original pride in a different form. When her brother and lover dies in attempted penance, she tries to spite God by refusing all suitors and denying her womanhood. On the tablet she writes to put next to her son before he is put out to sea in a barrel, Sibylla makes the nature of their sin clear beyond any doubt. It is self-love. Pride is the love of self; it is an excessive self-consciousness and self-assertion. Thus, even though Sibylla is a distillation of feminine beauty, she is also a representation of the male principle. Her openness to another individual is illusory—the twins love themselves in each other.

"Be mindful, shouldst thou live, of thy parents, whom I may not name by name, not with hatred and bitterness! Far too much they loved each other, and themselves the one in the other, and that was their sin and thy begetting. . . ." [13]

When she is half-knowingly drawn to young Gregorius it is again a love based on resemblance. It is half knowing because Sibylla is presented with hints of the identity of her knight—outward hints in the material of his clothing, made from brocade she had left with the infant, and internal stirrings of suspicion. But she does not pay heed to either. As she prays to the Virgin, feeling she might have in her spite cut off access to God, she claims that she must have Gregorius because he alone is her equal.

Their awareness that pride is the essential sin does not keep these sinners from perpetrating it again and again. When mother and son discover their incest they try to rival with each other in their share of the guilt. Sibylla then spends years in poverty and supposed humility, tending the sick and doing menial chores. But as she speaks to her helper Gudula about a plan to see the new pope and confess to him, this pride is still intact. The pope should find out about her, she says, because he probably never heard of a sin so great. Gudula asks her to get absolution for a sexual transgression of her own. It is really not worth bothering about, replies her mistress. The pope would smile indulgently and wonder that she found it worth while coming to him because of such a trifle. Even in the climactic audience with Pope Gregorius Sibylla insists on the greater share of sin, arguing that her sin was more conscious.

This pride, as I suggested, is another name for self-love. When Wiligis or Sibylla, or even Gregorius, are pleased with their beloved and seem to reach beyond the self in love, they are actually merely approving of themselves and confirming their inability to get out of the self. The more they try to establish contact with the outside world, the more involuted they become. Physical distance does not help— Gregorius is set adrift and then makes a long journey in seemingly arbitrary direction only to find the first woman he meets to be his mother. Unlike the pleasing effect of variation that the double image

[13] *The Holy Sinner,* p. 68.

produces in Krull, both for Felix and the reader, this double saddens the narrator monk and makes the reader share the frustration of sameness in apparent variation.

How far does this variation go? Willigis and Sibylla are exactly alike except in sex. The variation involved in their sex difference, however, includes not only diversities in their bodies but also aspects of their character, feelings, and actions. As the twins compare their varying physical charms and invariably find the other sex more beautiful, Wiligis tries to penetrate what he considers the most important psychic difference between the sexes:

"Glorious," he answered her, "are you, Sibylla, quite of yourself and with no buhurd at all! My sex, it must bestir itself and do something, to be glorious. For yours one need only be and bloom and is already glorious. That is the most general difference between male and female, aside from the more particular." [14]

This is an important statement and pertinent to an examination of the male-female dialectic. It explains Clavdia's contempt for self-development and self-cultivation. It goes along with the greater openness and relaxation of the female principle. On the other hand, it explains the concentrated, tense striving, the concern with accomplishment (*Leistung*) of the male characters.

Gregorius does try to live up to the implied distribution of male and female roles. As man, as husband he feels that he should make all important decisions, not only those governing his own life but also arrangements for the future of his wife and mother. After they have inescapably faced their relationship, he goes away to do extreme penance and gives Sibylla precise and specific directions about how to arrange hers. The largest burden, he says, is reserved to him not because of pride but because he is the man (which may still be pride of a sort). When she protests his harsh dispositions, he says that Sibylla is speaking like a woman. She has, he believes, remained a woman, while he grew from boyhood to manhood. This is no mere play with words. If a woman's growth is an organic unfolding, as it is asserted to be in Wiligis' statement, then she never really changes. Again, this confirms the special relationship of the female principle to time and explains the woman's disdain for conscious self-improvement. A man, on the other hand, is defined to a greater extent by what he does. Sybilla's role in the initiation of both incestuous relationships is a passive one, one that

[14] *The Holy Sinner,* pp. 26-27.

fits well with Peeperkorn's idea of the female role. The brother seduces her though she is not unwilling. It is again her son who, though at least half unknowingly, comes to her and asks to be her knight. In repentance she always turns to brother or son for guidance. At times Sibylla thinks of her role in the conventional terms that recognize the woman's need to hide her superiority in situations where she might feel she has the upper hand. We would not be women, she says to Gudula, if we did not know how to use wile. And in the interview with the Pope she lets her son play the revelation scene without showing that she has recognized him long since. Yet, at the end it is Gregorius again who establishes a pattern for the whole family's future. The inherent passivity of woman is confirmed by this relationship.

There is also some confirmation of other themes that have been connected with the male and female principles earlier. Although the double image of brother and sister seems to lead to an almost hopeless solipsism, some hope emerges from the child that it produces. To be sure, only God's grace, only a miracle can undo the gates of imprisonment in the self. But the woman is the one that bears the child, the one who loves him even before his birth, something that Wiligis cannot bring himself to do. Any hope to get out, then, rests with her.

Indicating this potential for escape, Sibylla, like so many of Mann's female figures, has especially lovely hands. In general, hands are again important. The son earns her love and gratitude by conquering a persistent suitor in a duel. But Gregorius accomplishes this feat in an unusual manner—he pulls his opponent inside the walls of the castle by grabbing his sword, and, no matter how painfully the weapon cuts into his hand, holding onto it. Sibylla, to the consternation of her women, kisses this hand when she first meets him. When the son marries his mother, the monk describes the event as a symbolically fraught scene with Gregorius ascending the throne by her hand. As they part to do penance, he will not let her kiss him on lips, forehead, or hand. It all started with the hand, he says.

The steady hand is another expression for a special gift of Gregorius. Even in childhood he could frequently accomplish the seemingly impossible by an unusual power of concentration. In competitive games or fights with boys he won when he wanted to because he could focus all his powers on any one thing at any moment. The closed fist around his enemy's sword summarizes this ability. It signifies, as I have shown earlier in other contexts, a state of being closed and introverted, a high degree of individuation, and, finally, the male principle.

This state not only sums up Gregorius' early years; it also describes all the relationships in the novel. Along with it goes a fear of being open and undefined. Thus, Gregorius is at first happy when he is told that he is not the child of Mahaute, his adoptive mother. This discovery has, he feels, opened the gate of possibilities to him. But he does not set out to do great deeds and define himself. His plans, heroic as they are, always turn around discovering who he is by birth. He feels compelled to find out his inherited identity, not to form a new one. The experiences of heavy sin and repentance are necessary to bring him out of this self-imprisonment. First, he is to go through the utmost focussing and concentration of his individuality when he survives the hard penance by shrinking to a tiny plantlike ball of a creature. But from there on the movement is reversed. The small ball in its shrivelled state seems to have preserved the essence of Gregorius. He flowers out physically in hardly any time, and spiritually his contact has now broadened to Christendom. As pope, he is tolerant, receptive, and understanding. The child Gregorius has finally formed a synthesis between the pure masculinity of his father and the potential openness of his mother. Loosing, it is said of him, seems more important to him than binding.

In the double image of incestuous twins Mann can best portray sameness with a difference pulled irresistibly but narcissistically toward the "other." An earlier version appears in *The Blood of the Walsungs*. In *Felix Krull* the brother and sister pair are set apart from their surroundings by their foreign exoticism. Wiligis and Sibylla are isolated by high birth. It is their Jewishness that alienates Siegmund and Sieglinde in *The Blood of the Walsungs* from others and turns them inward to each other. These pairs are doomed to ever-growing self absorption in any case, but the initial distance from others motivates that necessity realistically. Mann harps on their "racial characteristics" and tends to forget those of their equally Jewish family.

Siegmund and Sieglinde first appear as they descend the stairs to a late and richly appointed breakfast. The youngest in the family, they are 19, but their bodies seem immature. Painstaking description of their appearance follows. It is kept parallel: her dress is depicted, then his suit; his hair, then hers; her diadem that is a gift from him and his golden bracelet that is a gift from her. At first, differences predominate, though even here subtle connections are established. Siegmund's raspberry colored tie echoes the red of Sieglinde's dress. His hair is black, luxuriant, and rebelliously curly, forced into a side part in a quest for suave elegance. His brows are black and grow together in the center and his dark beard grows fast and heavily so that, in addition to the frequent ablutions that his compulsive cleanliness dictates, he must shave twice a day. Later, we learn that he has much hair on his chest. His mark of distinction, his masculinity, is well established. The only practical outlets for this virile power are a cruel wit and constant preoccupation with grooming. He shares the aggressive wit with his twin. They also have the same noses, the same lips, cheekbones, and eyes. But, significantly, most alike are their hands, long and slender in both, his differing only in their reddish hue. And they constantly hold hands, even at table. Occasionally their eyes meet in an "understanding to which there was no way nor admittance from the outside."

Throughout the story, this isolation is reiterated in many ways. On their walks, they avoid others. Driving to the opera to attend *Die Walküre* together for the last time before Sieglinde's impending marriage, they arrive late in order to miss the rest of the public and after intermission return to their loge seconds before the curtain rises for the same reason. The loge keeps them safely apart from the rest. So does the carriage that brings them to the opera and back and that becomes a metaphor for their sheltered existence. It is softly upholstered, hung with brown silk curtains, gently warmed. Well appointed and efficient, soundless and fast, it carries them elastically over the occasionally rough road while they sit inside, safe from the busy vulgar city life outside. On their return, the servant escorts them back to this haven directly and quickly shuts them in again.

In many ways, they are like the pair in *The Holy Sinner*. Like those, they are exceedingly proud, insufferably arrogant. Male and female, though carefully distinguished to display the physical charms peculiar to each, are not as subtly elaborated in their existential possibilities as they are in the later work. Yet even here the girl is slightly more open to the outside world than the boy. He might break out of his isolation either through love or through art. He ponders these possibilities while sitting with his sister at the *Walküre* performance that instils both with a fever of incestuous sensuality and finally inspires them to imitate their Wagnerian namesakes, down to choosing a bear rug for lovemaking.

Respectfully, Siegmund feels the presence of a work of art. But how does one make such a work? Siegmund too dabbles in art. For two thousand marks a month, his father buys him instruction from "an artist of European reputation." But what he paints is trivial, and Siegmund whose sharply critical wit gives no quarter to others' productions, is well aware of the worthlessness of his own. The conditions of his existence, he thinks, do not make for creativity. Surrounded by luxury, he spends all his energy preparing to do anything and has none left for the work itself. Neither do those around him expect anything more of him than enjoying himself and dressing with the exquisite taste that takes up much of his time. Mann's real artists are always under some hardship. At the very least, there is a self imposed asceticism in their surroundings. Only a Spinell is inspired by yellow velvet opulence. Siegmund lacks a *Trotzdem,* a goad, internal or external. He does not share Aschenbach's "heroism of weakness." Thinking in similar terms, he admits to himself that he is "no hero." His yearning finally focusses on two words— creativity and passion. Listening to Wagner's music he senses that creativity derives from passion and finally assumes passion's shape. What he lacks is experience [*Erlebnis*]. Whether it should lead to good painting or to the consummation of passion he does not know. Settling on a strange and sterile mixture of both by sleeping with his sister in emulation of the operatic pair, he achieves nothing.

Passionately stammering to Sieglinde, he reminds her of how similar they are. Possibilities of escape exist for both. The "Erlebnis" thing in me, he says, is in you balanced by "that with Beckerath," her convenient fiancé who works in the ministry and sports a "von." His futile yearning for experience sees a possible outlet in art. Hers is the avenue of sex, the conventional female one. Sieglinde does not love Beckerath. She has nothing but mocking contempt for him. But there is a compliant sensual expectation, a willing openness about her. At the breakfast table she suddenly looks at her fiancé; her gaze is "large and black, probing, expectant, questioning" and it speaks "like that of an animal." Ever since her engagement, she has been wont to do that. Sieglinde has some share in the female principle. It is a small share. Even while staring at Beckerath she holds her brother's hand.

Other associations, small but significant, contribute to the impression that the girl has a slight foothold on the female aspect. One is her passivity. She defers to Siegmund in large matters as well as small. At the opera, she tentatively (and negatively—'I'd like to get one if it weren't sure to be so inferior') suggests buying an ice, expecting his snobbish rejection and immediately agreeing with him. Apparently he has had some say in the decision to give Sieglinde to Beckerath: "And even Siegmund, *to whom she was subject,* had part in this outcome, he despised himself, but he had not been against it because von Beckerath worked in the foreign office and was noble. . . ." [15] Her brother's opinion matters to her; she accepts the family decision; she is passive.

Other suggestions of a wider association can be found in descriptive detail. We saw how important Clavdia's clothing was in tracing the implications of her character. Sieglinde's dress may also be telling, especially through its color. For breakfast, she wears Bordeaux-red velvet. Without assigning set values to Mann's colors, one could suggest that the choice is significant (wine, blood, communion), and one should remember that Siegmund on the same occasion wears grey. For the opera, she dons a sea-green gown. And for the climactic orgy she appropriately wears a white robe. The suggestive power of white clothing was made clear with Clavdia.

But all those suggestions remain unfulfilled possibilities. In *The Holy Sinner* they lead to an eventual breaking of the narcissistic spell. Here they do not, and there is no release or transcendence. Instead, introversion is sealed by incest which here, unlike in the later work, occurs at the end of the story, thus leaving no opportunity for expiation. The cloying sessions of mutual admiration, replete with kissing and petting, are merely adorations of the self in the other. It is constantly the same physical quality that one loves in the other at any moment—while she is kissing his *soft* cheeks, he adores her *soft* arms; they breathe in each other's fine perfume; they love each other for the sake of "their select uselessness." Sieglinde is to her brother "his sumptuously adorned darkly lovely likeness." They mirror each other. And mirrors play a part in introducing the climactic scene. Before Sieglinde comes to him, Siegmund looks at himself in the mirror, then in three mirrors at the same time. It is in the mirror that he sees the bear rug, and now the mirror images proliferate. For the rug inspires him to imitate the operatic love scene, and the opera itself is a mirror of their love. No transcendence from love into art occurs here. Instead, a slavish and literal aping of art dramatizes inversion and futility. To make it more oppressive, Siegmund and Sieglinde become more alike in the course of the novella. Their hands were said to be strikingly similar in the initial description. His were distinguished not by any difference of form but by their more ruddy coloring. Toward the end of the story, *her* hand is described as narrow and ruddy.

The double images in *Krull* were clearly indicated as such by the narrator. In *The Holy Sinner* and *The Blood of the Walsungs,* not only

---

[15] My translation and emphasis.

the family ties but also the irresistible incestuous attraction between brother and sister, mother and son made it evident that they were pairs. But there is yet another kind of double image in Mann's work. These are pairs of overtly male figures, frequently friends, at least one of whom is usually strongly attracted to the other. This attraction may be highly ambivalent, as it is in *Doctor Faustus* where the narrator Zeitblom at the same time admires and resents his friend Leverkühn. In some instances, the complementarity of the two is so strongly indicated, that they are actually one character split in two.[16] Usually, the predominating characteristics on one side are those we have associated with the female principle.

The pair of Hans and Joachim in *The Magic Mountain* represents this type of double well. I have already suggested that Hans partly embodies the female principle and I have also indicated why he must do so. When Hans, in confirming the femininity of Clavdia, cast doubt on his own masculinity, we did not take this as mere humility, or indeed as a value judgment of any kind. Hans can be male enough when he wants and needs to be, but he also needs to be something else. If he were an incarnation of male potency, or of the kind of single minded devotion to that potency that Peeperkorn represents, he could not fulfill his function in the novel. Peeperkorn does not learn anything. He learns nothing because he has neither the need nor the ability to learn, and he lacks those because he is pure physical masculinity. But Hans needs to learn. Hence receptivity and a certain amount of passivity, an openness to people and things outside himself are absolutely necessary to him. And these are the attributes of the female principle. In examining this double image, however, it is not enough to determine what each of its members is like. To understand the dialectical process underlying that device, one must also ask what their relationship is and how they feel about each other.

When Joachim meets Hans at the Davos railway station, a cousin (adopted cousin, as it turns out) supposedly come for a three-week visit, their relationship seems one of easy comradery. They talk excitedly; Joachim serves as knowing guide to the strange world of Berghof. Obviously, they like each other. The only bothersome note is their studied avoidance of calling each other by their first names. "Thou" is

---

[16] In *The Story of a Novel*, pp. 89-90, Mann explicitly describes this splitting device. Among other works he read while writing *Doctor Faustus*, the author lists *Dr. Jekyll and Mr. Hyde* (p. 19).

their common form of address, and they meticulously observe it, with one dramatic exception. North German coolness and reserve is given as the reason for this estranging habit, but it also serves to draw attention to the identities of the two as problematical. At least they do not seem to be closed off neatly into two compartments labelled "Hans" and "Joachim." After all, when they call each other "Thou," they are using the same "name." Occasionally, other appellations, also anonymous and generic, such as the colloquial "man" crop up. In any case, the easy comradery is something that has been worked at and is not really easy at all.

The physical appearance of Hans and Joachim indicates a polarity that is confirmed by their intellectual and emotional natures. Hans is blond and blue eyed, with a slim but by no means athletic body that has a tendency to careless and slumping postures. Joachim, on the other hand, has a dark complexion, soft black eyes and the powerful and well proportioned body of an athlete. His posture is ramrod stiff, and in his single minded desire to be a soldier he acknowledges orders from the Berghof doctors by clicking his heels.

It is this atmosphere of controlled tenseness that is described by the adjective that always accompanies Joachim—"military"—rather than just the young man's striving to join his regiment. Again, in clear contrast, Hans is described as civilian. Doctor Behrens' professional eye immediately recognizes in Hans the material of which good patients are made, and he associates this talent with Hans' civilian status. Military and civilian, then, in this context carry more weight than the meanings conventionally assigned to those terms.

Joachim is predictably Spartan. He takes care of his body because he needs it in the service of his country. It is only for that purpose that he devours the large meals at the sanatorium and meticulously obeys the rest cure rules. All that Joachim does is seen in the light of duty. As his chances for a cure become more remote, he does not flag in his effort, and Hans is probably correct in surmising that the therapeutic ritual itself becomes a substitute service. The punctiliousness and devotion that he expends upon it is really meant for the army, but, since the military is a way of life rather than a substantive aspiration, its object is interchangeable. As Settembrini points out in a conversation with Hans who has been praising the military, the existence of a soldier is pure form. As such, the humanist claims, it cannot be discussed meaningfully unless one knows for what the soldier is fighting. But what appeals to Hans is precisely the formal aspect of Joachim's militarism.

If Hans likes the soldier in Joachim, it is because there is none in him. Unlike his cousin, Hans enjoys the heavy food and breakfast beer; he even takes great sensual pleasure in the clever construction of the lounging chair in which the patients take their rest cure. Music produces a similar sense enjoyment in him, though it also touches deeper chords. Joachim, on the other hand, considers it part of his round of duties to appear at the occasional concerts arranged by the staff. Smoking is another of Hans' civilian pleasures—the satisfaction he derives from his Maria Mancini cigar is important to him. When, in the process of acclimatization, he loses taste for it, he is seriously concerned. While enjoying himself, Hans occasionally thinks about Joachim who cannot share these pleasures. Perhaps the greatest difference between civilian and military emerges in their reaction to sexual desire which is heightened by disease and the attitudes of those surrounding them.

On the first day of his visit, Hans in the easily joking manner of down below comments to Joachim on Marusja, a buxom giggly Russian girl who sits at their table. The cousin's attempt to master his frighteningly violent reaction betrays an erotic attraction the he cannot fully contain. Yet he refuses to satisfy it. This desire is the single flaw in Joachim's military armor, the one, Hans feels, through which susceptibility to disease and death can find access. Refusing to believe in Krokowski's lessons, Joachim would deny such a connection, but denial does him no good. The erotic attraction has taken possession of his body, and his body has taken charge—no amount of good will to stay down below and serve the army can keep Joachim healthy. Yet, the mind refuses, and it is this determined effort to close himself off that makes him a representative of the male principle.

The susceptibility to Eros is the one thing that the cousins share. What is more, there is a striking parallelism in the form that this susceptibility takes. Like Hans' love Clavdia, Marusja is Russian. As part of the Russian community at the Berghof, Marusja is in Clavdia's orbit—they converse and even go on excursions together. Beyond the connection of the objects, there is also an empathetic association between the cousins' romantic feelings. As they sit at table, Hans furtively glances at his cousin, fearing to catch the violent tortured look he had assumed earlier at sight of Marusja. The look he sees shows complete forgetfulness of self, an impression that Hans perceives as "civilian." This establishes the connecting link, the common element of the cousins' natures as erotic—this is Joachim's solitary civilian trait. It is because of this deep empathy that Joachim's love can serve as a springboard and preparation for Hans'. As the latter watches his cousin, he feels his heart hammering. This is before he has seen Clavdia.

It seems ironic that Joachim's influence on Hans would exert itself in this way. Civilian Hans might profit more from the cousin's military side, and he realizes that. Temporarily, Joachim's example does help to hold Hans' behavior within socially respectable limits. Eventually he is to let himself go completely and find pleasure in the other patients' ridicule of his passion-blinded state. For the moment, however, the heroic restraint of his cousin shames him into a modicum of self-control. Even though Hans finds ways to get by this control, there are evidences all through their association that Joachim continues to function as a check and restraint.

In speaking of the connotations of militarism, it should be noted that even in its more conventional associations militarism does not only mean reserve and discipline. After Joachim's death, phonograph records of *Carmen* and of Valentin's prayer from Gounod's *Faust* become important to Hans in evoking the loved cousin's presence at first spiritually, and finally, in the occult session, spiritualistically. In these operas the soldier meets death. So does Joachim; like the other two, he does not die on the field of battle. And this connection with death, along with discipline and an emphasis on ritual, is what attracts Hans to the military personality.

But for all that, and aside from my personal inclinations—or even, perhaps, not altogether aside from them—I have some understanding and sympathy for a military life. It has such an infernally serious side to it, sort of ascetic, as you say—that was the expression you used, wasn't it? The military always has to reckon on coming to grips with death, just as the clergy has. That is why there is so much discipline and regularity in the army, so much "Spanish etiquette," If I may say so; and it makes no great difference whether one wears a uniform collar or a starched ruff, the main thing is the asceticism, as you so beautifully said.[17]

Civilian and military attract each other. Hans and Joachim are constantly together from the moment that the former arrives. Almost forcibly, the impression results that they are literally inseparable—parts of one person. They are said to form a "miniature society" apart from the rest of the patients. This isolation results partly from Joachim's aloofness, but the sense of their inseparableness is rather strengthened than weakened by Hans' occasional reluctance to keep his distance from the others. Even when he does not want to retire from the patients'

---

[17] *The Magic Mountain*, p. 378.

evening sociability, he feels compelled to follow his cousin. As he sits on a lonely bench with Joachim, Hans complains to himself that the other dragged him away from society. He thinks of Joachim as something of a tyrant. Yet it does not occur to him that he could have stayed by himself. "After all, we are not Siamese twins," he says to himself. But he behaves precisely as though they were Siamese twins. So does Joachim. He feels that Hans is often using him to cover up for himself. On a morning walk, Hans literally drags him along to speed up their pace sufficiently so that he can meet Clavdia at a desired place. Though he does not care for the mixed motives of the visits Hans makes to the moribundi in the sanatorium, Joachim feels he must go along if Hans is set on them. Such examples could be multiplied indefinitely.

People surrounding the two are also aware of them as a single unit. Usually they are not referred to by name but simply as "the cousins." In a joking reference to Hans' name [18] Doctor Behrens calls the two Castorp and Pollux.

Another hint at the special relationship between the two cousins is the wordless understanding between them. They rarely discuss the important things. All reference to either Clavdia or Marusja is avoided. So is love generally, especially as it is discussed in Krokowski's lectures. As I suggested, their personalities merge primarily in this area. Even in the similarity of the choices of love objects, the cousins may be expressing the deeper kinship and the attraction for each other which they dare not communicate directly. So charged with meaning are the subjects, and so well do the cousins know each other's mind and heart, that they dare not even look at each other. Eyes are carefully cast down lest a moment of embarrassing truth und closeness result, such as that produced by Joachim's addressing Hans by his first name.

The event occurs in the station as Joachim is leaving, without the doctors' blessing, to join his regiment, doomed to return within the year. It is a moment of despair, especially for Joachim who feels that without him Hans will lose all restraint and will never have the strength to leave the mountain. This fear impels him to break the usual tacit understanding reserve. To Hans, who is normally more open, this is deeply disturbing, but he is not ready to reciprocate because in this

---

[18] There is disagreement among commentators as to whether the name "Castorp" was chosen by Mann to convey this aspect of the Hans-Joachim relationship. Maurer, "Names from *The Magic Mountain*."

instance he needs the veil of silence. He has not yet satisfied the various longings associated with Berghof. It is also fitting that Joachim should finally say "Hans" and hence recognize the other as a separate entity precisely at the moment when they part.

Whether they want to know each other's secrets or not, Hans and Joachim always recognize the hidden thoughts of each other. Thus Hans is sure that Joachim knows of his carnival night meeting with Clavdia. He also knows that Joachim will construe it as a personal betrayal. Knowledge is always assumed. An osmotic communication seems to take place between their psyches. Perhaps the relationship between the two is best signified by the spatial relation of their rooms. Except for a brief period after Joachim's return to the mountain, while they have to wait for the present occupant to die, they always have adjacent rooms. Much of their time is spent on the small balconies opening up from each room. This is where the important rest cure takes place, winter or summer, in the fresh air. As they lie on their deck chairs, Hand and Joachim can talk—even a whisper can be heard. Each can also hear conversations between the other and any visitor. The balconies are separated only by an opaque glass partition. This opacity also accurately describes the permeable wall between the cousins.

To show the fundamental identity of Hans and Joachim is to point to the importance of their relationship. Its dialectical nature can be seen as a magnification and clarification of the dialectic that is usually confined to the mind of a single individual. Additional evidence for seeing them as one individual can be found in the author's wording. Speculating about the mysteries of time, Hans is described as questioning himself and his cousin about it:

He asked himself, inwardly, and also by way of asking Joachim....[19]

An inspection of this statement indicates that Joachim is equated with "himself," that is, with Hans. Asking Joachim is simply another way of asking himself. On another occasion, a similar identification occurs. When Clavdia enters the foreroom of the x-ray cabinet where the cousins are already waiting, Joachim speaks to her. Hans feels that this is almost the same as though he had spoken with her himself:

For his cousin to speak to Frau Chauchat was almost the same as his doing it himself—and yet how altogether different![20]

[19] *The Magic Mountain*, p. 219.
[20] *The Magic Mountain*, p. 212.

Joachim, though a very different person, is also another side of the entity Hans-Joachim.

These differences have so far been discussed under the general category of military against civilian. That is the way they are most often described by characters in the novel. But rather than constituting an additional and separate antithesis, they correspond to the fundamental dialectic of male and female principles. Hans' civilian nature is merely another way of indicating the preponderance of qualities we have ascribed to the female principle. Joachim's militarism is really a concentrated essence of his masculinity. The two are always mentioned in conjunction. Hans' manliness, on the other hand, is at times jokingly undermined. He does it himself. Others do it also at times—thus Settembrini remarks that his young friend looks like a little nun, having finished her novitiate. But the adjectives most commonly associated with Joachim are "masculine" or "manly." As Hans watches his cousin's bare chest in the examination room he admires its athletic form.

He has always been more inclined than I to the things of the body—or inclined in a different way. I've always been a civilian and cared more about warm baths and good eating and drinking, whereas he has gone in for manly exertion.[21]

Joachim's masculinity is especially emphasized as he lies dying. It is as though in suffering and waiting for death he were reduced to that which is essential about him. In typically brusque manner Behrens chides Hans for not showing sufficient composure on finding out about the inevitability of Joachim's death. Joachim knows of it, he says, and Joachim also knows how to face it.

Your cousin's a different sort, quite another pair of shoes. He knows. *He knows* —and keeps quiet. Understand? He doesn't go about hanging on to people's coattails and asking them to help him pull the wool over his eyes! He knows what he did, and what he risked, and he is the kind to bite his teeth together on it. That's that kind of thing a man, that is a man, can do: unfortunately it isn't in the line of a fascinating biped like yourself....[22]

A "fascinating biped," Behrens calls Hans in order not to say "man." But "biped" may also be a sly reference to his dual nature, both as a Siamese twin and as a sexually ambivalent being.

Joachim's sef-control in the face of death is in the last stages of the novel constantly described as manly. At the very end he becomes

[21] *The Magic Mountain,* p. 178.
[22] *The Magic Mountain,* p. 530.

an apotheosis of manhood—the severe and beautiful expression on his face is always called masculine.[23] In death, he can no longer show his manliness in behavior, but this is compensated for by his looking like a quintessential embodiment of manhood itself.

Shaving had grown burdensome to him, for some eight or ten days it had not been done, and he had now a strong growth of beard, setting off with a black frame his waxen face and gentle eyes. It was the warrior's beard, the beard of the soldier in the field; they all found it manly and becoming. But because of this beard Joachim had suddenly grown from a stripling to a ripe man—though perhaps not because of it alone.[24]

To hold one's tongue, Doctor Behrens said, was one of the pre-requisites of manhood. This requirement fits well with the conception of the male principle as representing a more rigidly separated identity, while the inherent openness of the female principle allows it to com-municate with others easily. Surely Hans is female in this respect as well. He talks a lot. Joachim, on the other hand, is always tight-lipped, and it is usually Hans' knowledge of the cousin's reserve that keeps them from intimate discussions. The guarded, enclosed nature of Joachim can be seen also in his stubborn refusal to submit to Krokowski's psycho-analysis. Hans, on the other hand, becomes one of the analyst's regulars. He feels guilty about going to the sessions and tries to hide his visits from Joachim. The latter finds out by accident and, as Hans knows he would, feels betrayed. Hans has again opened himself up.

That the usage of such terms as open and closed is relevant can be shown by citing Mann's use of those terms for a similar purpose. Here they describe the posture of the two, and they seem as pertinent to their mental as their physical posture. They are standing in a cemetery that they have visited with Karen Karstedt, one of their moribundae:

Involuntarily the three paused here, the young girl first, to read the mournful incrip-tions; Hans Castorp stood relaxed, his hands clasped before him, his eyes veiled and his mouth somewhat open, young Ziemssen very self-controled and not only erect, but even bending a thought backward. . . .[25]

This inwardness, the desire to close and to concentrate, is characteristic for Joachim. Just before he dies, he performs a strange ritual. He

---

[23] Phrases such as "beauty of early manhood" recur.

[24] *The Magic Mountain,* p. 537.

[25] *The Magic Mountain,* p. 322. Mrs. Lowe-Porter here renders "gelöst" as "relaxed" and "geschlossen" (literally "closed") as "self-controlled," thus losing some parallelism and the closed-open connotation that is relevant here.

makes sweeping movements on the bed covers with his right hand, toward himself, as though he were collecting or gathering something, perhaps the fleeting essence of his own life. It is characteristic of him as an embodiment of the male principle that he would still try to keep himself in, to husband this essence.

The attraction Hans and Joachim feel for each other and the constant watchful fear of betraying too much emotion indicates that this sexual identification exists not only on the philosophical level but also on a practical human one. Flowers are tokens of love, and they are used as such in the repeatedly mentioned aria of Don José from the second act of *Carmen*: "La fleur que tu m'avais donnée, dans ma prison m'était restée." [26] Joachim is clearly connected with the opera later. He is also associated with flowers. Thoughtfully he has placed mountain flowers in a vase in Hans' room when his cousin arrives for his visit. When Hans returns to his place in the dining room after being confined to his bed for three weeks, it is Joachim who has instructed the servants to place some flowers near his cousin's plate. Out on a walk in the mountain spring, Hans is enchanted by the variety of flowers. He draws Joachim's attention to one kind especially. It is the Ranuncula, and it may be no accident that this plant is, as Hans points out, bisexual. The aquilegia, one of the varieties of this family, grows in large quantities near a bench in the secret nook where Hans had his first nosebleed and his first vision of Pribislav Hippe and where he goes to think about important things.

The clearest sign that Hans, at least subconsciously, thinks of Joachim as the male element in their pair occurs in another musical identification. In naming the chapter which deals with Joachim's death "A Soldier, and brave," Mann has established a connection between Valentin in Goethe's *Faust* and Joachim. After his cousin has died, Hans forms a special attachment to Valentin's prayer in Gounod's *Faust*. Again, it is quite clear that he identifies the soldier with Joachim. But how does he see himself? Valentin prays to God that when he goes to heaven he might be able to look down and watch over his sister. The pronoun used is the second person singular—"dich." Hans, the narrator tells us, knew full well that this "thou" was Gretchen, but nonetheless the passage moved him very deeply. He is equating himself with Gretchen. And, in view of the male-female associations we discussed, this should not be surprising. There is, then, some erotic attraction between Hans and

[26] *Carmen*, p. 200.

Joachim. But its depth and charm consists in its very vagueness and ambiguity. They are, at least to some extent, really parts of one entity, or of what is to become by the end of the work one entity. Hans absorbs Joachim as he incorporates Clavdia. At the end of the work, there is a synthesis of the two, and Hans even wears the military uniform that Joachim so desired and prophetically wore in his materialization in the séance. Given their identity, it may not be essential to establish precisely the nature of their attraction. What remains significant, however, is the identification of Hans with the female principle, of Joachim with the male. If Hans and Joachim together form a bisexual plant, then it is Hans who carries the prevalently female characteristics.

The boundaries between Hans and Joachim, then, are not as solid even as the glass wall separating their balconies. The limits tend to shift. In the pair of mother and daughter in *Felix Krull,* individual boundaries were clear. They became confused only when Felix wanted them to do so. The doubleness of the image existed in Felix's mind. It was primarily an aesthetic satisfaction that he derived from looking at Maria Pia and Zouzou as one entity. He felt no grief at the physical separateness of the two, no frustration at not having before him in the flesh the perfect woman who would combine the charms of mother and daughter. On the contrary, the enjoyment of being able to think of them in conjunction was enhanced by his ability to separate them again and to contemplate the beauties of each type. But for the members of the double image their relationship is an existential problem that requires solution. When the author looks at the question from the inside, from their point of view, the double image is not an aesthetic game but a search for a way out of the self and toward a synthesis. In *The Holy Sinner,* only the grace of God could rescue son and mother out of an ever increasing tangle of inversion. Hope for redemption rested singly on the child of sin. The child as a metaphor for the possibility of true synthesis will occupy us in the next chapter. Here we are dealing with the dialectic itself.

The dialectical relationships exemplified in these pairs are diverse, and the purpose of the double images themselves varies. The ones discussed above do not exhaust the many possibilities of the double in Mann's work. The combination of sameness and variation can take many forms. As we saw, mother and daughter stand for an idea of female beauty. Hans and Joachim complement each other as male and female principles. Other, related but not identical, correspondences could be pointed out in their relationship. They are also two faces of Germany whose correct synthesis becomes a vital problem for the author. The kind of doubles that are repetitions of an identity with slight variation seem doomed to love themselves in each other unless a miracle happens. The complementary halves are well described by Hans' remark to Clavdia on carnival night: "We love what we have not—that is proverbial." The various ways of mixing individualities and constructing doubles can be demonstrated in rather schematic ways at times, for instance, in the colors of the pairs' eyes.[27] Thus, Hans' eyes are as different from Joachim's as possible. Wiligis and Sibylla both have eyes that are "blue in their blackness," thus indicating that these are the qualities of two persons there, but these are combined in such a way that each has his half of everything.

The nearly identical pairs have small chance of finding contact with another—in loving each other they love themselves, and their pride makes it impossible for them to seek contact elsewhere. The complementary halves, when they are conscious of being a pair, attract each other and have a chance of coming together. Hans incorporates some of Joachim's identity into himself after the cousin dies. Finally, he finds sufficient discipline within himself to leave the sanatorium, though he had felt on the eve of Joachim's departure that with the cousin went away any chance of his own return down below. Now he does find the strength to leave even though Joachim is dead. He can do so because he has been able to absorb within himself some of the control that he occasionally admired in Joachim.

But whatever the chances of a contact or synthesis between the members of a pair, in the double image these possibilities are given. They are built into the way the pair is constructed, and effort has only limited efficacy. Hans does work at his synthesis, and it is at least partly to his merit that he achieves one. He could have chosen not to make use of the chances he has. But he does have these chances because of the complementarity built into his character and Joachim's. One might call this way to obliterate the limits of individuation the naive way. In most cases, there is no clear consciousness of separation, followed by a conscious and active struggle to overcome it. Yet one has to separate first in order to unite truly.

---

[27] Eyes are always important in Mann's work. In *The Genesis of Doctor Faustus*, he speaks of the erotic motif of the blue and the black eyes. Eyes are the carriers of wordless communication, ways out of the self and into the other.

Ideally, this kind of union would be achieved in love. There was mention of love in this chapter, but love between members of a double image is affected by their membership in that pair. Does love carry the possibility for meaningful communication, when it is not limited in this way? Love and death are both ways out of the self. But Hans' preoccupation with death showed him a way of live. Love was importantly connected with this way, but it was also closely associated with death. In his openness, Hans partly represents the female principle. But, as we saw in the dangers of his attraction to Clavdia, the openness should not be total—love is not identical with death. These were the risks involved in Hans' road to a richer life. For love to be an agent in the opening of the self, it needs to take such risks. As Hans remarks to Clavdia when she accuses him of selfishness, it is not easy to separate self-renunciation from self-enrichment.

In the double image, even when there seems to be a possibility of real contact between self and other, such communication is usually based on an illusion. Either the other turns out to be an almost mirror image of yourself, or he is in actuality a part of you. As a structural device, the double image is an attempt to show unity within diversity. Any insights into the overcoming of personal boundaries derive from the way the pairs are, not from what they do. To see how one might through his own efforts attain contact, we have to look at what Mann's characters feel and do about their sense of isolation.

CHAPTER VII

LOVE: A POSSIBLE SYNTHESIS

Love, in Mann's world, can be said to refer to any attempt to break down the barriers that isolate individuals. Since the female element implies this ready outlet to the outside world, an ease of contact with others that the male lacks, love is closely related to it, but the final aim is of course a meeting of the two. Why the concept of love is so inclusive, what it means in various contexts, and what kinds of love there might be—the answers to these questions will have to emerge from the following discussion. Justification for making it so inclusive comes from the author himself. Thomas Mann tends to see all relationships in an erotic light, even tensions between conceptual entities. Thus, the antithetical relationship between life and spirit is, in his scheme, governed by erotic attraction. Even irony is erotic.[1] It should be evident from this scheme that erotic attraction makes the dialectic a process and gives it impetus toward synthesis.

Clearly, then, a term of such wide application involves some danger of vagueness. So far, I have defined it most generally as a desire to escape one's specified, confined existence.[2] Such striving can take many forms. Hence, under the general heading of a discusssion of love, I will speak first of the erotic attractions between men and women. Then, other attempts to get out of the self, activities that are not obviously

---

[1] Thomas Mann, "Betrachtungen eines Unpolitischen," *Gesammelte Werke,* XII pp. 568-569.

[2] Freud singles out love as the only non-pathological state in which the boundary of self that has been gradually, and in most cases irrevocably, established since infancy melts away. *Civilization and its Discontents* (New York, 1961), p. 13. The connection is also made by Ignace Feuerlicht in *Thomas Mann und die Grenzen des Ich* (Heidelberg, 1966). Feuerlicht deals very thoroughly and insightfully with Mann's unindividuating processes. Some of the topics of his discussion closely parallel mine—he deals with love and the double image, for instance—but his emphasis and context are different.

connected with love will be discussed—images, dreams, and art. They belong in an examination of the role of love in Thomas Mann's world— first, because they have the same purpose, and secondly because they are frequently associated with love.

At the outset, love is not attached to an object. The attraction is given the name of love even when it is not known what the striving is toward. At first, as we have seen in our discussion of *The Magic Mountain,* there is only a heightened state of expectation, a receptive readiness for love. Hans' heart beats without reason, but after meeting Clavdia he feels that now a reason and a content has been given to the state. Yet we will also see a movement in the opposite direction— from the attachment to one specific love object to feeling him or her to be a representative of a whole class of objects that one loves, and sometimes beyond any class or category to an all-inclusive affection.[3] This generalizing tendency exists in *The Magic Mountain.* Hans' love for Clavdia eventually transcends its object so that he can do without her. First, the state of expectancy is needed, and it is a universal and general condition. But it is empty, a form that needs some content. This content is provided by a specific personality, who then serves as a springboard for a wider and more generalized feeling. If this process is to be worth while, the final stage must differ from the similarly general quality of the preparatory one. But, in order to determine whether they differ, we have to look at the two stages and also at what is between them. What does Mann make his characters say, and what does he occasionally say himself about what love is and what it does? What can we deduce about it from what the characters do, and from the way they develop? That Mann does indeed think of love as the striving out of one's self can be seen in his own pronouncement. In a discussion of Goethe's *Werther*[4] he speaks of love as "the highest and strongest form of the expansion of the soul." At its base is the desire to move from personal determination, from what he calls the prison of individuality, toward the undetermined and the infinite. Significantly, Mann sees this desire as the explanation of the behavior not only of Werther but also of Faust. Werther, like Hans, is ready for love before he meets the beloved.

---

[3] This movement is called transcendence here. It is part of the "love of love" complex of which Denis de Rougemont writes, and anyone interested in its broader historical and social implications should read his *Love in the Western World.*

[4] Thomas Mann, "Goethes 'Werther'," *Gesammelte Werke,* IX, pp. 649-650.

If men need to feel passion first and then find an object for it, this is not true of most women. Mynheer Peeperkorn's observation about the woman's need for being awakened by the man's passion seems to apply. Awakenings are very important. Thus, Lotte's beauty which enchanted young Goethe blossomed as a result of Kestner's interest in her. In *Doctor Faustus* Ines Rodde shows unsuspected depths of passion after Helmut Institoris proposes to her and thus makes her conscious of herself as woman. Even Eni, Potiphar's wife, who eventually comes to feel that as mistress she must have the initiative, admits that the slave Joseph started it all.

If Peeperkorn is right about the initial passivity of woman, he may not be correct about the way she chooses her mate. Her interest aroused by Institoris, Ines immediately turns to another man, Rudi Schwerdt- feger, whom she woos aggressively. Lotte is grateful to Kestner and respects him but cannot help falling in love with Goethe. The theme of wooing by proxy which becomes important in *Doctor Faustus,* with all its inherent complications, pertains to this problem. A woman starts from a latent state, is aroused by a particular person, one who happens along by chance, and then may direct her passion at another, more specific individual (more specific in the sense that he is more consciously her choice). There is, thus, an increasing specificity of direction in her development. If this is true, it need not cast doubt on the thesis of the greater openness and lesser individuation of the female principle. If woman is indeed less individuated and more vaguely defined, she need not fear the specific and particular but may find definition for herself through her mate. Even passivity is still maintained to some extent— Ines, though she loves Rudi, marries Institoris. Lotte, for understandable reasons, though evidently stirred by Goethe's courting, stays with Kestner.

Thus, it might be said that women, insofar as they represent the female principle, are not conscious of the imprisonment of individuality. A woman like Clavdia finds it easy to slip in and out of affairs, main- taining her openness or "freedom." Others do not feel their communication and contact with the rest of the world as threatened in any way by their commitment to an individual. There is another reason for this lack of fear—as we will see later, to a woman who bears children the man is also a springboard, a catalyst that brings her into her own. By bearing children, she escapes any feeling of imprisonment that she may have— part of the openness of the female principle consists in its privileged relationship to time. And the direct sense of a chain of generations that a woman has is produced by her more intimate association with birth.

It has been said before that the female principle is by no means equivalent with woman and the male principle with man. This distinction is especially necessary here because one can speak of the varying uses of love only by male and female characters. These figures are mixtures of varying and changing amounts of the male and female ingredients. In order to be concrete, one must speak of specific men and women in Mann's work. But every time one does so there is a tendency to obliterate categories. Love is close to the female element because of the latter's openness, but it is also associated with the male one because the desire to seek communication and union is the result of feeling oneself to be in need of it, to be isolated. This is only to say that love happens between people, or characters in a novel, not between principles.

A pure incarnation of the male principle would be incapable of love. If Mann believes that pure masculinity is inhuman, it is so in its incapacity to empathize, to get out of oneself and understand the other—to love. Characters who represent largely the male principle have little relationship with the world. Leverkühn is surrounded by an atmosphere of cold. In an essay, Mann describes Nietzsche, the most striking prototype for this character, as having a "monstrous masculinity."[5] Adrian's relationship with others, even with his biographer Zeitblom, who is really a complementary part of him, is strained, unnatural, and often based on misunderstanding on at least one side. When he thinks of marrying Marie Godeau, a lovely young Swiss woman, he clumsily assumes that it is an affair to be decided by him alone and that once he has made up his mind, the matter is settled. There is no sense of mutuality. Though he seems to have feelings for her, he is incapable of communicating them to her or even to Zeitblom, in whom he tries to confide. Rudi, who incorporates more of the female principle,—he is even outwardly somewhat feminine—becomes the intermediary, with tragic results.

Adrian does find contact with the world, but he does it only through art. As I will propose later in the discussion, artistic productivity is itself a way out of the imprisonment in the self, an alternative to love. But for the moment, one can say that Adrian, being more "male," is less capable of love than other male figures who include more of the female principle. Hans, we have seen, incorporates several aspects of it. He is capable of love for a woman, for a schoolboy friend, and for his cousin

[5] In *Betrachtungen,* [Reflections of a Nonpolitical Man], p. 83.

Joachim. More than that, love becomes the answer to all the ultimate questions he learns to ask on the mountain. Another male figure who is closely associated with love is Felix Krull. He becomes an advocate of love, defending its rights in front of outspoken and stubborn Zouzou. Felix is truly bisexual—he attracts both men and women. He is operatively a potent male and is himself sexually attracted to women only, though aesthetically sensitive to the beauties of both sexes equally. Yet he does not resent the homosexual passions that he arouses. There is a good deal of the female in Felix, and especially of the receptivity and openness of the female principle. He is never imprisoned in an individuality—he changes identities several times, not by superficial pretending but by a total commitment to the new identity, accepting it with great joy and devotion and even adopting the past that goes along with it. Thus, he has both an openness to things and people outside himself and the special relationship to time (implied by the notion of an interchangeable past) to a very high degree.

On two occasions, we have seen Hans incorporate qualities of people he loves—Clavdia and Joachim—and be able to do without their physical presence when he is forced to do so. In both cases, the feeling of love itself, and the expansion of soul that it engenders seem to be the desired end. The specific love object is transcended. After Joachim dies, Hans finds the strength to leave the mountain. He can do it because he has internalized his cousin's self-discipline. Even though the two have always been aspects of the same entity, the two sides have, on the fictional level, been divided into seemingly separate personalities. After Joachim's death, Hans has to combine both. At the climax of the séance, urged by his companions to question the returned Joachim, Hans whispers "forgive me!" and switches on the light. This action may well rest on Hans' realization of how unnecessary and merely external it is to call his cousin back in this way, when he is really and permanently a part of him.

Clavdia, we hase seen, is transcended in a similar way. Hans' intense preoccupation with her body gradually acquires another dimension. The body becomes more and more transparent and reveals insights of ever increasing importance. A whole complex of ideas revolves around Clavdia. Her erotic attraction and association with Pribislav Hippe mediate insights that further Hans' education. Her body which holds such attraction for Hans owes this attraction to disease and death, stations of the dangerous road to life. The group of ideas that is associated with her deals with tensions between body and spirit and the relationship of each of them to disease, to life and death. There has been ambivalence so far in Hans' interpretation of what that body means to him. The body which appears to Hans in a vision is still part Clavdia but already partly an idealized image, a symbol. It suggests death. But it is also an image of life and the symbol of a unity achieved not by the obliteration of death but by human work on this earth. That the scales are being tipped in favor of life is indicated by the term Hans uses to describe the vision—it is the image of life. In the great vision that Hans has while skiing during a snowstorm, love is already seen as being clearly on the side of life. "Death and love—no, I cannot make a poem of them, they don't go together. Love stands opposed to death. It is love, not reason, that is stronger than death." [6]

The frequency of visions and dreams is striking even in a brief look at Hans' thoughts about love, and it is more so in a thorough examination of his actual love for Clavdia. The climactic snow vision takes place when Clavdia is absent not only from Hans' side but from the mountain. Yet it is the culmination of a train of thought started by his feelings for her. By then, he is on the way to assimilate the meaning of Clavdia to the extent that her presence is not absolutely necessary. But from the very inception of their relationship. Mann tends to present the events of the affair indirectly. Even the physical details of the lovers' encounters are usually conveyed after the event through Hans' recollection.

Except for the Walpurgis Night scene, one of two important confrontations where we actually see Clavdia and "hear" her voice, most encounters between the two are relayed to the reader as Hans relives them. Thus, early in the work, it is evident that it is Clavdia's image that concerns Hans. The look Clavdia directs at him in the dining hall, nudging him to the doctor's appointment that is to justify Hans' staying at Berghof is recollected later. In his memory Hans pieces the whole experience together. That is the reader's only source of information about it. One might object that this is the only way to see any experience as a whole and to understand its meaning. But the writer is in this position in regard to the experiences he describes in any case, and he may well choose to present the chaotic momentary impressions of his hero. If Mann chooses to acquaint us with Hans' experiences after they have occurred, in Hans' thoughts about them, then this indicates that it is Hans' thoughts and feelings that matter, not the experiences.

[6] *The Magic Mountain*, p. 496.

Examples of this manner of presentation could be cited all through *The Magic Mountain*. The meeting in the corridor is also savored at great length later, as Hans painstakingly recalls the details of Clavdia's face. This is clearly part of what I have called the process of internalization. As a result of it, Clavdia can be both "invisibly-absent" and "invisibly-present" after she has left.

In addition to the narrative device of presenting meetings with Clavdia in the past and in Hans' mind, there are other clues to this process. I have talked at length of the importance of pictorial representations of Mme Chauchat, though the emphasis was on specific aspects of these, such as transparency. But the frequency of the representation itself is significant. Though it is Clavdia's flesh that haunts Hans, we rarely see Clavdia in the flesh. She is remembered, her painting is detailed as Hans carries it about in Behrens' apartment and fondles it, her x-ray slide is the physical symbol of her presence in absence. The need for tokens is a hint that complete internalization has not yet taken place. At first, only a temporary absence of short duration can be tolerated— Hans' memories need periodic refreshing. Then longer parting can be endured, but there is not yet full transcendence of the physical, even though the physical is a representation, an increasingly abstracted symbolic object. Progressively, the value of the representation is downgraded, that of the inner meaning raised. In order to achieve complete internalization, Hans has to deal with the "real" Clavdia. His desire for her needs to be faced, expressed, even satisfied to some extent. He needs to find out what this real Clavdia is like, how she feels about him and, as it turns out, how she feels about Peeperkorn. Also he has to renounce the chance of laying claim to Mme Chauchat in order to purify the experience for its new existence in the mind. If he had avoided the real Clavdia or failed to deal with the actual situations involving her, the transcendence could not occur. The transition to spiritual associations would then appear as escape and illusory compensation.

Hans recollects Clavdia in tranquility; he worships images of her. A third level of evidence for the process of transcendence is the frequent use of the word "image" (*Bild*) in association with Clavdia. This is the use of the term in an abstract way—not to denote the painting of Behrens or even the slide, but as a description of what goes on in Hans' mind. The symbolic body of his vision, we have seen, is the "image" of life. "Her image had floated before him . . .", the narrator tells us. It is her likeness that appears to him constantly as he is falling in love. Clavdia standing in the doorway on carnival night forms a picture, conveniently framed by the doorway. This may be another reason why she is often associated with doorways.

The image of Clavdia is frequently seen in a dream. Dreams are very important in *The Magic Mountain*. There is a range of dreamlike experiences from the clearcut and complex elaborations of Hans' dreams at night that combine identifiable elements of his waking existence through waking dreams or day dreams to marginal experiences that are predominantly dreamlike. Thus, Hans says that his conversation with Clavdia on carnival night is like a dream. And, even though we are in this instance told their exact words, the situation and the words themselves do have a trancelike quality. It is only on these terms that we can accept Hans' sudden flood of eloquence in French, a language of which he previously seemed to have only the most elementary control.

Especially vivid are Hans' erotic daydreams. The detail is graphic and the presentation is not at all "abstract" in the sense of being palely intellectualized. It is very concrete. This is not a contradiction to the thesis that Hans' internalization of Clavdia is a progressive abstraction. It is an abstraction of an aesthetic nature. Though Hans is not an artist, the syntheses and abstractions, the conclusions that he reaches, are broadly aesthetic—they are not clearly analyzed in terms of ideas. Instead, they are intuitive and apprehended concretely. Hence his insights are visions. His dreams are so concrete that they can be smelled—Clavdia, as image of life, bends to kiss him, and Hans senses her "organic scent."

In contrast to the vividness of erotic dreams and visions, actual love scenes are very spare. The narrator makes an ironic, teasing point of ringing down the curtain on the consummation of all these anticipatory dreams. Now, this surely is a matter of irony and teasing.[7] It may also be a matter of discretion. But it may be more than that. It may mean that Hans' anticipation and recollection is indeed more important than the objective event. The dream and the image of Clavdia are more important than Clavdia herself. She is a mediator of feelings and insights.

There is a similar conjunction of the dream and the image with love in other works of Mann. It seems that love, from the frankly and devotedly physical to the almost objectlessly spiritual, is constantly associated with dream, vision, and image. This can take the simple form of daydreaming of the beloved or it can reach a point where the

---

[7] Hermann Weigand believes the practice to be dictated exclusively by irony and discretion.

making of images itself becomes the essence of the love relationship. When the object is sufficiently transcended the image crystallizes its best qualities. The image is also timeless. Occasionally, in such instances, the object itself may become something of an embarrassment. This is true especially when the image maker is very successful—when he is a professional image maker, that is, an artist. The would-be artist and practising aesthete Spinell in Mann's *Tristan* novella makes an idealized mental statue out of the tubercular Gabriele. Yet he is not artist enough to create an independent and separate artistic entity that can exist apart from the physical Gabriele. Thus, he ends up by helping to accelerate her death. He needs to enlist the help of death to stop the ravage of time and disease. Since he cannot successfully embody the loved one into a work of art, the work of art needs to be performed on her body itself. This body cannot be permitted to continue to exist and change and thus belie the image.

What happens when a real artist, one who knows his craft well, makes an image out of a loved woman? In *Lotte in Weimar* Goethe has also transformed a living girl into a work of art. Forty-four years later, Lotte still lives in the middle of the episode that is incorporated in *The Sorrows of Young Werther*. Even though she knows that the attendant celebrity has made her life difficult in many ways, she enjoys it. Goethe has, in making her image so vivid, somehow deprived her real life of intensity. There have been many pleasures and much suffering, a whole brood of children—a full life, it would seem. Yet she feels more real as Werther's Lotte. At times she catches herself "remembering" something that Goethe invented about her past. There is no distinction in the reality of events that actually happened and those that were invented once they form parts of an artistic whole. It seems that even a successful artist may be a Pygmalion in reverse. Lotte, by temperament a lively and responsive woman, describes herself with some satisfaction as being henceforth a "madonna in the niche of a cathedral." She busies herself researching her own genealogy, to facilitate matters for future researchers, and arranges a museum for posterity. Even though she cannot help feeling a twinge of jealousy and competitiveness, she recognizes the deliberate pattern of repetition that governs the love affairs of the poet. The poignancy of the situation increases when the reader becomes aware that for old Goethe it is embarrassing to face the continued real existence of Lotte, an existence that has been subject to change in time. The essence that he looked for in young Lotte is not limited to the individual Lotte. There is no need to search for it in the traces of beauty that are still left in the face of old Lotte. He has found it again and again in other faces, different in many ways but carrying a resemblance which he intuitively recognizes and that he needs for the celebration of love. No wonder that the impatient genius comments peevishly that the pink ribbons Lotte has fastened to her gown in a whimsical allusion to a literary and real past have been hung on the wrong self.

If this sort of attitude seems to be characteristic of the male principle, it is not limited to men. For comparison, let us look at a woman who seems to think in terms of mythical recurrences, who pursues a constant type of male beauty, and who makes images of a sort.

She is Diane Houpflé, or Diane Philibert, as she prefers to be known under her nom de plume. For she is a writer, a producer of novels that are, as she tells Felix Krull, "pleins d'esprit, et des volumes de vers passionnées." [8] It is significant that she refers to herself constantly as a woman of esprit. She claims to represent the spirit in its search for humiliation by Life. Spirit is, in Mann's scheme, a male principle. Pure maleness is pure spirituality and hence inhuman. Diane is more concretely masculine because she is, like Potiphar's wife, a woman in pursuit, an aggressive woman. Krull's own openness, his participation in this sense in the female principle tends to reinforce the impression that she is the male half of their affair. In a traditionally male role, she adores Felix's body that, in its resemblance to Hermes, comes close to being the essence of all the young bodies that she craves. But she needs the bodies. Whatever the quality of her art (and the paucity of references to it as well as the tone of the few existing ones implies that it is marginal or minor art), it has not taken the place of the actual body.

Diane, in her masculine role, and in a delightful and not unkind parody of Tonio Kröger's search for love from the uncomplicatedly dumb, looks for stupid beauty. Felix is far from dumb. As it turns out, she can extract her quota of humiliation from him and also satisfy her aesthetic sense in the identification of Felix with Hermes by having him steal from her. But he refuses to cooperate in the fiction of his stupidity. Felix's menial occupation and lack of literary knowledge helps somewhat. Along with the thrill of being robbed by her lover, it keeps up the fiction of the spirit's self-abasement.

[8] *Krull*, p. 174.

"...And yet the intellect—oh!"—and once more she knocked our heads together, somewhat harder than before—"how could you understand that? The intellect longs for the delights of the nonintellect, that which is alive and beautiful *dans sa stupidité*, in love with it, oh, in love with it to the point of idiocy, to the ultimate self-betrayal and self-denial, in love with the beautiful and the divinely stupid, it kneels before it, it prays to it in an ecstasy of self-abnegation, self-degradation, and finds it intoxicating to be degraded by it—"[9]

Like Hans, Diane Philibert deals in images. She calls Felix a "statue of beauty" ("Standbild der Schönheit"). This is the appellation that Aschenbach uses in *Death in Venice* for Tadzio who incorporates his own ideal of Greek beauty and love.[10] In a lengthy and literate outpouring of her feeling that ends in a rush of Alexandrine verse, Diane alternates between "Du" and "ihr," the singular and plural second person pronouns. Felix stands for many. She loves an image of a young man and tries to realize it with a changing partner. Not being a good enough artist, she cannot transcend the actual object once and for all. Her image is not strong enough to live on its own. Hence it needs to be revitalized constantly by ever new encounters with ever new and ever young men. Again, Felix becomes an image—"Wunschbild" she calls him now. But there is no progressive ascent from man to image, from object, through successive stages of abstraction, to vision, as there was with Hans. Rather, Diane alternates between image and object. If her compulsive search and evident lack of contentment are not themselves sufficient evidence for Diane's failure, then the testimony of form—the alternations between singular and plural "you," and those between the references to actual boy and ideal construction should strengthen that impression. That she does not achieve a transcendence with Felix, can be seen in the persistence of such alternations in her farewell speech to him:

Adieu, Armand! Farewell, farewell forever, my idol! Do not forget your Diane, for in her you will survive. After years and years when—*le temps t'a détruit, ce cœur te gardera dans ton moment béni*. Yes, when the grave covers us, me and you too, Armand, *tu vivras dans mes vers et dans mes beaux romans*, every one of which—never breathe this to the world!—has been kissed by your lips. *Adieu, adieu, chéri....*[11]

---

[9] *Krull*, pp. 174-175.

[10] "Standbild und Spiegel"—the terms of Aschenbach suggest the greater complexity of his feelings.

[11] *Krull*, p. 181. Mr. Lindley renders as "kissed by your lips" a phrase that really means "kissed from the lips of all of you."

Though she promises him immortality in her work, Diane does not seem to have a great deal of faith in its efficacy. While she is alive it is surer for him to live in her heart. Goethe, the perfect artist, is so successful in making images that the continued physical existence of the model can become an embarrassment to him; Diane Philibert cannot get beyond the model itself.

Why is the making of images so frequently associated with love? When lovers are artists, good or bad, they think of their love and their work in close connection. To Aschenbach, love for Tadzio is not only a pathetic personal rejuvenation but also an infusion of needed artistic vitality. Goethe's *Werther* is brought alive by the experience of love. To the aesthete Spinell, affection for Gabriele becomes inextricably intertwined with his desire to see life artistically. Diane does not know where eroticism ends and art begins. The dream is closely connected with this problem. The association of art with dream is an old one (Plato, for instance, and later Nietzsche). The dream is also a concrete and direct embodiment of feeling and thought, or felt thought. It, like art, deals in images. When a Mann hero is not an artist, he expresses the same needs in dreams. As we have seen, Hans does that. But what are the needs that have to be satisfied by such means?

The driving force is primarily the need to get out of the boundaries set by individuation. That the dream can do it, and that this is indeed the importance of the dream for characters in Thomas Mann's works where dreaming is so frequent and prominent, can be seen in *Felix Krull*. The significance of the dream, says Felix, is the obliteration of insurmountable barriers between people. The dream is irresponsible; it is the place where the other is our own creature and where we can use him for our wishfulfillment:

> ... dreams, where our "I" associates with shadows that have no independent life, with creations of its own, in a way that is after all impossible in waking life where one flesh-and blood being exists in actual separation from another.[12]

The occasion that brings Felix to such conclusions is not a fullfledged dream. It is a conversation with the prostitute Rozsa that has the strange directness and primitive wishfulfillment qualities of the dream. Different in many ways, this conversation is still reminiscent of the one that Hans has with Clavdia on carnival night. We are sitting here as in a dream, he tells Mme Chauchat.

---

[12] *Krull*, p. 113.

"... it is like a dream for me, that we are sitting like this—comme un rêve singu-
lièrement profond, car il faut dormir très profondément pour rêver comme celà....
Je veux dire: C'est un rêve bien connu, rêve de tout temps, long, éternel, oui, être
assis près de toi comme à présent, voilà l'éternité." [13]

Thus, not only are dreams associated with love but a whole varying
gradated cluster of dreamlike experiences grows around it as well.

An image, even though it may not form part of a dream, is like
a dream because it tends to erase the flesh and blood boundary between
self and other. The making of images that gives him this power of playing
with individuation is the main prerogative of the artist which makes him
the supreme dreamer and connects art and dream. Mann makes use
of this power in creating types which he can then vary in a multiplicity
of proportions and combinations, by celebrating striking recurrences or
reincarnations, and, in a more easily and clearly identifiable, striking
way, by constructing the double image. All of these constitute sovereign
play with individuation. But it is play. The final metaphor for an
obliteration of boundaries is love. Ideally, the union achieved in love
would be a more solid one, a synthesis that might be permanent but
is, in any case, not restricted to the realm of the imagination. The
tendency in the works we have examined in this connection always to
associate love (both substantively in having lovers say they are as in a
dream, and formally—by relaying love scenes to the reader obliquely
as in anticipation or recollection) with dream and image may show a
failure of love. But first we must see what love means to the heroes in
Mann's work and what it might be when it is successful. We have seen
its effect on Hans Castorp, as a communion and finally an incorporation
of the loved one. What does he think of love itself?

Hans' conception of love changes in the course of *The Magic Mountain*.
When he concerns himself with it at all in his earlier existence down
below, love to him can be summed up in a harmless little song lyric,
sentimental and straightforward. The existence at Berghof deepens his
sensibilities also in this respect. Thoughts of love get confounded with
meditations on disease and death. Like disease and death, love is a
yielding up of the self, a willing renunciation of individual separation
and even existence. (Disease, is, after all, shared, especially the con-
tagious diseases Mann usually chooses to describe.) No wonder that
they tend to form one complex whole that is hard for Hans to separate
and examine. But he tries to do it nonetheless. The carnival night talk

---

[13] *The Magic Mountain*, p. 336.

with Clavdia marks the high point of Hans' dedication to the emotional glorification of the love-disease-death-complex. In his miraculously proficient French, he shares this view with Mme Chauchat:

"Oh, l'amour n'est rien, s'il n'est pas de la folie, une chose insensée, défendue et une aventure dans le mal. Autrement c'est une banalité agréable, bonne pour en faire de petites chansons paisibles dans les plaines."[14]

The sentimental little lyric is haughtily rejected. Love, to Hans, now is one with death and with the body which to him at this stage symbolizes both lust and disease, which again are really one. On the verge of freezing to death during his excursion in a snow storm, he again tries for synthesis. He has thought, stimulated both by his feelings for Clavdia and by Settembrini's talk, about love and life and death constantly. The constellation in which he now sees them is a different one. Death is important even in life and it wants to be respected, but man must not let his concern with it control his life. Man, or the "homo Dei" as he appears to Hans in this vision of harmony, stands in the middle and thus can feel that the extremes exist through him, that he can control them rather than be dominated by them.

The dialectic does indeed exist through man, as does thought itself. Another version of this dialectic is the juxtaposition of individual and community. ("Mystical" community, Hans calls it and "windy" separatism—an allusion to the mystical Russian soul that Clavdia represents and to the "windbag" Settembrini.) Again, man's place is in the middle. Thus, love is no more a passive surrender, a melting away like death. In contrast to his carnival night conviction, Hans now sees love not only as separate and different from death but opposed to it. A new distinction has been introduced—that between love and lust. It is lust that is an equivalent of death. Thus, there has been a separation, a refinement of thought. Love has been distinguished from one of its aspects that earlier seemed inseparable to Hans, the part that is directed to the body merely as body. But there has also been a widening. Love has also come to include a dedication to community and state.

... death is release, immensity, abandon, desire. Desire, says my dream. Lust, not love.... And from love and sweetness alone can form come: form and civilization, friendly, enlightened, beautiful human intercourse—always in silent recognition of the blood-sacrifice. Ah, yes, it is well and truly dreamed. I have taken stock. I will remember. I will keep faith with death in my heart, yet well remember that faith with death is evil, is hostile to humankind, so soon as we give it power over thought

[14] *The Magic Mountain*, p. 341.

and action. *For the sake of goodness and love, man shall let death have no sovereignty over his thoughts.*[15]

The widening of love is clearly evident in its pairing, twice within the passage, with goodness or kindness. But while we note Hans' growth and the maturing and broadening of his idea of love, we should not forget that it occurs in a dreamlike vision; that these thoughts are explications of an insight presented to him in a conjunction of concrete images, and that, even while congratulating himself on the interpretation, Hans says it was "clearly [or distinctly] dreamed." The phrase is accurate enough as a description of the concreteness of anybody's dreams, but when applied to philosophical insight it is at the very least ambivalent. When Hans says "Oh, this is distinctly dreamed and well governed!", "governing" to him means a blend of metaphysical speculation and wishful dreaming. This private and special meaning of the word has been established earlier.

Nor should we take the distinction between love and lust as a precise and absolute one. In abstract thought it may be so. In an actual relationship such insistence would chase away all charm. Thus, even after the vision, Hans' love for Clavdia retains both aspects. The kiss they exchange as part of their pact to protect their friend Mynheer Peeperkorn is the best example of this ambivalence. It is described as a Russian kiss, the kind that are given in Russia, say at Easter, without much prejudice as to the sex of the recipient—a spiritual kiss of sorts. For Hans and Clavdia it is even more spiritual because it is a kiss of renunciation. Yet the narrator suggests that the precise nature of the kiss is better unexamined. If it was more fleshly and passionate than spiritual, that would be quite understandable knowing the two, he tells us, and, in any case, this ambivalence is the very essence of love.

To try to make a clean-cut distinction between the passionate and the soulful—that would, no doubt, be analytical. But we feel that it would also be inept—to borrow Hans Castorp's useful word—and certainly not in the least "genial." For what would "clean-cut" be? The subject is so equivocal, the limits so fluctuating. We make bold to laugh at the idea. Is it not well done that our language has but one word for all kinds of love, from the holiest to the most lustfully fleshly? All ambiguity is therein resolved: love cannot but be physical, at its furthest stretch of holiness; it cannot be

---

[15] *The Magic Mountain*, pp. 496-497. The new opposition of love to death should not be taken too literally. Hirschbach, for one, (p. 74) calls it a mistake. Love and death, as we have pointed out, both obliterate individual barriers and thus are not totally opposed. The newness of the discovery of their significant differences may prompt Hans to state the distinction as an opposition.

impious, in its utterest fleshliness. It is always itself, as in the depth of passion; it is organic sympathy, the touching sense-embrace of that which is doomed to decay. In the most raging as in the most reverent passion, there must be *caritas*. The meaning of the word varies? In God's name, then, let it vary. That it does so makes it living, makes it human; it would be regrettable lack of "depth" to trouble over the fact.[16]

Since such delicate hovering and masterful ambivalence marks his whole existence, it is no wonder that Felix Krull should be the great spokesman of love. His disquisition on the subject is a canonical text of what this whole complex of themes means in Mann's dictionary and in his philosophy. Themes that we have noted earlier and that reappear persistently in the author's work, singly or in smaller or larger groups of varying combinations, are now finally seen all together, and their meaning as well as their relationship to each other becomes clear.

Thus, Mann's obsessive preoccupation with skin here explicitly receives the meaning that we suspected it to possess implicitly. It is the skin that physically defines the limits of one individual against those of another. Hence it becomes the symbol of mental and spiritual separation as well, a sign for individuation.[17] It was correct, then, to suggest that Hans' interest in Clavdia's skin and his obsession with transparency was motivated by his desire to erase these boundaries and incorporate Clavdia into himself. In *Krull*, this preoccupation is clarified. It is highly appropriate that Felix, who has perhaps best solved the problem of solipsism, who is open and "female," and never bound by any one identity, should also be described as having a thin skin. It is so delicately sensitive, Krull tells the reader, that, even when he was poor, he was forced to buy fancy soap—cheap and utilitarian brands would damage his skin so that it bled. Zouzou suffers from an obsession that appears to be the negative counterpart of Hans' skin complex. Her arguments tend to be based on a sort of squeamishness. Love in its physical manifestations, she feels, is a ludicrous and unclean matter. In her opinion, men constantly try to seduce women into their dirty game, while women have no natural tendency toward it. Zouzou is a devil's advocate. Secretly, she desires nothing more than to be converted. But even this differentiation of the sexes with regard to sexual passion is merely a sharpening of other statements about the problem—Peeperkorn's disquisition about female passivity, for instance. Even to Zouzou, love remains a metaphor for the

---

[16] *The Magic Mountain,* p. 599.

[17] Nietzsche also sees a thick skin as a sign of spiritual isolation. In *Ecce Homo* he says: "Solitude has seven skins which nothing can penetrate," (p. 105).

blending of two individuals. The difference is simply that she pretends to want none of it.

And what do you want? What is the purpose of your melting words and melting glances? Something that is unspeakably laughable and absurd, both childish and repugnant. I say "unspeakably," but of course it is not at all unspeakable, and I shall put it into words. You want me to consent to our embracing, to agree that two creatures whom Nature has carefully and completely separated should embrace each other so that your mouth is pressed upon mine while our nostrils are crosswise and we breathe each other's breath. That's what you want, isn't it? A repulsive indecency and nothing else, but perverted into a pleasure by sensuality—that's the word for it, as I very well know; and the word means that swamp of impropriety into which all of you want to lure us so that we will go crazy and two civilized beings will behave like cannibals. That's the purpose of your flirtatiousness.[18]

Against this attack, Felix needs to defend his own conception of love. Even though Zouzou concentrates her venom on sexual love, or lust, as we might distinguish with Hans, it is important to Felix to construct a good defense. To him, by this time, love has come to mean a universal sympathy, and he might simplify his defense by retreating into the walls of this higher conception. But, like Hans, he realizes that such a rigid distinction would deprive the concept of all its charm. The continuity and co-existence of the various forms of love, their organic growth into an almost inseparable knot, is the very essence of love. Her attack, he tells Zouzou, is untrue because it is "excessively true," that is, it tries to separate clearly where the act of separation does violence to the object. This object is, as we said above, an intricate growth, and cutting it one could not help but cut into flesh. The imagery that Felix uses is not organic, but it implies the same danger that cutting would destroy its form. He uses the imagery of fabric. His heart, he tells Zouzou is "enwrapped" or "spun around" (*umspinnt*) by his love for her. It is wrong to say that love is the calculating means to some end, he retorts to her suspicious accusations; it is an end in itself—it is "totally woven into itself."

Zouzou is not so easily persuaded. Without following the whole argument whose outcome we know in any case, let us listen to part of her retort to Felix's eulogy of the kiss. It will confirm our assertion that, like Hans, she is preoccupied with the human skin.

Pfui, the kiss—that tender exchange! It's the beginning, the proper beginning, *mais oui*, or rather, it is the whole thing, *toute la lyre*, and the very worst of it. And why?

---

[18] *Krull*, p. 354.

Because it is the skin that all of you have in mind when you say love, the bare skin of the body. The skin of the lips is tender, you're right there, so tender that the blood is right behind it, and that's the reason for this poetry about the mutual discovery of pairs of lips: they in their tenderness want to go everywhere, and what you have in mind, all of you, is to lie naked with us, skin against skin, and teach us the absurd satisfaction that one miserable creature finds in savouring with lips and hands the moist surface of another.[19]

Felix responds in kind. Love is a miracle, he says, and the miracle consists precisely in the erasing of the physical boundary. Surely, he admits, men do live separately. He even takes up the skin preoccupation of Zouzou. We are isolated from each other, living in our own skin, he says, and the other, in his skin, usually repels us. But in love, this normal physical revulsion disappears. And it disappears because the other is no more felt as other. The transformation begins in the eyes. The lover's gaze, while still perceiving the other as distinct, sees him not as something indifferent or disagreeable but as an object of intense desire. The limits of the bodies then try to fuse more closely in the kiss. In a world of individuation, it is "the seal of the miraculous abolition of isolation." Now the kind of physical closeness that was irritating earlier becomes the aim.

The kiss interests Mann because it is still just barely individual. In *Krull* it is its tendency to erase the individual barriers that is important. But it hovers between two worlds. In *Lotte in Weimar* Goethe contrasts it with the sexual act and finds it ". . . spiritual because [it is] still individual and highly discriminating. . . ." It is a unique head you cradle in your hands. The kiss says: "I love and mean *thee*, *thee* God's sweet singularity, expressly thee in all of creation." The sex act is basically unselective, hidden by the night—anonymous. Art is mentioned along with eroticism. The distinction between kiss and procreation parallels that between art and life. The human fullness of life which is equated with the making of children is not the share of art which is rather a "spiritual kiss on the raspberry lips of the world." Whether Mann is justified in ascribing such an opinion to Goethe does not really matter here. It points to Mann's own association of art and love and his consistency in attributing meaning to the proximity.

Even short of closer physical union, Felix sees traces of love seeded everywhere in the contacts of daily life. The original nausea against the physicality of the other is overcome in the simple act of the handshake that to Felix becomes a celebration, a victory of nature's impulse to love

---

[19] *Krull*, p. 356.

over her own barriers. And here another preoccupation of Mann comes to light and is placed in context—the constant dwelling on hands and arms, especially those of women.

People shake hands—that is something very ordinary, everyday, and conventional; no one thinks anything about it except those who are in love, and they enjoy this contact because as yet no other is allowed them. Others do it unfeelingly and without considering that it was love that originated the practice; but they do it. Their bodies remain at a measured distance—not too great proximity on any account! But across this space separating two closely guarded individual lives they extend their arms, and the strange hands meet, embrace each other, press each other. . . .[20]

If Felix speaks best about and for love, he is also best aware of its limitations. Even to Zouzou, he must admit that the total union that the lovers always seek can never succeed. The complete fusion of two beings and two lives is impossible. But to admit that this is what is desired is to provide yet more proof that love to Mann means a whole range of phenomena, where the sexual is by no means disdained but where it tends to become a metaphor for all meaningful contact between self and other. The sex act is pathetic, as Zouzou claims, even to Felix, but it is pathetic in the original sense. It has pathos—it is both sad and funny because it is doomed in the final analysis. Nature, though she fosters love, does not feel that her ends would be served by total fusion. At best, such union may be symbolized by the child, Felix suggests. But that, he feels lies outside his topic of discourse. It may not lie outside mine, and I will return to that possibility. First, let us briefly draw the consequences of the preordained failure of the love impulse. This may be the answer to one wondering why love scenes in Mann's works are most frequently shown in recollection, anticipation, dream or image. If love is, as Felix says, the closest thing to a real union of separate individuals but can never in actuality achieve that union, then to show the act of love would be to clearly admit defeat. As long as it remains only vaguely adumbrated, no demystification need take place, and sexual love can still endure as a metaphor for total success.

Zouzou may not have been entirely wrong in claiming that men seem to be more vitally interested in love than women. She said that women were by nature less disposed toward it. On one level of analysis this is quite true. It may refer merely to female passivity and thus denote a difference in degree or manner. But Zouzou says that women are "by nature" not inclined toward seeking love. If one is to give such a statement serious consideration, it may well substantiate my view of the

[20] *Krull*, p. 365.

female and male principles. Love is the most dramatic and most nearly successful way to break out of solipsism. The male principle is the more confined, the more specified, and rigidly individuated one. It, then, needs an escape from individuality much more than the female does. Such an escape becomes an existential matter. Hence those in whom this principle dominates must seek love, and naturally they are the initiators of any love relationship, the pursuers. This is true also of women who incorporate the male principle. Diane Philibert and Mut-em-enet are active and aggressive in love. Diane is also exceptional in her attempt to work with images, regardless of her success. And, except for Eni, we are not shown the dreams of women. The making of images and even the dreaming of dreams seems to be the prerogative of the male principle.

Love is often associated with dream and image because it tries to achieve more permanently what dream and image hold out in momentary vision or illusion. Apart from seeking love, then, the male principle tries other ways in its desperate desire for contact. The same impetus can be seen behind the tendency to ban women into an image where no flesh and blood, no skin boundary exists between self and other. There are attempts of varying success and value. Spinell, in the *Tristan* novella, makes an image of Gabriele, but it is as unimaginative as a death mask and like it requires the death of the subject. Goethe, on the other hand, makes the Lotte in his *Werther* so alive that she drains the vitality of the "real" Lotte. In art, no individuation barriers exist between the artist and his characters—they are, after all, wholly creatures of his mind. Art is, in this way also, a dream. Most artists in Mann's work are male. If there are female writers (Diane Philibert or Jeanette Scheurl in *Doctor Faustus*), they are usually merely clever and practice narrowly prescribed entertainment genres. To them, literature is not an existential matter. The female principle is not so confiningly individuated, and it can get out of the self in other ways.

There is another reason for the paucity of female artists, besides this lack of dire need. In Thomas Mann's world there reigns a law of conservation of energy, an implicit assumption that one possesses a limited reservoir of creative powers. If these energies are used in one endeavor they will not be available for others. This principle of economy is evident in *Doctor Faustus* where Adrian's attempts to make closer human contact inevitably lead to a diminution of his artistic production. When I said above that the female has other avenues of escape if it needs them, I meant that women bear children. The child, as Mann had Felix Krull say, is perhaps as close to a symbol of meaningful human contact as any.

If no children result from poems as from kisses, then it is so partly because the poem is an alternative expression of the productive instinct. Men can have both—poems and children. But men are not involved in the birth of children the way women are. The female artists in Mann's works, such as they are, never have children. Of those we have mentioned, Jeanette Scheurl is a spinster, and Diane Philibert expressly connects her amorous activities (and her writing is a direct outgrowth of them) with her lack of a son.

Childbirth is in Mann's world a counterpart for artistic creativity. A vivid demonstration of its equation with spiritual creation occurs in the séance in *The Magic Mountain*. Here it is not a work of art that is brought forth but the materialization of spirits. The labor pains of the medium Ellen Brand are described in detail and at length. Her movements are identical with those of childbearing. The author's preoccupation with female creativity matches his enduring interest in the artist and the artistic process.[21] Thus, Lotte is aware of the parallel when she sadly speaks of how long since it is that she bore her last child. The kind of creativity in which she excelled is over now, while Goethe's powers as writer are not diminished by age. In the Joseph-novels, the obsession with fertility is realistically and historically explained by the needs of Israel, but the author's emphasis on the psychological aspects of the problem, especially with Rachel, goes beyond those requirements. Even in the earlier novellas, there are indications of this concern and of the view of childbirth as one alternative of creativity, one that excludes others. Thus, in *Tristan*, Gabriele's small reserve of strength has been sapped by the child who grows at the same rate at which she wanes. When Spinell kindles a renewal of her musical interest, her concern for her child dwindles. A grotesque version of the same complementarity can be seen in the same novella. The leitmotif that accompanies Frau Höhlenrauch, a minister's wife, states that she had borne nineteen children and had not a brain left in her head. This is a character conceived grotesquely and hence the statement is an extreme one. We need not take it literally. But the equivalence and complementarity that it describes does exist in Mann's world view, and it can be detected in subtler incarnations in many other places in his work.

---

[21] There may be deep psychological roots for the relationship of artistic creativity and the motherly element. Charles Mauron in *Des Métaphores obsédantes au Mythe personnel: Introduction à la Psychocritique* (Paris, 1963), sees artistic creation as a rediscovery of the mother, after the child has gradually lost his memory of his original oneness with her (p. 233).

Like art, birth is a way out of imprisonment in the self. As he is consistently concerned with art, so Mann shows a recurring interest in birth. Its frequent mention and its explicit comparison with artistic production testify to that concern. Yet another kind of evidence can be adduced. It is the way in which the author speaks of birth. Hard births interest him especially, and he dwells lovingly on every detail (with Rachel, especially). And it is not the outcome so much that seems to preoccupy him. It is the process itself. In birth, as in art, he is deeply interested in the how. And the way in which the process of birth is described is at times surprisingly close to the way one would normally describe artistic creation. Dame Eisengrein in *Der Erwählte* is an artist of birth. Her single and consuming interest is devoted to what is here described as the female realm.

... except for God (she was very pious and wore a large jet cross on her mountainous bosom) she was interested in nothing at all but what has to do with women's life, in the most pious, most physical sense of the word, and thus in particular in female burdens and needs and sacred fertility rich in pain; in arrested menses, gravid bodies, chokings, strange cravings, childbed, solemn shrieks and writhings, tapping movements in the belly, labour pains, birth and afterbirth and sighs of bliss and hot cloths and bathing of the mucus-covered fruit, to be stroked smartly with rods and held by the feet upside down if it did not at once show life by screaming.[22]

Having outlived her own fertility, Dame Eisengrein now concerns herself as passionately with that of others. Not content with supervising the births around her own castle, she goes out in the villages to look for an exercise of her skill. She has borne six children herself. Four died early, but, the narrator says to his surprise, her grief was not as great as had been her joy in bearing them. It is the bringing forth, he concludes significantly, that mattered to her. The words that the author puts in Dame Eisengrein's mouth when she speaks of birth clearly indicate the aesthetic nature of her concern. When she consoles frightened Sibylla, she does not do so by downgrading the seriousness of the process but instead by emphasizing its beauty:

"Just wait, that will be very fine and is at bottom much finer than a lytel embracing."[23]

---

[22] *The Holy Sinner,* p.59.
[23] *The Holy Sinner,* p. 61. "Lytel" is the rendering of a regional form of "little" in German. Mrs. Lowe-Porter translates the German "schöner" as "fine" and "finer." "Beautiful" would not only strengthen my point about the aestheticism of the lady's approach but is also more accurate.

Not only is birth compared to the artistic process. Artists are sometimes equated with women in more direct ways. In *Death in Venice* we saw Aschenbach imagine himself speaking to Tadzio as Socrates did to Phaedrus. What to Socrates was a problem of philosophy had taken on the form of the fundamental problem of the artist. Love for the physical beauty of another person, says Socrates, is an impulse and even a pre-requisite for the love of absolute truth or beauty. But man, in his weakness and imperfection at times misunderstands the mediating nature of the lover and not only does not get beyond him but becomes attached to the lover in a beastly physical, possessive way. In art, the danger is even greater. While making the object transparent to a higher truth, the artist still needs to retain the physical dimensions, the specificity, and the concreteness of it. Susanne Langer[24] thinks of works of art as "images of the forms of feeling." They are not models showing how feeling works; this is the significant difference between art and science and art's vital contribution. An image, she says, shows how something appears and how it feels. Art seeks to retain not only a graphic abstraction of reality but a feel of the totality of a phenomenon, the shape of the reality itself. Thus an artist has to transcend and not transcend the object at the same time. Transparency seems to be a good way to transcend the object and yet to retain it. Its frequent recurrence in Mann's work testifies to his constant preoccupation with the special and difficult way in which an artist must work.

But Aschenbach has not yet come to the tranquil acceptance of the difficulty which may let one play with it and put it to one's use, though he is aware that this aspect of art constitutes not only its curse but also its blessing. He alternates between cool detachment and hot erotic pursuit. And it is this attachment to the body which he feels to be demeaning to the artist that equates him with woman:

For you know that we poets cannot walk the way of beauty without Eros as our companion and guide. We may be heroic after our fashion, disciplined warriors of our craft, yet are we all like women, for we exult in passion, and love is still our desire—our craving and our shame.[25]

His longing has to take the form of love, says Aschenbach. That is, both the woman and the artist, in order to fulfill themselves, are dependent on another. An artist, I said, needs to be concrete. The woman's creativity is more concrete yet. But both are firmly rooted in the world of phenomena.

[24] *Mind, An Essay on Human Feeling*, xviii.
[25] *Death in Venice*, p. 146.

A child may be the closest that love can come to solidifying into an image. To a writer, the image that his work is must still retain the shape and feel of the model. Huij, in the Joseph-novels, saw the primeval swamp, a female element, as the prototype of creativity. Woman would have to purify her kind of creativity to approach art. But the artist needs contact with the swamp in order to have something to form, to purify, and finally to turn into art. The danger for him lies in getting caught in the swamp. This danger, however, needs to be braved because such periodic descents to the fruitful chaos are necessary. The woman needs a man to come into her own. The artist also needs some relationship of an erotic nature —the body Tadzio, for instance, or the succession of women in the life of Goethe. The artist may then discard the person who served as his springboard, at times showing a great deal of reluctance to even see him or her. Lotte senses this reluctance in Goethe's relationship to others as well as to herself. She blames him for it with a hidden vehemence and plaintively claims a failure to understand, though in truth she prefers not to admit her understanding. Dame Eisengrein, the birth artist, shows the same contempt for the person who made her kind of art possible. She tries to make that clear to Sibylla who laments her departed brother and lover.

"Let be," said the lady-in-waiting, "and let him go. When they have made us women and given us our own, then they are of no more use and all the rest is just women's matters. Let us be glad that we are now among ourselves, we women ..." [26]

In *Lotte in Weimar* Mann puts a similar comparison in Goethe's mind. The poet's gift is his "sign of purity." The woman (he is thinking about the woman in a projected poem) is lost when she is seduced. The poet, much seduced as he is (and it would seem that the more seduced the better a poet), always retains his talent and with it the assurance of continued purity.

To assert that an artist is in some important ways like a woman is, of course, not to identify the two completely. It is highly relevant to our context to show the large share that an artist may have in the female principle. This emphasizes the dialectical process inherent in art. Yet this share varies. Some of Thomas Mann's artists are almost totally masculine, in my sense of the term. Aschenbach, who compares artists and women, is himself in danger of being so trapped in his own individuality, so cut off from the rest of the world, that the forming instinct may become

---

[26] *The Holy Sinner*, p. 61.

sterile without revitalization and new content brought up from the "swamp." The balance is precarious. The dialectical dynamism must be retained even within a synthesis. Adrian Leverkühn is perhaps even more masculine. It may be that the motherly love he constantly seeks out is the mediating principle, the vital contact with the female element that keeps him alive and sane as long as possible. Both Aschenbach and Leverkühn create some good work, but neither finds any sort of tenable balance between life and art, some accommodation that would let them live and create at peace with themselves. They cannot survive.

Balance, then, is what is needed, a balance of male and female elements. But this balance implies the continued existence of a creative tension; it is never static. An artist creates out of bisexuality. God has it—he also creates. In *Lotte in Weimar*, Mann has Goethe in his morning ruminations give this quality another name—"androgynous art" he calls it.

Originality! That kind is just crazy, distorted, art minus creation, barrenness, vanity, petty dried-up spinsterishness! I loathe and despise it. What I am after is the productive, male-female force, conceiving and procreating, susceptible in the highest degree. Not for nothing do I look like that sturdy brown ancestress, I am the Lindheymer in male form, womb and seed, androgynous art, quick to receive, yet myself begetting, enriching the world with that I have received.[27]

A woman "artist" can be as lacking in participation in the female element as a male one. Andromache, the woman acrobat in *Felix Krull* is more artist than some of the women writers that appear in Mann's work. The latter, with the possible exception of Diane Philibert for whom life and art bear a very special relationship, are occasional writers. Even when they are successful, art to them is not an existential matter. To Andromache it is that. In accordance with Mann's law of conservation of energy, she gives all she has to her art, and hence has nothing left for life. It would be unimaginable to see her as wife and mother, feels Krull. Indeed were she to conform to Felix's fearfully jealous imaginings and take Mustafa, the equally accomplished animal trainer, as lover, she would immediately come tumbling down from the perch she uses in her daring netless balancing act. This act Felix perceives right away as being unnatural for a woman. He concludes: "She was not a woman; but she was not a man either and therefore not a human being." [28]

To Andromache, her art represents her communion with men, or, indeed, with the world. The public is important to her. But her com-

---

[27] *Lotte in Weimar*, p. 338.
[28] *Krull*, p. 194.

munion with it is not verbal. She defies gravity and thrills the audience with her consummate acrobatic skill, but she refuses to even smile at them. To Felix, she seems an angel in her perfection and severe remoteness. But the appeal of her high trapeze act depends on a different sort of perfection than does that of the writer's art. She is beyond words and, seemingly, beyond human experience. The curves that her trained body describes in the air appear to have nothing to do with human feeling. She is called "fille de l'air." The patterns and images that a writer creates, however, must harken back to human experience and feeling in some form, at whatever remove, if his art is to mean anything to its readers. If Andromache can afford to be inhuman, the poet cannot. This is why the artist needs some infusion of the female element. But what he needs most is a balance of male and female qualities that is at times described as bisexual or androgynous.

A metaphor that can be used for such a combination of male and female principles is marriage. Since for Mann the woman's fruitfulness and that of the artist are very close, it is natural that when he speaks of art rather than of the individual artist he would compare it to the institution of marriage rather than to an androgynous being. When he is concerned with the artist, as he is more often, the problem has to be solved either through a clear attribution of spiritual bisexuality, as it was for Goethe in *Lotte in Weimar*, or by making him part of a double image. When art is the subject, such complexities are not necessary. The two halves do not need to be seen as essentially one. Art can be seen as an institution. Hence marriage, the closest possible institutional binding of male and female, is the perfect metaphor. In 1925, answering an inquiry about his views on marriage, Mann twice compares it with art. To those who see in the emancipation of women and other modern developments the doom of marriage, he says that art also seems at an end and yet it will survive. It is, like marriage, a sacrament, something spiritual with a bodily foundation.[29] Responsibility is inherent in both. Anyone who tries to escape that responsibility, as Mann believes that Thomas Buddenbrok and Aschenbach do, arrives at "metaphysical individualism" or the orgiastic freedom of the individual. A true artist, to produce and to survive, needs a "morality of life" ("Lebenssittlichkeit"). The artist is necessarily connected with the other sphere—that of pessimism and death, but, like Hans Castorp, he must not allow it to control him. The artist is in this

---

[29] Thomas Mann, "Über die Ehe," [On Marriage], *Gesammelte Werke*, X, especially pp. 206-207.

too a mediator. He needs, Mann writes, a whole list of attributes that have to do with life—"Lebensbefehl," "Lebensbürgerlichkeit," "Lebensfreundlichkeit," "Lebensgutwilligkeit," "Lebensgutwillige Bravheit."

These life-affirming attributes are frequently connected with the female element. In the male it is an acceptance and a commitment to life to marry and have children. Man shows his good will toward life by associating himself with a woman. But the woman, when she is a good representation of the female principle, has this readiness for life as part of her nature. This is especially so when she is or wants to be mother. Thus, for instance, Lotte and Rachel are frequently described as having a "readiness for life" (Lebensbereitschaft). So is Joseph's bride Asnath. A readiness to expose herself, an openness to people is perhaps the most striking characteristic of Lotte. Her daughter, who is a closed, reserved, repressed woman, resents this quality and thinks that people impose on her mother, preferring to ignore the mother's eagerness to be imposed upon. This attribute becomes more prominent in women figures that approach the mythical (here again, the mythical is meant in a broad sense, including the Biblical women of the Joseph-story as well as Lotte, of whom Goethe made a myth). These figures can be used more readily as incorporations of the female principle because, no matter how well characterized, they are already symbolical—creatures of tradition and not only "real" women.

The artist's readiness for life may also be expressed in marriage and children. Mann points out, in this connection, that he married soon after creating Thomas Buddenbrook and Aschenbach.[30] But he need not be a bourgeois in the narrow sense. What matters is that he maintain his ties to life, that he feel responsible and loyal toward it. What gives permanence to art as to marriage is the constant interplay between the physical and the spiritual. An art that loses its foundation in human feeling is easily uprooted.

> ...what gives marriage the ineradicable stamp of sacrament and institutional permanence amid changing times is the peculiarly reciprocal relationship of spirit and flesh, their mutual grounding in each other, strikingly reminiscent of the essence and relationships of art.[31]

The opposite of such loyalty and responsibility on the part of the artist is an attitude that consists in an admiration for death, the beauty of death, and sterility. In Spinell, the would-be writer in the *Tristan*

---

[30] "Über die Ehe," p. 200.
[31] "Über die Ehe," p. 202. My translation.

novella, we are shown a sterile aesthete, a lover of style in bric-a-brac, letter-writing, and furniture, who can not maintain literary productivity because of his exclusive adulation of the beauty of death. In the marriage essay, Mann connects homosexuality with this unproductive aestheticism. It has the impermanence, the sterility, and also the seductive appeal of aestheticism. Fruitless love can be very appealing. Thus, Clavdia's enforced barrenness sharpens Hans' pleasure in watching her body as he sits listening to Krokowski's lecture. It pleases him that the social accept-ance of women's attempts to make themselves desirable which is based on its goal in procreation should also extend to Mme Chauchat's seductive dress. An involuntary association with his homosexual attraction to Pribislav Hippe forces itself on him. For other reasons, the love of Diane Philibert for her succession of young men is also sterile. So is Aschenbach's irresistible passion for Tadzio—it does kindle one essay, but it cannot support lasting productivity. Articulate Diane may be the most persuasive advocate of such an attachment.

Love is perversion through and through, it can't be anything else. Probe it where you will, you will find perversion.... But it's admittedly sad and painful for a woman to be able to love a man only when he is quite young, when he is a boy. *C'est un amour tragique,* inadmissible, not practical, not for life, not for marriage.[32]

Diane seems to be right—one cannot marry Beauty. But, in a sense, this is precisely what the artist needs to do. In mediating between a timeless ideal realm of Beauty and daily human experience and feeling he must achieve a productive union—a marriage.

It is this mediation of the artist, however, that brings up a caution. Having made his vision fruitful, he must not forget the way back to the higher realm. Whether the artist lacks permanent association with others because he avoids commitment or because he has learned to renounce, the lack is a needed condition of his artistry. This is one source of the sense of superiority in Mann's artists; it also contributes to their feelings of guilt, stronger in some than in others. Though, in *Lotte in Weimar,* Mann attributes a great burden of this human guilt to Goethe, he does not make him feel guilty. "Well set-up, gifted young fool," he con-gratulates his younger self on a *Werther* scene. Even then, he feels, he "knew as much about art as about love and privately meant one when

---

[32] *Krull,* pp. 176-177. The translation omits (as needless repetition?) the following sentence that constitutes an emphatic and necessary generalization of the specific situation:—"One cannot marry beauty."

he made the other," even at that age ready and willing "to betray love and life and human beings to his art." [33]

Another version of this requirement is the transparency of the loved object. It is part of an all pervasive tendency in Mann's work toward the generalizing of love. From attachment to one individual to love for community or world, from a purely sexual desire to a warmer and more spiritual feeling—the movement from particular to general is evident. Hans' love for Clavdia brought to him an understanding for many things. It widened his mind and his senses. For Hans this feeling remained a vague benevolence because he was not given a chance to show his love for his fellow man actively, as we lose him from sight in the mêlée of World War I. But, even on the mountain, he was capable of compassion, for instance in his reaction to Mynheer Peeperkorn. Even though we have said that Hans, for his development, does not need the physical presence of Clavdia any more, he himself surely feels that he does. He wants her; he was waited for her many years. Yet, he renounces his claims in honor of the suffering "personality" Peeperkorn, in respect and sympathy. When he finally complies with the long standing petulant request of Mynheer that he should give a kiss to Mme Chauchat it is a kiss of renunciation. After Carnival night, Hans' desire to obliterate this separation had, for the moment, fully succeeded. To kiss her on the forehead, as Peeperkorn wants him to do, would be to go back to an earlier stage of intimacy and erase the subsequent closeness. It would bring him back into the intermediate "normal" realm of social intimacy that he has heretofore carefully avoided. The Russian kiss they exchange, that unanalyzable mixture of sacred and profane, is already half renunciation as it climaxes an agreement to protect the feelings of a third person. After Peeperkorn's death, when his presence is, as Hans puts it, more symbolic than real, Hans complies with his request. This kiss that he plants on Clavdia's forehead marks the final stage in the generalization of his love. It is not really for her any more—it is for what she has meant to him in the widest sense. As he appropriates these wider implications of his love, he must take leave of its original object, and to make it clear that he is relinquishing any remainder of possessiveness he addresses her in the polite "you" form.

Love and goodness appeared to Hans as the answer to all questions in his vision in the snow. There are equivalents for this generalized good will in other works. Elsewhere too it is indicated that love for one person,

---

[33] *Lotte in Weimar*, p. 318.

erotic attraction, is a first step in the process of such generalization. In the Joseph-novels, the final generous feeling is called "sympathy." Joseph asks the Pharaoh to let him live in Menfe, a symbol to him of the interweaving of life and death. As a boy, he had stood on a hill not far from the city of Hebron near the burial place of his ancestors. The grave inspired him with respect for the dead and death itself. Yet he has equal affection for the busy activity of the people below in the city. This early ambivalence initiates Joseph's desire to live in this city of graves which is nevertheless a very lively and elegant city. And this pleasure, the narrator says, betrays a vital part of Joseph's nature—the will to keep faith with both life and death, a desire very close to that of Hans Castorp as he promises to keep his attraction to death in check during his snow-bound vision. Hans calls the feeling love; in the Joseph-novels the wider implications are recognized by making the term less possessive yet and more inclusive—sympathy.

And this pleasure was almost Joseph himself, it revealed the deepest depth of his nature. We call that feeling of his by the name of sympathy, a rather tame word for so profound an emotion as it actually is. For sympathy is a meeting of life and death; true sympathy exists only where the feeling for the one balances the feeling for the other. Feeling for death by itself makes for rigidity and gloom; feeling for life by itself, for flat mediocrity and dullwittedness. Wit and sympathy can arise only where veneration for death is moderated, has, so to speak, the chill taken off by friendliness to life; while life, on the other hand, acquires depth and poignancy.[34]

From love in the guise of sexual passion to love as good will toward all people and things to a recognition of the need to register the change in the content of the feeling and hence to call it sympathy—the process of generalization is quite clear. In *Felix Krull* it reaches a high point. Felix's good will toward other people knows no limits. He never comes close to concentrating all this desire and good will on one person. Generously, he lets many bask in his admitted beauty. There is no danger of the tendency toward universality to be arrested at any one individual, but the feeling changes as Felix matures. This development can be seen in the content of what Felix calls the "great joy." Even as a small child he had great interest in sexuality, and not knowing what to call all the pleasurable phenomena associated with it, summed them up under this inclusive name. The concept, though vague enough to accommodate growth, was at that stage filled with a content almost exclusively sexual. The older Krull writing his memoirs can look back upon this narrow

[34] Thomas Mann, *Joseph the Provider*, pp. 257-258.

conception and appreciate the lack of definition that let it grow. Sexual love, he feels, is only the crudest way of fulfilling this need, and, by giving too much satisfaction it bribes us and keeps us from being lovers of the world. Felix needs to remain open to the world. His longing, he sees now, always was for the wide and the faraway; it was ever "little specialized or exactly determined." After Kuckuck gives him knowledge of natural science, evolution, and insights into the unity and continuity underneath the apparent spatial and temporal discontinuities of the universe, this feeling expands still further. Now, his love or sympathy includes the whole universe, not only men and women, but animals, including prehistoric ones, and inorganic nature. A visit to the museum of natural history in Lisbon later dramatizes these insights, but even before that Felix emerges with an almost painful expansion of feeling. It may be surprising to the readers, he says, but this expansion was actually the same thing that he had unknowingly as in a dream, but even then with a providential vagueness called "the great joy." It is Kuckuck who gives yet another name to this feeling, a name that fits into my progression and clearly shows the impulse to generalize—"universal sympathy" he calls it. All-sympathy—a step beyond the plain sympathy of Joseph even, includes concern for and empathy with the contentment of a moss covered rock in a mountain stream. Man, having consciousness, must feel the pleasure and pain of those parts of creation that cannot feel themselves. This expanded feeling, however, does not result in disdain for the simpler, cruder forms that made it possible. Felix's universal love tolerates and perhaps even encourages his courtship of Zouzou and her mother. For Felix the development is not a climb along some narrow path with higher stages cutting off return. It is exactly what I called it—a widening. If the "great joy" was originally sexual and then came to mean something more inclusive, this does not mean that sexual pleasure is henceforth irrelevant and relegated to some garbage heap for cruder feelings. The book ends on a note of joyful abandon with Signora Kuckuck. Love between man and woman, though we now know it as a metaphor for intercourse with the world, still remains important in its own right.

CHAPTER VIII

CONCLUSION

In the Introduction, some characteristics were proposed to indicate the primal differences between male and female in Mann's scheme. The female principle, on this basis, seemed to be distinguished by passivity and by a different relationship to individuality and time from that of the male. To verify the hypothesis and mainly to see whether theoretical statement is implemented in artistic practice—in the construction of character and the structuring of relationships between characters—, one female figure from a major work was examined. Clavdia, in *The Magic Mountain,* was investigated first as a substantive embodiment of the female qualities, and the actual character did confirm the principles I had proposed. Secondly, the functional implications that were tentatively stated in the Introduction—the facilitating and "barometric" or "thermometric" nature of the female element—were also reinforced. The ambiguity of the dialectic and the continuity of the male and female realms was also apparent in Clavdia who is partly a reincarnation of the boy Pribislav Hippe. There was an association with death, at times direct, at times implied in her general tendency to destroy the self—in her negative attitude toward individuation.

To show an almost totally male character I chose Gustave Aschenbach in the novella *Death in Venice.* He is an artist and thus needs some relationship to the female principle. The examination, thus, became at least partly one of the attempt of a representative of the male realm to escape into the other element. Adrian Leverkühn, of *Doctor Faustus,* also an artist, is a still purer distillation of the male. If he has any desire or hope to reach out toward the other pole, it occurs in his art rather than his life. The dialectical tension works itself out in his musical compositions. With a look at Mann's view of Goethe and Schiller the investigation of this aspect of the artistic sensibility was expanded. The dialectic entered more clearly as the attraction and repulsion between two different types of artists was concerned. Mann consistently presented Goethe as the female side of the polarity and Schiller as the male one. But what interested him most was the relationship between the two.

It is this complex relationship between the male and female principles that governs a striking and persistent device of Mann—the double image. This is a game with individuality: two as one or one as two. In it, the varying distribution of male and female qualities could be shown better than in a single figure. Five pairs, chosen for their varying combination of these qualities and for the varying purposes to which their doubleness is put, were followed in some detail. The antithesis of male and female here became a vividly illustrated dialectic. The double image represents an attempt to combine the two in a desirable totality. But this kind of a synthesis is primarily an aesthetic one. A wholeness that exists in the eye of the beholder, narrator, or reader.

To look at a synthesis that really involved a conscious union, worked at and achieved by members of the pair on a existential level, I spoke of love. Since love is seen as a metaphor for any successful union of self with world, other attempts at achieving it were included under that heading—the image, the dream, and, finally, art itself. The successful synthesis ought to be productive; it is, however, the female principle within it that is primarily the fertile one. As the sexual union produces children, so the aesthetic synthesis results in art. The artist, in order to be productive as artist and also to survive as man, needs an infusion of the female principle.

As sexual love is the prototype for all exchange between the self and the rest of the universe, so the dialectic of the sexes can itself be considered a prototype for all dialectic. It is, at least, the primary antithesis. In *Love's Body,* Norman Brown assumes this primacy and sees all dual organization as sexual organization.[1] This basic character of the sexual opposition can be seen in the pair of Yin and Yang, for instance, which is a cluster of antitheses built around but not limited to the male-female one.[2]

The interplay of male and female principles is one of many antitheses in Mann's work. Others impinge upon it in various ways and may at times resemble it without being identical with it. Even when the author specifically disavows any intention to equate another dialectic

---

[1] *Love's Body* (New York, 1966), p. 23.
[2] Brown, p. 23, citing Granet, *Chinese Civilization.*

with the male-female one, he still refers to the latter. He does so, for instance, in speaking about the all-important polarity of Life and Spirit.

It is longing that mediates between spirit and Life. Life too clamors for spirit. Two worlds whose relationship is erotic without one representing the male, the other the female principle—life and spirit. Therefore there can be no union between them, only the brief intoxicating illusion of union and understanding, an eternal tension without resolution....[3]

Why is it necessary to associate the other dialectics with the male and female principles? There may be many independent antitheses. When, however, one speaks of the possibility of combining the two opposites into a new and richer whole, a dialectical process results. And to describe the dynamism of that process, the relationship of male and female seems to Mann the best one. I said in the introduction that Mann sees many relationships in an erotic light, among them some that are not usually thought of in that way. Thus, in the above description, the attraction between life and spirit is erotic, though they do not necessarily represent the male and female elements. The union of male and female in love, we saw, becomes a metaphor for the best possible synthesis and as such it stands for the potentiality inherent in all other dialectics. Through this, the male-female dialectic itself acquires high generality and wide application.

It would be not only naive but wrong headed to claim that Thomas Mann was alone in recognizing this generality of appeal. We do not need to trace the power of the primal dialectic from Yin and Yang through its varied Western versions. But, without sorting out parallel from influence, a task that would be time consuming and take us too far from our main concerns, I should at least mention what amounts to a vogue for such explanations in the early part of the twentieth century because Mann's writing is contemporary with it and because Mann himself was aware of some of it. The dialectic of the sexes appears in psychoanalytic theory. Freud often speaks of male and female, or masculine and feminine attitudes when he means active and passive. In "The Claims of Psycho-Analysis to Scientific Interest," for instance, he writes:

We speak, too of 'masculine' and 'feminine' mental attributes and impulses, although strictly speaking, the differences between the sexes can lay claim to no special psychical characterization. What we speak of in ordinary life as 'masculine' or 'feminine' reduces itself from the point of view of psychology to the qualities of 'activity' and 'passivity'—that is, to qualities determined not by the instincts them-

---

[3] "Betrachtungen eines Unpolitischen," *Gesammelte Werke*, XII, p. 569.

selves but by their aims. The regular association of these 'active' and 'passive' instincts in mental life reflects the bisexuality of individuals, which is among the clinical postulates of psychoanalysis.[4]

I have already had occasion to refer to the fundamental importance that Jung attaches to the male/female dialectic. He also sees it as the paradigm for all other oppositions:

> Although man and woman unite, they nevertheless represent irreconcilable opposites which, when activated, degenerate into deadly hostility. This primordial pair of opposites symbolizes every conceivable pair of opposites that may occur: hot and cold, light and dark, north and south, dry and damp, good and bad, conscious and unconscious.[5]

The opposition appears in Jung's syzygies, paired opposites—heaven and earth, day and night, male and female, animus and anima.[6]

Explicitly or by implication, the dialectic also appears in much literature and other art of the time. To mention two prominent and very different examples, there are the plays (and the paintings) of the Expressionist Oskar Kokoschka and the novels of Hermann Hesse. The former's short plays *Murderer the Women's Hope* and *Job* are built on the dialectic as battle of the sexes. The question of who is the true creator, man or woman, occupies Kokoschka again and again. And the question seems to be answered in the summary of an interview with the artist.

> A vision is a light which never left him; but in the background behind the light was the female principle, the significant, the reason for life. It reminded him of the scene when Faust descends to the mothers, and the passage where Hamlet addresses his uncle. . . . The female principle of life is more than an idea, it is a fact, a vital force. Woman is eternal. Life is like the earthworm. Parts die and rot and are replaced. But it is still the same organism—the essence of life, not a mechanical process. . .[7]

Hesse also tends to glorify the female principle, at least in his earlier works. The sexual tension is more often expressed in terms of love and

---

[4] "The Claims of Psycho-Analysis to Scientific Interest," *The Complete Psychological Works of Sigmund Freud,* ed. James Strachey (London, 1955), XIII, 182. For one of many other examples, also see "Jokes and their Relation to the Unconscious," *The Complete Psychological Works,* VIII, 98.

[5] C.G. Jung, *Psychological Reflections.* Ed. Jolande Jacobi, Bollingen Series XXXI (New York, 1953), p. 94.

[6] See C.G. Jung, *Aion. Researches into the Phenomenology of the Self.* Bollingen Series XX, *The Collected Works of C.G. Jung,* (New York, 1959), IX, Pt. 2.

[7] J.P. Hodin, *Oskar Kokoschka. The Artist and his Time* (London, 1966), pp. 4-5.

friendship than in the battle imagery of Kokoschka. "We all share the same origin, our mothers," he writes in the prologue to *Demian,* "all of us come in at the same door." [8] And this is not a mere truism; it is rather the affirmation of his allegiance to the female element. In *Demian,* the female principle is incorporated into the "goddess" Frau Eva, Demian's mother who brings insight and at least temporary peace to the searching, struggling Emil Sinclair. As in Mann's work, the dialectic produces characters that have a double aspect, who are sexually ambiguous or hermaphroditic (Demian himself and later Hermine in *Steppenwolf,* for instance) or characters who appear to be two sides of a single full personality, such as Narcissus and Goldmund. It is in the latter novel that Narcissus summarizes the polar tension between them, the relationship in which he represents the masculine aspect.

Natures of your kind, with strong delicate senses, the soul-oriented, the dreamers, poets, lovers are almost always superior to us creatures of the mind. You take your being from your mothers. You live fully; you are endowed with the strength of love, the ability to feel. Whereas we creatures of reason, we don't live fully; we live in an arid land, even though we often seem to guide and rule you. Yours is the plenitude of life, the sap of the fruit, the garden of passion, the beautiful landscape of art. Your home is the earth; ours is the world of ideas. You are in danger of drowning in the world of the senses; ours is the danger of suffocating in an airless void. You are an artist; I am a thinker. You sleep at the mother's breast; I wake in the desert. For me the sun shines; for you the moon and the stars. Your dreams are of girls; mine of boys. . .[9]

In *Steppenwolf,* Harry Haller has to immerse himself into various aspects of the female element—its earthy sensuality, its timelessness, and finally and most importantly its shattering of the conventional and narrow sense of individuation. The dialectical tension, however, is evident because the road back to the Mother, "back to God, back to the all" [10] is seen as the way of the "suicide" (a metaphysical rather than literal suicide more often than not, one that would kill the self). Though man's "innermost longing draws him back to nature, the mother," not onward to "the troublesome primal father Spirit"—"back to nature is a false track that leads nowhere but to suffering and despair." [11] Apparently one must partake of both realms, although the rewards sound more like those the primal mother is likely to give: "The return into the All, the dissolution

[8] Hermann Hesse, *Demian* (New York, 1966), p. 4.
[9] *Narcissus and Goldmund* (New York, 1969), p. 45.
[10] *Steppenwolf* (New York, 1969), p. 55.
[11] *Steppenwolf,* pp. 70-72.

of painful individuation, the reunion with God means the expansion of the soul until it is able once more to embrace the All."[12] The motherly pole, thus, seems to be stronger, though the atmosphere becomes more masculine in the later work of Hesse, especially in *The Glass Bead Game.*

Indeed the male/female dialectic seemed to be in the air. Much of it settled down in literature, some in metaphysical speculation, and some in psychoanalytical thought. The Jungian anima stands behind Hesse's female characters, inviting a union with the feminine aspect of the self. But perhaps the most influential and the richest common source, working directly or through commentators and admirers, is Johann Jakob Bachofen whose extensive study of mother right was published in 1861.[13] He saw the dialectic of the sexes as a moving force behind the development of the religious and political structures of civilization. Societies could be distinguished by the dominance of either the male or female principle in them, and this dominance colored all their institutions. The female element is associated with primary matter and with the earth. It is "telluric", though in a higher manifestation it can become "uranic", emancipating itself from the swamp and hetaerism to a purer state of monogamous life associated with Demeter. No more tied to the earth, it is at this stage connected rather with the moon which represents a "heavenly earth" rather than a chthonic one.[14] The male power is represented by the sun. Even in its purified state, the mother's tie with her world and child is sensual, visible, concrete, whereas that of the father is more spiritual and abstract. The female principle is still one of matter and of nature. This material character ties it to the pain of the cycle of becoming and death, and thus it stands for sorrow as opposed to the joy of the solar-spiritual father.[15] The mother is heavy, weighted with the gravity of matter; the father weightless as light.[16] The male is the principle of movement, the winged phallus, while the female rests

---

[12] *Steppenwolf*, p. 73.

[13] Many similar ideas already appear in the treatise "Versuch über die Gräbersymbolik der Alten," of 1859. The complex matter of the correctness of Mann's Bachofen borrowings and of his attitude to the Swiss theorist is exposed and clarified most helpfully in Dierks, *Studien*, in the chapter on "Thomas Mann und Johann Jakob Bachofen: Mythos und Ideologie."

[14] Note Mann's use of the moon in *The Magic Mountain* and especially the Joseph-novels.

[15] "Versuch über die Gräbersymbolik der Alten," in *Johann Jakob Bachofen's Gesammelte Werke*, IV, 121.

[16] "Versuch," p. 133.

in itself, "an image of eternal peace."[17] The male becomes; the female is—she represents that which is "given."[18] Since she exists in such close harmony with nature,and since she gives life that is subordinated to the natural cycle, she is also closely identified with death, the peace of the grave.[19] Other associations made by Bachofen, and often by Mann as well, are that of left as against right with the female as opposed to the male principle; also of night against day; the struggle of the material against the non-material principle within history, and, finally, that of Orient or Asia (representing the material perception of the world) against the Occident.[20]

The appeal and influence of Bachofen's work to artists might have been based not least on his solid grounding in myth and the compelling potency of his vision and statement. Alfred Baeumler (whose long introduction to an anthology of Bachofen's writings Mann read and praised rather highly)[21] sees Bachofen as a Romantic and compares the latter's work on the ancients' grave symbolism to the almost contemporary culmination of musical Romanticism—Wagner's *Tristan,*[22] the work to which Mann had an ambivalent but irresistible attraction all his life. Like it, Bachofen's work is saturated with the sense of death, along with a preoccupation with the other side of the cycle—the erotic as embodied here in the sexual symbolism of the grave decorations.

Yet Mann, aware as he is of the danger of seduction in Wagner's music, is even more alert to the political and intellectual temptations of this aesthetically alluring scholarship. In *Pariser Rechenschaft* (1926), he ponders the wisdom of Baeumler's admittedly fascinating selection and introduction to Bachofen—especially its timing. The "Germans of today", he feels, are already too drawn to facile theorizing about historical recurrence, too willing to clutch any pseudo-scientific excuse for crude

---

[17] "Versuch," p. 186.

[18] *Der Mythus von Orient und Occident,* p. 127.

[19] See "Versuch," p. 186, for instance, or *Der Mythus von Orient und Occident,* CCLIV. "... there the woman, here the man; there the material primary ground, here articulated life; there the concept of material fullness, here that of energy and power; there the one of peace and preservation, here of acquisition, strife, multiplying, battling in attack and defense; there Fortuna at the hearth, here the serpent genius, totally devoted to life, generating, preserving, and dominating it." "Versuch,", pp. 190-191.

[20] *Der Mythus von Orient und Occident* and "Versuch," passim.

[21] "Pariser Rechenschaft," in *Gesammelte Werke,* XI, 48, "Great and brilliant", he calls it.

[22] *Der Mythus von Orient und Occident,* CC.

reactionarism posing as new and revolutionary. They are only waiting for "scholarly fictions" to justify a romantic nationalism against a humanism that appeared to them dull and worn out. To focus on Bachofen in whom Baeumler sees the climax of the "true" Romantic movement[23] at this time may be a pedagogical disservice indeed. To make it worse, Baeumler is doing so with the "silent insinuation" of present relevance and future promise. What he propagandizes is a "revolutionary obscurantism", an explosive mixture of "soil, folk, nature, past and death."[24] Here Mann takes up the defense of Nietzsche whom Baeumler had compared unfavorably with Bachofen, both as interpreter of antiquity and thinker. Nietzsche, Mann agrees, represents manly will and the future, not what Mann calls "the great return", immersion in the motherly night element of the past.[25] And, to Mann, this Nietzschean heroism should be the foundation for the future of Germany and for the new humanism, not a romantic reaction in the guise of the new and revolutionary.

Mann's attitude to the female principle, then, is neither unchanging nor free of ambivalence. The male/female tension in his work thus remains ever in motion, adjusting, changing—truly dialectical. The political implications of the motherly element tend to drive him in the opposite direction. This can also be seen in an exchange of letters with Hermann Hesse. In a letter to Mann on March 1932,[26] Hesse sets himself on the side of the female. He has read a new edition of Mann's essay on Goethe and Tolstoy and aligns himself with the latter: "I stand on the same side, my origin is motherly and nature is my source

---

[23] According to Baeumler, Novalis, Schlegel, and Tieck fail to reach the true insights, the "blue flower" finally incorporated into the motherly element which is fully realized by Joseph Görres, Brentano, Grimm, and especially K.O. Müller and Romantic natural philosophy. See the Introduction to *Der Mythus*.

[24] "Pariser Rechenschaft," p. 48.

[25] "Pariser Rechenschaft," pp. 48-51. There is some question here about Mann's explication of Baeumler. The latter, at one point, says that Nietzsche, though a representative of the male principle, strove toward the dissolution of individuality, to the Dionysian, to darkness, death, and the night, whereas Bachofen actually aimed toward articulation and considered the Apollonian light the highest goal. In any case, we are concerned with Mann's views rather than those of Bachofen or Baeumler, and with the further working out of these views in his art rather than their correct or incorrect derivation from their sources.

[26] *Hermann Hesse-Thomas Mann Briefwechsel*, ed. Anni Carlsson (Frankfurt/Main, 1968), p. 19.

and reliance." [27] The unquestioning tacit acceptance of these categories by both correspondents shows how much they can be taken for granted as part of their contemporary intellectual and emotional baggage. But Mann's response indicates how much his assessment of them is affected by the current cultural situation in Germany. He writes: "It does not behoove me, it would be a kind of snobbism for me, to join up with the side of the motherly and 'the Queen of the Night.' Between us, today one gets into terrible company that way, and out of disgust with that I have preferred the lesser evil and gained the reputation of a drily humanitarian rationalist." [28] We know what sort of company he means —it was indicated in all its irrational national mysticism and archaic radicalism in *Doctor Faustus.*

The changing value of the male and female poles does not impair the dialectical nature of the opposition. Rather, it enhances that quality by preventing stabilization and rigidity. Neither is the representation of male and female characters and attitudes in Mann's work, persistent as it is, fixed or schematic. The apportioning of male and female qualities remains shifting and intriguing. In fact, in the discussion of specific characters in specific works the sexual continuum often seems to overshadow the sexual dialectic. The view of the distribution of male and female elements as a continuum, we saw, does not contradict the dialectical approach. In dealing with concepts, the principles can be separated with some clarity. But in their embodiments, they are never as clear-cut and unmitigated. Thus, even though the male physiognomy is more particularized and the male principle involves the danger of solipsism, the openness of the female attitude must not become total or anonymous. Female characters such as Clavdia may be associated with death because that is what total openness and dissolution of form means. But, usually, even in their transparency, the female figures show a core of continuity, a record of past events. It is the record of the race—Hans sees through Clavdia's body, to early forms of life; a woman's arm clearly shows its ancestry in the prehistoric bird and fish. A man's arm has the same ancestry. Why, then, is it never used as a symbol? It is because the record is not as visible; it is because the male is not transparent. Yet transparency is not emptiness or total anonymity. It is still individuation of a sort, but the widest possible one. The body is often

---

[27] The editor points out the fundamental importance of the mother/father opposition in Hesse's work, along with its origin in Bachofen. P. 20.

[28] *Hesse-Mann Briefwechsel,* p. 21. My translation.

thought of as a record of past events and activities, not necessarily only those of the individual himself.

What makes an organism look individual is not the possession of unique features, nor of many slight deviations from a standard, e.g., a known type specimen, but the fact that the ontogenetic processes of its individuation, which may be perfectly normal, are encoded in its bodily form. That is the basis of "living form" in nature; and this projection of dynamic pattern into relatively fixed material pattern holds good to the most elementary level of cellular and even molecular structure.[29]

The individuation of the female principle, then, is wider and more general, sometimes even a universal identification. In its embodiments the female principle is already to some degree a synthesis. But that may be stretching the sense of individuation too far. Holding fast to the accepted meaning of the term, this dialectic is very close to the one which Susanne Langer considers "the great rhythm of evolution"—the alternation between individuation and involvement.[30] They are extremes and tendencies; actual characters and events are in the middle, approaching one or the other pole, but, in order to survive, maintaining some balance. The tension between form and disintegration that Heller[31] sees as the fundamental dialectic of *The Magic Mountain* and that appears in various guises all through Mann's work is also related to the male-female one. The female principle, as pure abstraction, would mean dissolution and obliteration. The attraction of states that border on formlessness can be seen in Mann's interest in symbols of those states such as sleep and the ocean. In the essay "Süsser Schlaf" [Sweet sleep], Mann sees the dialectic in which the artist must find a synthesis as one between concentration and abandon. I have frequently associated concentration with the male principle and its emblem of the closed fist. On the other side is "freedom," and it seems to be the kind of freedom that Clavdia sought.

The artist's morality is a focussing, it is the power of egoistic concentration, the commitment to form, articulation, limitation, solidity; to a denial of freedom, infinity, the slumbering and stirring in an unlimited realm of sensation,—it is, briefly, the willing of the work....[32]

But the female principle is also necessary: "The artistic morality is

[29] Langer, p. 331.
[30] Langer, p. 355.
[31] Heller, p. 186. (See Introduction)
[32] "Süsser Schlaf," *Gesammelte Werke*, XI, 338.

abandon, erring, and self-loss. . . ."[33] The essay is a confession of the attraction that Mann has always felt for the formless side of the anti-thesis and his dislike for organization and measure. Sleep, that is sleeping for pleasure and beyond the minimal need of the body, has been a well nigh irresistible temptation. The bed is a metaphysical piece of furniture (birth and death occur there). The root for his love of sleep, says the author, is the same as that for his love of the ocean. It is the attraction of the unconscious, of the formlessly infinite. The sea, though it is often used to symbolize entirely different attitudes, is here expressly associated with the relaxation of rigid boundaries, rendering those boundaries "fluid." The ocean is an image of the relaxation of individuation. In this, it is related to the female principle. Use of the ocean in this way suggests Freud's similar connection of the sea and diffusion of identity in the conception of the "oceanic feeling."[34]

It is the attitude to individuation that remains the main theoretical point of distinction between the male and female principles. Other characteristics cluster around it, especially in the concrete artistic em-bodiment of these principles, but they are philosophically subsidiary. Of the fundamental and irreducible nature of individuation, Susanne Langer testifies:

> . . . the process of individuation runs through the whole realm of life, and is the thread of Ariadne that guides our understanding from one level to another, where the shifts formerly seemed to be breaks: from inanimate nature to animate, from physiology to psychology, from animal life to human.[35]

Thomas Mann persistently sought links to unite inanimate and animate, plant and animal, animal and human. Seeing the simulation of structures characteristic of one realm in another fascinated him; so did the appear-ance of any phenomena which reinforced his notion of fluid boundaries. It is no wonder, then, that he felt the connecting power of individuation, and that this thread of Ariadne should govern the fundamental dialectic of male and female principles.

---

[33] "Süsser Schlaf," p. 338.
[34] Freud, *Civilization and its Discontents*, pp. 11-20.
[35] Langer, p. 312.

A SELECTED BIBLIOGRAPHY

Primary Sources

Hermann Hesse-Thomas Mann Briefwechsel. Ed. Anni Carlsson, Frankfurt/M., 1968.

Mann, Thomas. *Gesammelte Werke,* 12 vols. Oldenburg, 1960.

Mann, Thomas-Karl Kerényi. *Gespräch in Briefen.* Zürich, 1960.

Translations of Mann's Works

Novels and Novellas

Note: I have used the best available translations. Where revisions were necessary because the translator's rendering obliterated some distinction that I felt needed preserving I have registered my objections in a note; when I have made my own translation, that is clearly indicated.

The Beloved Returns. Lotte in Weimar. Transl. H. T. Lowe-Porter. New York, 1940.

Confessions of Felix Krull, Confidence Man. Transl. Denver Lindley. New York, 1955.

Death in Venice. Transl. H. T. Lowe-Porter. New York, 1930.

Doctor Faustus. The Life of the German Composer Adrian Leverkühn as told by a Friend. Transl. H. T. Lowe-Porter. New York, 1948.

The Holy Sinner. Transl. H. T. Lowe-Porter. New York, 1951.

Joseph and his Brothers, 4 vols (*Joseph and his Brothers, Young Joseph, Joseph in Egypt*). Transl. H. T. Lowe-Porter. New York, 1935.

The Magic Mountain. Transl. H. T. Lowe-Porter. New York, 1947.

Stories of Three Decades. Transl. H. T. Lowe-Porter. New York, 1938.

The Transposed Heads. A Legend of India. Transl. H. T. Lowe-Porter. New York, 1941.

Essays and other work

Essays of Three Decades. New York, 1937.

Last Essays. Transl. Richard and Clara Winston and Tania and James Stern. New York, 1959.

Past Masters and Other Papers. Transl. H. T. Lowe-Porter. Freeport, N.Y., 1968.

A Sketch of my Life. Transl. H. T. Lowe-Porter. New York, 1960.

The Story of a Novel. The Genesis of Doctor Faustus. Transl. Richard and Clara Winston. New York, 1961.

Secondary Sources and Other Texts

Altenberg, Peter. *Die Romane Thomas Manns. Versuch einer Deutung.* Bad Homburg, 1961.

Bachofen, Johann Jakob. *Gesammelte Werke.* Ed. Karl Meuli. Basel, 1954.

Bachofen, Johann Jakob. *Der Mythus von Orient und Occident.* Ed. Manfred Schroeter. München, 1926.

Bizet, Georges. *Carmen* (words by H. Meilhac and L. Halévy). New York, 1958.

Blume, Bernhard. *Thomas Mann und Goethe.* Bern, 1949.

Brann, Hellmut Walther. *Nietzsche und die Frauen.* Leipzig, 1931.

Brown, Norman. *Love's Body.* New York, 1966.

Bürgin, Hans. *Das Werk Thomas Manns.* Frankfurt/M., 1959.

Bürgin, Hans and Hans-Otto Mayer, eds. *Thomas Mann. Eine Chronik seines Lebens.* Frankfurt/M., 1965. Also the English version published by the University of Alabama Press in 1965.

Dierks, Manfred. *Studien zu Mythos und Psychologie bei Thomas Mann.* Thomas-Mann-Studien II. Bern, 1972.

Eloesser, Arthur. *Thomas Mann: Sein Leben und Sein Werk.* Berlin, 1925.

Freud, Sigmund. *Civilization and its Discontents.* New York, 1961.

Freud, Sigmund. *The Complete Psychological Works of Sigmund Freud.* Ed. James Strachey. London, 1955. Vols VIII and XIII.

Feuerlicht, Ignace. *Thomas Mann und die Grenzen des Ich.* Heidelberg, 1966.

Gehrts, Barbara. "Die Bedeutung der Frauengestalten im Romanwerk Thomas Manns," unpublished diss., University of Freiburg, 1958.

Girard, René. *Deceit, Desire, and the Novel.* Baltimore, 1965.

Goethes Sämtliche Werke. Jubiläumsausgabe in 40 Bänden. Stuttgart und Berlin, 1902-1912. Also Modern Library College Edition. New York, 1950.

Goncharov, Ivan A. *Obryv.* Moscow, 1946.

Graber, Paul Albert. "Female Characters in the Early Works of Thomas Mann," unpublished M.A. thesis, State University of Iowa, 1939.

Hamburger, Käte. *Thomas Manns Roman "Joseph und seine Brüder." Eine Einführung.* Stockholm, 1945.

Hatfield, Henry. *Thomas Mann.* Norfolk, Conn., 1962.

Heller, Erich. *Thomas Mann: the Ironic German.* Cleveland, 1961.

Hesse, Hermann. *Demian.* New York, 1966.

Hesse, Hermann. *Narcissus and Goldmund.* New York, 1969.

Hesse, Hermann. *Steppenwolf.* New York, 1969.

Hirschbach, Frank Donald. *The Arrow and the Lyre: A Study of the Role of Love in the Works of Thomas Mann.* The Hague, 1955.

Hodin, J. P. *Oskar Kokoschka. The Artist and his Time.* London, 1966.

Hofman, Alois. *Thomas Mann und die Welt der russischen Literatur.* Berlin, 1967.

Holthusen, Hans Egon. "The World without Transcendence," in *Thomas Mann: A Collection of Critical Essays,* ed. Henry Hatfield. Englewood Cliffs, 1964.

Jacob, Gerhard. *Das Werk Thomas Manns: Eine Bibliographie.* Berlin, 1926.

Jonas, Klaus. *Fifty Years of Thomas Mann Studies. A Bibliography of Criticism.* Minneapolis, 1955.

Jonas, Klaus W. and Ilsedore B. Jonas. *Thomas Mann Studies. Volume II. A Bibliography of Criticism.* Philadelphia, 1967.

Jung, Carl. G. *Two Essays on Analytical Psychology.* Cleveland, 1956.

Jung, C. G. *Aion. Researches into the Phenomenology of the Self.* Bollingen Series XX, *The Collected Works of C.G. Jung,* IX, Pt 2. New York, 1959.

Jung, C. G. *Psychological Reflections.* Ed. Jolande Jacobi. Bollingen Series XXXI. New York, 1953.

Kahler, Erich. *Die Verantwortung des Geistes: Gesammelte Aufsätze.* Frankfurt/M., 1952.

Kerényi, Karl. *Die Jungfrau und Mutter der griechischen Religion.* Zürich, 1952.

—. *Eleusis. Archetypal Image of Mother and Daughter.* New York, 1967.

Koopmann, Helmut. *Die Entwicklung des "intellektualen Romans" bei Thomas Mann (Buddenbrooks, Königliche Hoheit, Der Zauberberg).* Bonner Arbeiten zur deutschen Literatur, Bd. 5. Bonn, 1962.

Langer, Susanne K. *Feeling and Form. A Theory of Art developed from "Philosophy in a New Key."* New York, 1953.

Langer, Susanne K. *Mind: An Essay on Human Feeling.* Baltimore, 1967.

Lehnert, Herbert. *Thomas Mann—Fiktion, Mythos, Religion.* Stuttgart, 1968.

Lesser, Jonas. *Thomas Mann in der Epoche seiner Vollendung.* München, 1952.

Lion, Ferdinand. *Thomas Mann: Leben und Werk.* Zürich, 1947.

Lukács, Georg. *Essays on Thomas Mann.* New York, 1965.

Maurer, Warren R. "Names from the Magic Mountain," *Names,* IX (December, 1961), pp. 248-259.

Mauron, Charles. *Des Métaphores Obsédantes au Mythe Personnel. Introduction à la Psychocritique.* Paris, 1963.

Mayer, Hans. *Thomas Mann: Sein Leben und Werk.* Berlin, 1950.

Mayer, Herman. *Das Zitat in der Erzählkunst.* Stuttgart, 1967.

Nietzsche, Friedrich. *Ecce Homo,* in *The Complete Works of Friedrich Nietzsche.* New York, 1911.

—. *Also sprach Zarathustra,* in *Nietzsche. Werke.* Ed. Colli and Montinari. Berlin, 1967.

—. *Thus Spake Zarathustra,* in *The Complete Works of Friedrich Nietzsche.* New York, 1911.

Reichart, Walter A. "Thomas Mann: An American Bibliography," *MDU,* XXXVII (October 1945), pp. 389-407.

Schenck, Erna H. "Women in the Works of Thomas Mann." Unpublished M.A. thesis, University of Wisconsin, 1928. (Condensed version in *MDU,* XXXII (April 1940), pp. 145-164.

Scherrer, Paul and Hans Wysling. *Quellenkritische Studien zum Werk Thomas Manns.* Bern and München, 1967.

Strübel, Gustav. "Liebe und Geschlecht im Werke Thomas Manns: Eine Studie über ein anthropologisch-metaphysisches Grundproblem der Dichtung." Unpublished diss., University of Freiburg, 1949.

Weigand, Hermann J. *The Magic Mountain. A Study of Thomas Mann's Novel "Der Zauberberg."* Chapel Hill, 1964.

INDEX